PROMETHEANS IN THE LAB

Other Books by Sharon Bertsch McGrayne

Iron, Nature's Universal Element: Why People Need Iron & Animals Make Magnets (with Eugenie V. Mielczarek)

Nobel Prize Women in Science: Their Lives, Struggles, and Momentous Discoveries

Blue Genes and Polyester Plants: 365 More Surprising Scientific Facts, Breakthroughs, and Discoveries

365 Surprising Scientific Facts, Breakthroughs, and Discoveries

PROMETHEANS
IN THE LAB

*Chemistry and the Making of
the Modern World*

Sharon Bertsch McGrayne

McGraw-Hill

New York   Chicago   San Francisco
Lisbon   London   Madrid   Mexico City   Milan
New Delhi   San Juan   Seoul   Singapore
Sydney   Toronto

The McGraw·Hill Companies

Library of Congress Cataloging-in-Publication Data

McGrayne, Sharon Bertsch.
    Prometheans in the lab : chemistry and the making of the modern
world by Sharon Bertsch McGrayne.
        p.   cm.
    Includes bibliographical references and index.
    ISBN 0-07-135007-1
    1. Chemistry, Technical—History.   2. Chemists—Biography.
    I. Title.

TP18 .M34 2001
660'.092'2—dc21
[B]   2001030671

1 2 3 4 5 6 7 8 9 0   DOC/DOC   0 7 6 5 4 3 2 1 (HC)
1 2 3 4 5 6 7 8 9 0   DOC/DOC   0 7 6 5 4 3 (PBK)

ISBN 0-07-135007-1 (HC)
ISBN 0-07-140795-2 (PBK)

The publishers have generously given permission to use extended quotations from the following copyrighted works: Murozumi et al., "Chemical concentrations of ...," *Geochimica et Cosmochimica Acta*, 33: 1247-1294, © 1969 Elsevier Science; *Introduction to Kettering*, speech text by Thomas J. Midgley, Jr., from the Kettering University Archives, Flint, Michigan; Thomas Midgley, Jr., "How We Found Ethyl Gas," © 1925 *Motor* magazine, pp. 92-94; Thomas J. Midgley, Jr., "Man-Made Molecules," *Industrial & Engineering Chemistry*, 30: 120-122, © 1938 American Chemical Society; Thomas J. Midgley, Jr., "Accent on Youth," *Chemical & Engineering News*, 22: 1646-1649, © 1944 American Chemical Society; C. Patterson, "Contaminated and Natural Lead Environments of Man," *Archives of Environmental Health*, © 1965 Heldref Publications, courtesy of C. Patterson, *Archives of Environmental Health*, and Heldref Publications; Noell Deerr, *The History of Sugar*, fig. 33 by Norbert Rilieux, 2: 568, © 1950 Chapman & Hall, Ltd, with kind permission from Kluwer Academic Publishers; National Research Council, "Comparison of Relative Amounts of Lead in People," *Lead in the Human Environment*, fig. 1, p. 276, © 1980 National Academy of Sciences, permission of National Academy Press; papers of Clair C. Patterson and the oral history with Patterson by Shirley Cohen, by permission of the California Institute of Technology and courtesy of Lorna J. Patterson; papers of Wallace Carothers, courtesy of the Hagley Museum and Library.

Printed and bound by R. R. Donnelley & Sons Company.

 This book is printed on recycled, acid-free paper containing a minimum of 50% recycled de-inked fiber.

For George, Fred, Ruth Ann, and Tim

And in memory of Robert M. Secor

CONTENTS

PRELUDE

As far as the eye could see, strips of linen, hemp, and cotton cloth lay stretched over the fields. Dull gray from the loom, the fabric had been drenched repeatedly in stale urine, sour buttermilk, or sulfuric acid. Now it was being "grassed" on racks to bleach in the sunshine. In the eighteenth century, it took six months to bleach linen and up to three months to bleach cotton. Theft was a problem; stealing fabric from bleaching fields was a capital offense in England. Scottish bleachers augmented their insufficient supplies of sunshine and buttermilk by shipping semibleached fabrics to Dutch dairy farms for finishing. Grassed cloth, nowhere nearly as white or as bright as modern fabric, was a symbol of wealth and status.

In 1785, Claude-Louis Berthollet, a French chemist, demonstrated that chlorine bleaches fabric. His discovery was the first volley in a chemical revolution that has changed the everyday lives of millions of people. A humane and scrupulously honest man, Berthollet refused to patent his process; he knew it would release thousands of acres of farmland for food crops and speed up textile manufacturing 1000 times over. Berthollet shared his discovery with the English inventor James Watt, who told Mr. McGregor, the owner of extensive bleachworks near Glasgow. Together, Watt and McGregor tested chlorine on 500 pieces of cloth. By 1798, the Englishman Charles Tennant had patented bleaching powder, a highly irritating dust that was nevertheless much safer to transport and easier to use than a liquid.

Berthollet's chlorine bleach helped dress the world in sparkling white. Later it purified drinking water, saving lives around the world. His process solved two important problems, but it unwittingly created an unexpected one that came to light almost two centuries later. Only after modern chemists learned how to analyze and identify minute traces of chemicals could they discover that chlorine bleach produces tiny amounts of chloro-form and dioxin. Today, many paper-bleaching mills and European water systems are replacing Berthollet's chlorine bleach with other chemicals.

This book is about the scientific roots of our modern way of life. It tells the story of pioneering chemists like Berthollet whose discoveries solved critical problems in their lifetimes. Readers should be forewarned. The lives of these scientists tend to be dramatic. They are filled with the joys of dis-covery, the excitement of their times, and even the anguish of human tragedy.

Their discoveries—white clothes, cheap soap and sugar, brightly colored washable fabric, clean water, fertilizer, powerful aviation and automotive fuel, safe refrigerants, synthetic textiles, pesticides, and lead-free fuel and food—were enthusiastically embraced by the buying public. Few of us today would want to do without them.

In time, however, some of these scientific discoveries—even those that in their day made major reforms—produced their own set of difficulties. In each case where this occurred, the burden of identifying and solving the problem fell to science. Consumers clamored for new products, but they also demanded that governments and industry protect the air, water, soils, plants, and animals endangered by human-made chemicals. As pollutants became increasingly subtle and harder to detect, scientists became leaders in identifying harmful substances, in some cases before the public was even aware of their existence, much less their potential harm. In these stories, advances in science have both created new and needed products and dealt with pollution from the past.

Most of all, these are the dramatic stories of bold chemists who irrevo-cably changed our lives. They are indeed Prometheans who made our mod-ern world.

ACKNOWLEDGMENTS

This book is an outgrowth of a suggestion made by Otto T. Benfey when he and Anthony S. Travis were associate editor and editor, respectively, of a series of books about the history of modern chemical sciences to be published jointly by the American Chemical Society and the Chemical Heritage Foundation. That series is, unhappily, no more, but their encouragement eventually became this book, and I am greatly indebted to them for their help. Ted Benfey, for example, read and critiqued every chapter of this book, a record shared only by George F. and Ruth Ann Bertsch.

Many other experts also helped make this book as accurate and readable as possible. A number of them spent considerable time and thought helping me, and I thank them at the beginning of each chapter's bibliography. The history of science and, in particular, the history of chemistry, is enjoying a remarkable boom, and I hope that a book aimed at a general audience will alert readers to this interesting new field.

On a broader level, our everyday lives have been transformed by science. Yet many people remain deeply suspicious of science and, in particular, of chemistry. I hope that a balanced telling of the dramatic stories of some of the key people in the history of chemistry—people who permanently and irrevocably changed our lives—will help us understand the roots of our modern way of life.

Finally, it should be noted that my best editor has been, as always, George Bertsch and that I could not have written this book without the assistance of Cynthia Wolfe, Julie Coons, Alice Calaprice, Elizabeth Morrow Edwards, and my writer friends in "The Rejects."

1

Soap and Nicolas Leblanc

December 6, 1742–January 16, 1806

Nicolas Leblanc was a catch-as-catch-can chemist, a "wannabe" scientist hovering on the fringes of stardom. Poor and little known, he invented an industrial process to make pure washing soda for the manufacture of cheap soap, textiles, glass, and paper. For half a century, Leblanc's method epitomized large-scale chemical manufacturing; until synthetic dyes were developed, his process was virtually synonymous with the chemical industry. Before Leblanc, small family-run shops made and sold chemicals according to ancient recipes, and soap was a handmade luxury for the rich and a medicinal salve for the sick. After Leblanc, basic chemicals were manufactured in giant factories and traded worldwide, and professionally trained scientists could earn their livelihoods as chemists. When made into soap, Leblanc's invention formed the very gauge of human progress. The quantity of soap consumed by a nation is a measure of its civilization, declared the eminent German chemist, Justus von Liebig. "Artificial soda is one of the great benefits, if not the greatest, that modern science has bestowed on humanity," proclaimed the French National Academy of Sciences in 1856.

Unfortunately, the process that made soap produced a great deal of filth before it cleansed the happily unwashed populace at large. In fact, Leblanc's process polluted industrial regions so cruelly that it created an early rallying cry for environmental reform.

Nicolas Leblanc was born on December 6, 1742, in a village near Bourges in central France. His father, a low-level office worker in an iron forge, died when Nicolas was 9 years old. A surgeon friend of his father's educated the boy but when the surgeon also died, 17-year-old Nicolas was on his own.

The French Enlightenment had opened up access to learning and science, and for the first time talented young men from the provinces could dream of becoming scientists in Paris. The city was Europe's intellectual capital, and it pulsated with scientific excitement. To succeed, a young man would have to distinguish himself in school and convince an influential patron to give him money or letters of introduction to open the right doors. These were big ifs, but the Enlightenment valued talent, not privilege, and Nicolas Leblanc was eager to seek his fortune. Moving north to Paris, he studied surgery and, after earning a diploma, began to practice there.

At some point along the way, Leblanc fell in love with chemistry, which was an intrinsic part of upper-class culture in eighteenth-century France. Rich aristocrats studied chemistry and installed laboratories in their châteaus; even the king, Louis XVI, believed that the science could help solve a host of society's medical and technological problems.

Fortunately for a poor, would-be chemist like Leblanc, France's aristocratic passion for the physical sciences crossed economic, social, and political borders. Intellectuals such as Rousseau and Diderot cultivated the sciences with enthusiasm and compiled encyclopedias and dictionaries of natural substances. Local academies and institutes in the far-flung provinces sponsored chemical studies. Crowds flocked to hear chemists lecture and to watch their flashy laboratory demonstrations. Even the future revolutionary, Jean-Paul Marat, experimented with fire, electricity, and light and tried—in vain—to become a member of the Royal Academy of Sciences. In America, Benjamin Franklin abandoned his printing and publishing business for physics, and in England his friend Jane Marcet wrote *Mrs. Marcet's Conversations in Chemistry* for women and working-class men.

Chemistry was the most popular of all the sciences because of its obvious practical applications for manufacturing, pharmaceuticals, and mining. The lawyer and chemist, Guyton de Morveau, explained from his private Dijon laboratory in 1774 that "it is from chemistry that the dyer acquired all the processes for extracting, toning and fixing his colors; through it, the starcher, brewer, and distiller control their fermentations. It is chemistry that has allowed the cabinetmaker to vary the shades of his veneers, the varnisher to dissolve resins, the tanner to tan leather and soften hides. It is also chemistry that taught so many manufacturers how to remove the grease from wool and to smooth out silks. It alone can add some perfection to all these arts."

Far above Leblanc, at the very pinnacle of French science, stood Antoine Laurent Lavoisier, a government financier and reformer and the father of modern chemistry. Lavoisier was a fabulously rich tax collector. His net income hovered in modern terms somewhere between $2.4 million and $4.8 million a year, and he dedicated much of it to his scientific library and chemical laboratory.

His wife, Marie-Anne, studied drawing with the great painter Jacques-Louis David in order to transcribe her husband's laboratory notes and illustrate them. David's ravishing portrait of the Lavoisiers hangs in the Metropolitan Museum of Art in New York. The son of Marie-Anne's long-time lover founded the E. I. Du Pont de Nemours Corporation in Delaware. Marie-Anne later married the American physicist, Benjamin Thomson. Later ennobled as the Count of Rumford, Thomson demonstrated the mechanical nature of heat. Marie-Anne had an excellent eye for scientific talent.

In 20 years of scientific research, Antoine Lavoisier constructed a comprehensive and revolutionary chemical theory founded on quantitative analysis, the conservation of matter, his new definition of the elements, and his replacement of phlogiston by oxygen. Distinguishing between elements and compounds, Lavoisier showed that three of Aristotle's four elements—earth, water, and air—are compounds, and that the fourth—fire or phlogiston—is without substance. At the same time, he demonstrated that oxygen, hydrogen, nitrogen, and carbon are elements and that oxygen is responsible for combustion and respiration.

With Guyton de Morveau, Lavoisier devised the system of chemical terms still used today. For the first time, the names of chemical substances described their constituents and proportions; "astringent Mars saffron" became iron oxide, and "philosophic wool" became zinc oxide. Many contemporaries called Lavoisier's new chemistry "The French Science." Today Lavoisier is regarded as the equal of Isaac Newton in physics, Charles Darwin in evolution, or Albert Einstein in relativity.

Thanks to the range and depth of France's passion for chemistry, Leblanc was able to secure the introductions he needed to build a scientific career. First, he became a student of Jean Darcet, one of France's first chemistry professors. Darcet was a liberal-minded man who wore street clothes instead of academic robes as he lectured in French instead of the usual Latin. This was critical for Leblanc, who did not know classical languages. It was probably at one of Darcet's popular lectures that Leblanc met and became a friend of Claude-Louis Berthollet, a close scientific collaborator of the great Lavoisier. Professor Darcet and Berthollet were protégés of the extraordinarily wealthy Duke of Orléans. The duke maintained an extensive chemistry laboratory in his palace where he supported a number of young chemists, physicists, naturalists, and engineers who later became important scientists.

Professor Darcet had advised the Duke on several occasions, and either Darcet or Berthollet may have recommended Leblanc to the Orléans household as an up-and-coming chemist. At any rate, Leblanc got the chance of a lifetime in 1780 when he was invited to become a surgeon-in-ordinary in Orléans's scientific retinue. Joyfully, Leblanc renounced medicine with the hope of becoming one of Europe's first full-time, professional chemists. Five years later, when Orléans died, his son, the future Philip Equality, became the next Duke of Orléans and assumed responsibility for his father's scientific laboratory.

Although the new Duke of Orléans was the wealthiest man in Europe, he was wildly popular with the French public. The house of Orléans had been the liberal voice of France for 150 years. Cousins of the French kings, the dukes opposed the monarchy's absolute power and the Catholic Church's monopoly on education and supported the aspirations of the growing middle class. Radicals talked of making the new duke regent or even king.

As a member of Orléans' household, Nicolas Leblanc became a confirmed revolutionary. The orphaned son of an iron factory clerk must have felt reassured by Orléans' wealth and position, exhilarated by his radicalism, and positively starry-eyed at the possibilities for chemical discovery. Leblanc's scientific career was also progressing nicely. He reported to the Royal Academy of Sciences on the growth of crystals and, when a 25-foot-high pile of coal exploded in Paris, he studied ways to prevent the spontaneous combustion of coal. Above all else, he concentrated on winning a contest sponsored by the king and the Royal Academy of Sciences. Louis XVI was offering 12,000 livres—almost half a million dollars today—for the best way to turn common salt into washing soda for the manufacture of soap. For poor Leblanc, the contest represented a chance at attaining wealth, security, and professional acclaim.

Neither Leblanc nor the king was interested in using the soap to keep pristine and sweet smelling. People had been making soap as a medicinal salve for at least 2000 years, but they washed themselves and their clothes with other substances, if at all. The Greeks and Romans, for example, cleansed themselves with olive oil, bran, sand, ashes, or pumice stone and washed their linen in alkali-rich urine collected in pitchers at busy street corners. During the Middle Ages, public baths were fashionable trysting places, but the Black Plague closed them early in the sixteenth century; water was thought to open the body's pores to contagion.

The idea of cleanliness persisted, but a cold water rinse sufficed to clean face and hands, and the rest of the body was rubbed with dry linen or perfume. "To cure the goat-like stench of armpits, it is useful to press and rub the skin with a compound of roses." Linen shirts absorbed dirt and sweat under woolen outer garments. With the passing of centuries, the shirts were changed more often and sun-bleached linen began to peek out from wrists and collars to proclaim the wearer's position in society. Soap and water still did not touch the body, however. King Henry IV of France had dozens of linen shirts, but the ladies complained that he stank "like carrion." Thus, when the king of France offered a prize for an industrial process to make washing soda from table salt, he was not thinking about personal cleanliness. Louis XVI was promoting the textile revolution.

Today it is difficult to imagine that the production of sodium carbonate could bedazzle anyone, and we give the compound the commonplace name, "washing soda." But the future of the French and British textile industries—expanding neck and neck during the Industrial Revolution—depended on this scarce commodity. Fabric manufacturers launched the revolution by mass-producing cotton cloth for the masses instead of weaving costly silk, woolen, and linen goods for the rich. Cotton fabrics emerge from the loom dull gray, however, and must be cleaned, bleached, and chemically treated before they can be dyed or printed. As the public clamored for cheap fabric, the textile industry's hunger for washing soda to make soap became almost insatiable. Expanding paper and glass factories also demanded more washing soda. As a result, manufacturers did not call sodium carbonate washing soda. They called it "white gold."

Sodium carbonate is an alkali, a strongly basic compound that has a pH of 9 or more in solution. Boiling an alkali with fat makes soap. Chemically, soap contains a long chain of hydrocarbons that repels water but has an affinity for other fatty substances. When treated with alkali, the ends of the fatty chains are modified so that they are attracted to water. A molecule with one end that attracts fatty substances and another end that likes to dissolve in water is ideal for coating dirt particles and floating them away in water. Soap can be made from any kind of fat, whether from kitchen scraps or whale, olive, or palm oil.

The choice of alkali was more difficult. In Leblanc's time, the alkali was generally a carbonate (CO_3) or hydroxide (OH) of potassium or sodium extracted from the ashes of salt-rich plants. For example, northerners made an odoriferous soft soap by burning wood and boiling its ashes with animal fat or fish oil. In Spain, Marseilles, Genoa, and Venice, hard Castile soap was made by boiling olive oil with the ashes of seaweed and shore plants.

As demand for alkalis soared, more and more trees and plants were burned in Western Europe and North America. Each September, peasants along the coasts of Spain and southern France collected the highest quality alkali: coastal barilla grasses impregnated with sea salt. The peasants dried the barilla in the sun for a month and burned it in large pit kilns dug into the ground. The product, a rich 20 to 33 percent sodium carbonate, fused into 1.5-ton masses that had to be broken apart for shipment.

In western and northwestern England, Ireland, Scotland, and Norway and in the Hebrides and Orkney Islands, peasants neglected their farms and herds three months of the year to cut seaweed and haul it ashore. Instead of using it to manure their fields or overwinter their cattle, they dried and burned the seaweed, boiled the ashes, evaporated the liquid, and earned pennies for their pains. The result, called kelp, was only 5 to 8 percent sodium and potassium carbonate. Kelp made big landowners wealthy, but it impoverished peasant farmers.

By far the most important source of alkali for the textile industry came from New England. As settlers cleared primeval forests, they burned brushwood and small timber to make potash. Water percolated through the ashes made a solution that was boiled dry for shipment to European textile plants.

But not all the potash, kelp, and barilla in Europe and North America could keep up with the cotton textile factories of Britain and France. France was in a particularly dire situation. Even under normal conditions, her natural sources of alkali were insufficient. Then France supported the American War of Independence, and British ships cut off the French supply of American potash. With gunpowder and textile industries dependent on potash, France had to find a way to make artificial alkali.

Sodium carbonate—washing soda—was the best candidate. Chemists had long known that sea salt could be transformed into sodium carbonate, and French scientists understood that the two compounds are related. Later it was learned that they share the same base, sodium. No one could make the process work on a large, industrial scale, though. About a dozen laboratory methods were known and a few English and Scottish soap makers made their own washing soda, but no one could make sodium carbonate as cheaply as the barilla- and kelp-burning peasants. The hunt for a cheap technology was hampered by exorbitant taxes on salt and soap. In England, the tax cost more than the soap itself, and tax collectors locked soap makers' pans at night to prevent a black market in untaxed soap.

At the age of 42, Leblanc took up the challenge. He knew what the first step should be. As a chloride, sodium is extremely stable, but he thought he might be able to modify sodium sulfate. So Leblanc mixed salt with sulfuric acid to make sodium sulfate and hydrochloric acid:

$$2NaCl + H_2SO_4 = Na_2SO_4 + 2HCl$$

SALT   SULFURIC ACID   SODIUM SULFATE   HYDROCHLORIC ACID

Sulfuric acid had been readily available since 1746 when John Roebuck of Birmingham, England, began making it in lead-lined, wooden boxes several stories high.

The challenge was the second step. How could Leblanc break off the sulfur and oxygen from the sodium sulfate and transform the sodium into sodium carbonate? Today the answer might seem obvious, but at the time no one knew the chemical composition of even common substances like sodium carbonate (Na_2CO_3) or limestone ($CaCO_3$).

Leblanc wrestled with the problem for five years between 1784 and 1789. Then finally, somehow, someway, he stumbled on the solution. Ancient ironmakers had used carbon in the form of charcoal; when hot, the carbon is highly reactive and wrests the oxygen from iron oxide ores. As Leblanc heated his sodium sulfate with charcoal, he added a key new ingredient—common limestone (chalk)—as his source of CO_3. Almost miraculously, the transformation took place:

$$Na_2SO_4 \;+\; CaCO_3 \;+\; 2C \;=\; Na_2CO_3 \;+\; CaS \;+\; 2CO_2$$
$$\text{\footnotesize SODIUM SULFATE \quad LIMESTONE \quad CHARCOAL \quad SODIUM CARBONATE \quad CALCIUM SULFIDE \quad CARBON DIOXIDE}$$

Finally, he knew how to turn salt into pure alkali. Nicolas Leblanc had made white gold.

Sadly, one of the by-products from his first step was the powerfully corrosive hydrochloric acid, a potentially serious pollutant. But Leblanc may have been so excited at making sodium carbonate that he hardly noticed. He had found a way to synthesize a purer and thus more efficient substitute for the alkali traditionally extracted from plant ashes. When perfected, his method would make stronger, more consistent soda with far more alkali than the best soda made from plants. He must have felt utterly elated. He was a patriot about to save French industry and win a fortune, 12,000 gold coins.

Unfortunately for Leblanc, his process was not the only revolution to occur in France during 1789. That July, Parisian mobs stormed the Bastille and triggered the French Revolution. Leblanc's discovery was epoch-making, but his timing could not have been worse. The absolute monarchy was gone, and with it all chance of his winning the king's prize. And while Leblanc struggled to exploit his process commercially, events were beginning to swirl out of control.

Scientists volunteered en masse to help the revolutionary government. Eager for France to modernize and reform, many served on the wartime Committee of Public Safety. An astronomer became the first mayor of revolutionary Paris; a chemist was the first president of the Committee of Public Safety; mathematicians became senators and a naval minister; and so on. When after-work science classes were organized for Parisian workers, Leblanc, Lavoisier, Berthollet, and others volunteered as instructors. Few scientists emigrated, even during the Terror.

In the midst of the excitement, Leblanc told his former chemistry professor, Jean Darcet, the fabulous secret of his discovery. After running some tests and confirming Leblanc's discovery, Darcet recommended it to their patron, the Duke of Orléans. So far the process had worked only in laboratory crucibles, but Darcet declared optimistically, "I the undersigned, professor of chemistry at the Royal College of France and at the Royal Academy of Sciences, etc., certify that . . . with this same process, it will be easy to establish a factory." As is often the case, reality proved to be a trifle more complicated.

The Duke of Orléans was visiting London; so in February 1790, Leblanc crossed the English Channel on his first trip outside France. Orléans agreed to invest the equivalent of $8 million in a start-up factory to exploit Leblanc's secret process. On February 12, in the London office of a French-speaking notary public named James Sutherland, Leblanc signed a contract with the Duke, his agent, and Professor Darcet's assistant.

Hurrying back to Paris, Leblanc drafted a description of his discovery for Orléans. Folding two sheets of thick white paper in half, he made a little booklet and tied the pages together with red string. Dipping a thick quill pen in ink, he copied his draft into the booklet, careful to make no mistakes. He began: "To decompose entirely sea salt, take nearly the same weight of concentrated acid. It must be converted to . . . ," and so on. Then he carefully sealed the booklet inside a packet and on March 27, 1790, deposited it in the office of a Parisian notary public. There it remained unopened for 66 years, until a Commission of the French Academy of Sciences read it and confirmed the priority of his discovery.

Within a year of gaining the duke's support, Leblanc opened a small, walled-in factory beside a paved road and a barge canal outside Paris at Saint-Denis. At the entrance, he proudly nailed a sign, "N. Leblanc's Soda Factory." His first problem was to build a furnace capable of transforming his laboratory experiment into a large-scale factory. He modified his furnace design to create a hotter reaction that produced purer soda. He fitted a covered lead container with a pipe to release his dangerous by-product, hydrochloric acid. By trial and error, he figured out the best proportions of ingredients, a giant technological step forward that would make large-scale production possible. Finally, he applied for a patent under new legislation passed by the revolutionary French government to guarantee inventors the rights to their discoveries for 15 years. Under the monarchy, inventors' discoveries had been judged in open competitions and published for anyone to use.

One day three patent inspectors, including his mentor Professor Darcet, appeared at Leblanc's little factory and scrupulously examined his workshops and process. In their official report, they concluded that his invention was "different and very superior to everything that, until today, has come to our knowledge, in terms of the economy, speed, and sureness of the procedure, as by the richness and purity of the result." The inspectors warned, "The secret of his discovery should be carefully guarded."

On September 19, 1791, Leblanc became the fourteenth inventor granted a patent under France's new laws. For the next two years, Leblanc struggled to get his factory going amid wartime shortages of sulfuric acid and capital.

When the armies of Europe's monarchies threatened revolutionary France, Lavoisier, Orléans, and Leblanc found themselves in perilous circumstances. Orléans was the first to be arrested. During the revolution, Orléans had adopted the name Philippe Égalité, or Philip Equality, and become a member of the revolutionary National Convention. With the assembly equally divided for and against executing the king, Orléans panicked and cast the tie-breaking vote that sent his cousin, Louis XVI, to the guillotine. Orléans's cowardice shocked even radical revolutionaries, and he became one of the most despised figures in French history. Talleyrand said, "Orléans is the vase into which they threw all the excrement of the Revolution."

Eventually, one of Orléans' sons compromised his father's precarious position and the duke was arrested. From his jail cell a few days before his execution, Orléans wrote his mistress Agnes de Buffon, "The last letter received pierced my soul, for I learned that they have suspended the payment of the pensions and pledges of the people who were attached to me. I cannot tell you how I was affected by that. I put this sorrow among the biggest sorrows that I have suffered." Among his people was, of course, Nicolas Leblanc.

After Orléans' execution in November 1793, his vast properties became state property and Leblanc's factory was seized. Three months later, Leblanc faced even more distressing news. With war threatening, the Committee of Public Safety called for patent holders of soda processes to publish their methods: "A true republican does not hesitate to relinquish the ownership of even the fruits of his mind when he hears the voice of his country entreating for aid." Coming from the Committee of Public Safety, such a plea was tantamount to an order.

Hastening to comply, Leblanc submitted his discovery to the committee, which published a brochure describing his process in minute detail. The government wanted as many French artisans as possible to produce washing soda. Thus, within a few months of Orléans' execution, Leblanc lost his salary, the factory, and his patent. The revolution had already cost him his chance of winning the king's prize money. Meanwhile, Leblanc's wife had fallen ill, and he had four children to support.

Soon after Orléans' execution, Lavoisier was also arrested. On May 8, 1794, he and 27 other tax collectors were guillotined. Six months after Lavoisier's execution, the government ordered his former scientific collaborator, Berthollet, and two associates to inventory Lavoisier's chemical laboratory. Berthollet chose Leblanc to assistant him. The melancholy inventory occupied most of a week. Lavoisier had stocked his laboratory with $1.1 million worth of glassware, electricity-making machines, compasses, sextants, astrolabes, barometers, precision scales, and large quantities of chemicals, including, for example, 166 pounds of mercury. Many of his instruments were imported from England, but to encourage French technology and science, he had supervised the local manufacture of some apparatuses. To appraise all Lavoisier's precious equipment and supplies, Leblanc returned four times with a glass merchant and an apothecary. In his final report, Leblanc wrote that Lavoisier "as is well known, treated chemistry and many other branches of science and art with rare intelligence and success." This was probably more than many others would have dared to say at the time.

Leblanc had begun a frenzied period of his life, trying to support his family and the revolution while, no doubt, trying to avoid the guillotine himself. The government was sympathetic about the loss of his patent and appointed him to a patchwork of administrative and study posts, most of them unpaid. Offered a job as a teacher of natural history, he declined, noting realistically that he lacked the depth of knowledge required for the job. Instead, he joined France's scientific demimonde, trying to solve a host of practical problems for the wartime government. He investigated cotton spinning machines, naval construction, mining, library cataloguing, and canal and hospital construction. Like Lavoisier, he became a gunpowder commissioner at the Lesser Arsenal and moved his family into an apartment there. But while the great Lavoisier had studied the oxygen in air, Leblanc analyzed animal manures, cesspools, sewage-polluted millponds, and drains and concluded that ammonia is an essential ingredient of fertilizer. Then he asked—in vain—for a monopoly on manures and the night soil in cesspools and drains for recycling as fertilizer.

As his savings ran out, he considered emigrating to Russia and his two daughters opened a small notions shop. Each day the family watched as carts full of the condemned rumbled past on their way to the guillotine. The miseries seemed endless. Inexplicably, his beloved 17-year-old daughter became paralyzed and, six months later, died.

All through the Revolution and the Napoleonic Empire, Leblanc kept up a barrage of letters to various bureaucrats complaining about their lack of support. He regained possession of the factory in 1800, but he was never able to get it fully operational. Soap makers, for example, complained that his soda smelled of hydrogen sulfide. A modern historian who studied Leblanc found him "very exasperating . . . [with] a disposition to sulk, a certain querulousness, a tendency to nag, a proclivity for blaming misfortunes on the authorities or on the circumstances." When a board of arbitrators ruled against Leblanc's financial claims, he became deeply depressed. On January 16, 1806, at the age of 63, he committed suicide by shooting himself in the head.

Leblanc's process survived him. Within several decades, it was almost the only one used to produce washing soda for the textile, soap, glass, and papermaking industries. And eventually his synthetic sodium carbonate put the barilla and kelp collectors out of business.

Lamentably, Leblanc's method produced as much pollution as soda and devastated entire communities. For each ton of washing soda made, three-quarters of a ton of intensely acidic hydrogen chloride gas spewed into the air. Raining down as hydrochloric acid, it turned trees and hedges into gaunt skeletons and poisoned farmland. Tens of thousands of tons of sulfur compounds were piled around the factories. As hydrochloric acid poured into waterways, it combined with the sulfur to make hydrogen sulfide gas, spreading a rotten egg smell for miles around.

In France, local municipalities with one foul-smelling factory had the power to ban the construction of additional chemical plants. Napoleon also decreed that all factories emitting unpleasant odors should be rated according to the seriousness of the problem. When Leblanc factories got some of the worst scores, they were banned near human habitation. Later, however, both Leblanc and Lavoisier became French national heroes, martyrs of progress. Factory towns named streets after Leblanc, and industrialists commissioned his statue. In 1856—at the peak of the Leblanc pollution in

Britain—the French National Academy of Sciences concluded that "scarcely anyone has done so much for industry and received so little reward as did Le Blanc."

In Britain, Leblanc pollution went uncontrolled for decades. A visitor outside Liverpool, a major Leblanc factory center, described in 1846 "a sordid ugly town. The sky is a low-hanging roof of smeary smoke. The atmosphere is a blend of railway tunnel, hospital ward, gas works and open sewer. The features of the place are chimneys, furnaces, steam jets, smoke clouds and coal mines. The products are pills, coal, glass, chemicals, cripples, millionaires and paupers." An estimated 40,000 men, women, and children—many of them Irish escaping the potato famine—worked in British Leblanc factories. Until 1875, workers stirred batches of chemicals in a cloud of hydrochloric acid gas. Their teeth decayed, and their clothing burned. Inhaling deeply could make them faint and vomit.

Antipollution legislation was hampered in Great Britain by the fact that only the national government had power to act. By locating Leblanc factories in areas with ineffective local governments, manufacturers operated free of regulation for 30 years. The pollution from Leblanc factories mingled with the smell of privies, coal-burning stoves, and smoke from other heavy industry. When frantic property owners sued, judges ruled—correctly—that the harm caused by one company could not be separated from the damage caused by others. Factory owners argued that chemical fumes disinfected the air and benefited residents and workers.

Though workers died of industrial diseases, most Victorians considered Leblanc factories enormously beneficial, at least for the people who did not have to live or work near them. The public's demand for cotton clothing continued unabated and, not surprisingly, many Victorians viewed pollution as a necessary sign of progress for the greater good.

In response to conditions in Leblanc towns the beginnings of an environmental movement developed. Among the social reformers and writers who protested were Charles Dickens, Disraeli, Mrs. Gaskell, and Émile Zola.

Economics, aided by scientific and engineering advances, gradually cleaned up much of the Leblanc pollution. Early Leblanc factories varied widely in their ability to produce pure washing soda, so quality testing, especially after Dalton introduced his atomic theory in 1810, introduced quality control to the chemistry industry. Engineers designed seals to transport gases from one part of a factory to another without leaks and built tall chimneys to spread the noxious gases on Europe's prevailing westerly winds as far as Scandinavia.

The most effective antipollution measure, however, was recycling chemical wastes to lower the price of Leblanc soda and keep it competitive. Between 1815 and 1860, soda factory engineers gradually learned how to capture waste pollutants for recycling or sale. Using the by-product, sulfur, to make commercially valuable sulfuric acid became particularly important. Soon factories making glass, paper, sulfuric acid, hydrochloric acid, nitric acid, bleaching powder, various chemical salts, and other heavy chemicals sprang up around the Leblanc plants to take advantage of their by-products.

In economic terms, recycling Leblanc by-products established the first vertical or integrated chemical industry in which various factories derived raw materials from one another. As a result, the industrial map of Europe was shaped by Leblanc washing soda factories and their neighbors in Liverpool, Glasgow, and Tyneside, Great Britain; Marseilles, France; and Basle and Zurich, Switzerland. The United States had no Leblanc factories of its own, but participated in the trade indirectly as Liverpool's biggest washing soda customer. In a real sense, Nicolas Leblanc's process had become *the* chemical industry.

In 1863, the British Parliament passed the Alkali Act, which forced the LeBlanc factories to reclaim 95 percent of the hydrochloric acid gas that they produced. Angus Smith, the Alkali Inspector assigned to enforce the law, demonstrated that industrial towns suffered from higher sulfate levels than did the countryside. When Angus Smith also coined the term *acid rain*, air pollution became a public issue. By the 1870s, Leblanc factories emitted less than 0.1 percent of the hydrochloric acid gas they produced; the rest was reclaimed and sold.

Surprisingly, Britain's hard-fought reforms cost factory owners little. The summer after an industrialist spent £300 to install the towers required by the Alkali Act, nearby fruit trees that had not blossomed in years bloomed and roses grew. Unfortunately, reformers could not convince the government to ban the release of hydrogen sulfide too; new technology could control the release of hydrochloric acid gas, but not hydrogen sulfide gas.

As Leblanc factories were cleaning themselves up, people started to soap themselves up on a regular basis too. After centuries of avoiding soap, Leblanc's discovery was turning the product into an everyday part of modern life. In the end, it revolutionized personal cleanliness and made washable clothing available to all. Cheap soap also prevented scabies, an itching skin disease almost forgotten by modern bathers. To lay its eggs, a minute human mite, *Acarus humanus*, burrows into the skin between the fingers, under the breasts, and on the penis, wrists, armpits, and inner thighs. The creatures cause exquisite, almost uncontrollable itching. Open sores form, fester, and can be fatal. Scabies was a major public health problem and packed the enormous hospitals of Paris, Vienna, and other large European cities. When the British government removed its soap tax in 1853, the price of soap dropped, and for the first time in centuries, the incidence of scabies plummeted. Soap, water, clean clothes, and body-covering lotions treated scabies effectively and also reduced the incidence of typhus (Chapter 8).

In the United States—where the inhabitants were considered "filthy, bordering on the beastly"—basins, pitchers, and washstands did not become middle-class essentials until after 1850. During the American Civil War, the North adopted Florence Nightingale's nursing reforms to popularize hygiene and keep its soldiers disease-free.

By the beginning of the twentieth century, personal cleanliness was a veritable badge of respectability throughout the United States, and the line dividing the middle class from the great unwashed was covered with soap-suds. Nicolas Leblanc's washing soda was making soap as well as cheap cotton clothing available to the public at large, and finally, after decades of hesitancy, people were lathering it on themselves.

The Leblanc factories were finally shut down by two entirely new and clean methods of making alkalis. In 1863, a Belgian chemist, Ernst Solvay, designed a pollution-free tower to make washing soda from salt and limestone, the same ingredients that Leblanc had used. But instead of sulfur, Solvay used ammonium compounds as intermediates. Completely recycling the ammonia, Solvay's process outclassed Leblanc's on every front. Solvay made millions and gave them all away to charity before his death. In turn, Solvay's tower was replaced by the first clean *and* smokeless process after an American designed an electrolytic system in 1892. It used the hydroelectric power generated at Niagara Falls to transform salt into an alternate alkali, sodium hydroxide, called caustic soda. This clean process became the method used in the United States to produce alkalis. In 1918, the last Leblanc factory in Britain closed its doors for good, 123 years after Nicolas Leblanc discovered his famous process.

2

Color and William Henry Perkin

March 12, 1838–July 14, 1907

Nursing alcohol lamps and charcoal fires in his tiny home laboratory during the Easter vacation of 1856, a teenager slowly teased out the constituents of a black and tarry goo. Working nights, weekends, and holidays on chemistry, he was searching for a test-tube substitute for quinine, the antimalaria drug derived from plants. The black precipitate he had made was obviously not quinine, but the youth was well trained in chemistry, so he did not throw it out. Instead, he treated it with alcohol, and a fabulously intense purple appeared. Then he tested the purple on a piece of silk.

William Henry Perkin, an 18-year-old working in the back room and outdoor shed of his London home, had discovered in black coal tar a beautiful purple dye that would change the world. For the first time in history, color could be democratized. William Henry Perkin and his purple, later known as "mauve," rescued the poor and middle classes from their age-old austerity of hues. Natural dyes were expensive and, before Perkin's synthetic mauve, millions of poor people lived their lives in untreated drab and dingy fibers. Even for the middle class, pieces of brilliantly dyed cloth were treasures to be reused from garment to garment and from year to year. It was the schoolboy William Henry Perkin and his successors who would give the world the ample abundance of tints that only the rich had previously enjoyed.

While Nicolas Leblanc and his washing soda helped start the bulk chemical industry, Perkin's mauve spawned the world's dye and pharmaceutical drug industries. His synthetic dye was the first in a cascade of colors that institutionalized scientific research, professionalized chemists, changed the economies of vast regions, and helped make turn-of-the-century Germany the world's leading industrial power. Perkin was an adolescent college dropout, but his work dramatized the technological power of science and ushered in our uniquely science-oriented epoch. With the possible exception of Apple creators Steven Jobs and Steven Wozniak, college dropouts who developed the first ready-made personal computer in their teens and twenties, it is difficult to imagine a young person's invention that has started such an enormous revolution. And except for the games and cartoons that popularized computer software, it is hard to think of many other revolutions spawned by sheer frivolous fun, for it was the fashion tastes of women that powered the color revolution.

As a youngster growing up in London's East End, William Henry Perkin busied himself with carpentry, levers and screws, studies of steam engines, and painting. For a short time, he thought about becoming an artist. When a young friend showed him some simple chemical experiments involving crystals, the 13-year-old Perkin began dreaming instead about an apprenticeship in an apothecary's shop. Pharmacy was the closest field to chemistry that he could imagine.

Science was not a part of the regular educational curriculum in England, but a gifted teacher at Perkin's school gave twice-weekly chemistry lectures and demonstrations during the lunch hour. Recognizing William Henry's interest, Thomas Hall appointed the boy his lecture assistant, and together they worked happily through many a noontime meal. Two years later, Hall recommended that the youth attend the Royal College of Chemistry. One of Britain's first institutions devoted solely to teaching and research in chemistry, it later became part of Imperial College. At first, the elder Perkin was dismayed. He was an architect and a builder, and he wanted his son to become an architect too.

Although we do not know precisely how Thomas Hall convinced Perkin's father that chemistry was a laudable career, it is easy to imagine. Cloth making was the world's largest and most important manufacturing activity in the mid-nineteenth century. With the British textile industry expanding to dress the world, supporting industries and technologies were pushed to their limits. World demand for cheap and washable cotton fabric was insatiable, and it forced the invention of new technologies in machine tools, gas lighting, structural engineering, power generation and transmission, mass production, mechanization, marketing, and transportation. William Henry wanted to be a scientist, and chemistry was the closest science to the textile revolution and its remarkable ability to create great fortunes overnight.

Whatever Hall said to Perkin's father, the teacher was persuasive because the 15-year-old enrolled at the Royal College in 1853. Five years later, Perkin would be rich. At the college, he studied with August Wilhelm Hofmann, a German chemist who had come to London at the personal invitation of Queen Victoria's German husband, Prince Albert. The Prince and his agricultural and industrial allies wanted Hofmann to import Germany's new laboratory-based methods of teaching chemistry to England. Prince Albert hoped Hofmann could teach young Englishmen to use chemistry to solve important commercial problems concerning natural dyes, drugs, and other essential commodities. Thus, when Perkin finally got his father's permission to enroll at the Royal College of Chemistry, the boy entered the most up-to-date school in England for learning how to use chemistry to solve practical problems.

Like many chemists of his day, Professor Hofmann was analyzing and testing compounds extracted from natural sources. In particular, he was investigating the chemicals in coal tar, an abundant waste by-product of coke production and coal gas lighting. Coke was used to make the iron machinery that mechanized the Industrial Revolution. Coal gas made a brighter, safer, and cheaper light than either tallow candles or whale oil lamps. Because customers with gas lighting paid lower fire insurance premiums, its yellow glow was spreading rapidly through urbanized Europe. With gaslights, even the middle classes could read in the evenings, entertain, and enjoy bright and showy colors.

Located on the outskirts of big cities, coal gas factories produced enormous amounts of pollutants, particularly ammonia-rich water and coal tar. Some of the coal tar was used to make pitch to waterproof ships, roofs, and rope. Some was turned into creosote for preserving wooden railway ties, used by the millions during the railroad boom of the 1840s. But Europe did not have enough roofs, ships, and railroads to absorb all the coal tar that was being produced, so most of it was dumped, often into rivers. Hofmann was eager to learn more about its composition and find uses for it.

Coal tar intrigued early chemists because it was their main source of a host of complicated and stable organic chemicals that are made today from petroleum and natural gas. One of Hofmann's most gifted students, Charles Blachford Mansfield, developed the fractional distillation and freezing of coal tar. His techniques produced pure benzene, which started the dry cleaning industry, and phenol, which started Joseph Lister's antiseptic surgery. Mansfield himself was severely burned in a laboratory accident, and the young man died a slow and agonizing death.

Comparing chemicals that Mansfield obtained from coal tar with chemicals from other sources, Hofmann made a surprising discovery. Some of the constituents of coal tar were similar to a chemical obtained from the natural blue dye, indigo, called the king of dyes. The chemical, derived from the coal tar hydrocarbon benzene, was named aniline for the Portuguese word for indigo.

At the time, little was known about the internal structure of compounds or about how one compound was transformed into another. Chemists concentrated instead on the proportions of various chemicals in a substance. Hofmann realized that the proportions of ingredients in the anti-malaria drug quinine—"20 equivalents of carbon, 11 equivalents of hydrogen, 1 equivalent of nitrogen, and 2 equivalents of oxygen"—were almost identical to those in aniline. The difference was only "two equivalents of water." Hofmann speculated that he might be able to turn aniline into quinine. With European colonization headed toward the tropics, the drug was desperately needed.

Recognizing Perkin's ability and ambition, Hofmann made Perkin his research and staff assistant. The youth had his own ideas about how to make quinine, but his work for Hofmann left him little time at school to pursue them. So, over Easter vacation in 1856, Perkin decided to work on the problem at home.

Perkin began with a coal tar derivative with almost the same formula as quinine but without as much oxygen. Mixing the compound with an oxidizing agent, potassium dichromate, produced only an unpromising and dirty-looking, reddish-brown precipitate. The process sparked his interest, though, and he decided to try oxidizing a simpler base that would be easier to understand. He chose aniline, the coal tar compound in indigo dye. This time, adding oxygen and removing hydrogen produced a black precipitate. Treating it with ethyl alcohol, he discovered that it made a ravishingly beautiful purple dye.

Some historians have speculated that Perkin discovered his synthetic dye after spilling some of the solution on his worktable and sopping it up with a silk cloth. But an accident like that hardly seems necessary. Perkin and a young friend who was interested in art had already discovered one chemical with the properties of a dye. Moreover, the textile industry was the biggest employer of chemists, and the most scientifically advanced chemical industries involved dyes and cotton printing.

The natural dyes industry was also a large, sophisticated, and worldwide employer. Master dyers made a wide range of reasonably fast colors and handed down secret dye recipes to their apprentices. Europe's two staple dyes were madder red from the Mediterranean and indigo blue from India. Other natural dyes included violet from lichens; dark red from the forget-me-not family; brown from African aloe plants; and black from tumorlike plant galls. But natural dyes remained quite expensive, and colored fabrics were still a luxury for most of the world's population. Growers of natural dyes were also hard-pressed to keep up with the accelerating demands of the cotton textile industry. The need for more plentiful and cheaper dyes was fast becoming a bottleneck threatening the expansion of the entire industry.

As a result, many chemists were hunting for ways to synthesize artificial dyes during the 1850s. Some of these synthetic dyes were already in production although they were not fast; that is, they changed color when washed or exposed to light. A flashy synthetic canary yellow for silk and wool, for example, was one such "fugitive" color; here today, gone tomorrow, as it were. Another popular dye, a purple made from uric acid extracted from Peruvian bird droppings, faded fast in London's polluted acid air.

Thus, given the demands of the textile industry, a well-trained young chemist like Perkin would have been alive to the dyeing possibilities in a beautiful purple solution. After experimenting with the solution on silk, Perkin realized he had discovered a process for transforming the chemicals in coal tar into a colorfast purple dye.

That spring, Perkin mailed a precious sample of his purple to a Scottish dye firm. After exposing the sample to sunlight, the company's owner, Robert Pullar, wrote back that Perkin's mauve had kept its color better than any other lilac on the market. "If your discovery does not make the goods too expensive, it is decidedly one of the most valuable that has come out for a very long time. This colour is one which has been very much wanted in all classes of goods, and could not be obtained fast on silks, and only at great expense on cotton yarns."

Perkin came from a closely knit family, and that summer he and his brother, Thomas Dix Perkin, worked long hours together to produce a few ounces of the dye. By August 26, 1856, they had enough to apply for a patent. Perkin's father was not rich, but by this time he was excited by chemistry's commercial possibilities. He decided to gamble his modest savings on his younger son. Thomas, who had good business instincts, signed on full time as the family administrator.

"High-tech" start-ups were in the spirit of the times; the Perkins were starting their company during one of the most scientifically and technologically creative periods in human history. In addition to Lister's antiseptic surgery, Charles Darwin would publish *The Origin of Species*, the Atlantic telegraph cable would connect Europe with America, and Pasteur would show that microorganisms cause fermentation and disease. Anything seemed possible.

Curiously, William Henry worried that spinning off a chemical discovery for manufacture might be a bit beneath the dignity of a scientist like himself. That autumn, when he told Professor Hofmann that he was starting his own business, the professor was annoyed and downright discouraging. Perkin was a retiring sort of person, and at first he thought Hofmann might be right. Perhaps leaving science for industry would ruin his future. But instead of buckling under, Perkin dropped out of college and plunged ahead with his purple dye. He promised himself that later in life he would return to scientific research.

The Perkin family soon bought a rural property near a canal northwest of London, far from the city's new antipollution regulations. At this point, few of William Henry's friends or relatives had so much as glimpsed the inside of a chemical factory. Perkin's knowledge of manufacturing came only from books, but his ignorance was not a serious drawback. Because no one had ever built the kind of equipment he needed or planned such a chemical process before, there was little to imitate.

"It was, in fact, pioneering work all the way," Perkin said. When potential customers complained that his dye should adhere more tightly to fiber, Perkin discovered that adding tannin would do the job. When told that dyeing silk in large quantities made streaks, he figured out that dyeing in a soap bath produced a pure and even color. Although benzene was not yet mass-produced for the dry cleaning industry, he located a supplier. Finally, he struggled long and hard to design and build an airtight apparatus that was safe enough to handle benzene and highly concentrated sulfuric and nitric acids. Within a year and a half of discovering his mauve, the 19-year-old Perkin delivered a batch of his chemical to London's biggest silk dyer. Many of his technological breakthroughs would clear the way for the host of new synthetic coal tar dyes that was to come.

Yet the youth was far from satisfied. The big money was not in dyeing silk for the rich—it was in printing cheap cottons for the masses. Today it is difficult to imagine the excitement that cotton fabrics met in Europe. For more than 15 centuries the three main fabrics had been wool, linen, and—for the wealthy—silk. When European nations began importing goods from the East in the seventeenth century, cottons from India seemed quite exotic. In 1670, Molière's bourgeois gentleman announced proudly, "I have had these Indian fabrics made. . . . My tailor has told me that fashionable people wear such gowns in the morning."

Cottons could be finely woven, washed, and painted or printed with bright colors. They were novelties, as light and comfortable to wear as they were moderate in price. When French Protestant Huguenots began printing on white cloth from India, the fabric proved so popular that the government banned it in 1681 because it competed with French-made silk. The Huguenot dyers moved to Switzerland and continued printing calicos there.

The French aristocracy spent the next 75 years smuggling cotton prints. Customs officials patrolled the streets of Paris and ordered women to strip off their cotton dresses on the spot. Hours after 800 of her cotton gowns were confiscated and her four bales of cotton fabrics were burned, the Marquise de Nesle promenaded through the Tuilleries in Paris in yet another cotton dress. Even the king's mistress, Madame de Pompadour, decorated her apartments with cotton prints. Ladies dressed legally in silk as they rode in their carriages to parties; then they changed at their hostesses' into more fashionable printed cottons. When cotton printing was finally legalized again in 1716, the French had to relearn the craft from abroad.

Cotton factories were accustomed to using acidic vegetable dyes, however, and Perkin's mauve was a base that required different chemical processing. Only with great difficulty could the young man convince older, skeptical dyers to try his new product. And once he had convinced them of its worth, he had to solve a wealth of their production problems. Bankrolled by his father, Perkin set off alone on an exhausting tour of northern England and Scotland. Visiting one textile factory after another as a troubleshooter, he originated the kind of technical support that chemical companies routinely provide for clients today.

Ultimately, it was neither Perkin's technical skill nor his salesmanship that turned the organic chemical industry into a major economic force. It was mauve mania. Just before Perkin discovered his synthetic dye, the fashionable world was swept by a craze for a natural purple dye made from lichen plants. The color was supposed to be reminiscent of ancient imperial Rome and the mysteries of the Levant. Crinolines had been introduced two years before, and a natural French purple was the most elegant color to flounce over them. It was also the most fast and brilliant shade of readily available purple ever seen. A bright, clear pinkish lavender, it was named mauve for a French wildflower. As the American artist James Whistler put it somewhat disdainfully, "Mauve is just pink trying to be purple." Mauve was a special favorite of the French Empress Eugenie, and Queen Victoria wore it at her daughter's marriage and in a velvet train at one of her own levées. Mauve mania spread from the French and British courts through Europe, North America, and the Far East. The satiric magazine, *Punch*, joked that "Mauve Measles" was either a mild British form of insanity or a very catching French epidemic.

In any event, when Perkin's synthetic mauve became available in 1859, it brought the royals' natural lavender within the budget of the middle and working classes. A dyer wrote Perkin proclaiming, "I am glad to hear that a rage for your colour has set in among that *all-powerful* class of the community—the Ladies. If they once take a mania for it and you can supply the demand, your fame and fortune are secure."

At 21 years of age, Perkin was starting an entire industry based on coal tar products. His mauve represented the first multistep industrial synthesis of a completely new organic compound. New technologies were compounding the already enormous demand for brightly colored dyes and fabrics. Only a decade or so before Perkin discovered his purple, roller printing machines began mechanically printing more than one color at a time. Lock-stitch sewing machines invented in the United States were entering clothing factories, department stores were turning shopping into entertainment for the leisured classes, and the new transcontinental railroad would soon whiz mass-produced fabric and clothing across North America. The clothing revolution desperately needed synthetic dyes that were cheap, fast to sunlight and laundering, standardized and consistent, and quick and easy to apply.

Confident that he could supply such dyes, Perkin felt financially secure enough to marry Jemima Harriet Lissett. The first of their two sons was born a year later. The young father posed for a photograph. A bushy dark beard that stretched from the cleft of his chin to his ears made him look reassuringly older than 22.

Then, as suddenly as it had appeared, mauve mania was over and the elegant world whirled on to a new color. A magnificent red never seen before in dyes, the French hue was variously named fuchsia for the flower blossom and magenta for a northern Italian town where the Emperor Napoleon III had defeated Austria that summer. Like Perkin's mauve, magenta was a wildly popular synthetic dye with humble origins in coal tar, that is, in aniline and other similar compounds.

If Perkin's mauve launched the fevered race, magenta raised the stakes as three world powers—France, Britain, and Germany—competed fiercely for industrial hegemony. Within five years of Perkin's mauve, 28 dye manufacturers sprang up in France, Britain, Germany, Austria, and Switzerland. The predecessors of chemical giants—Hoechst, Bayer, Agfa, Ciba, Geigy, and BASF (the Badische Aniline und Soda Fabrik)—began their corporate lives making magenta. For the next 20 years, chemical dye makers competed through bribery, industrial espionage, patent fights, court suits, legal and illegal exports, cartel arrangements, industrial pollution—and a series of spectacular colors.

Shifting rapidly, the dye industry moved from Britain to France and then, after a few years, on to Germany. Fashion sped from purples through golden yellows to crimsons and finally to indigo blue. Along the way, color chemists produced a masterwork, the Belle Epoque palette of purples, greens, blues, yellows, oranges, and even brilliant blacks.

A kaleidoscope of sparkling colors emerged from coal tar's black sludge. How could an infant industry manufacture so many new products so quickly? First, by varying the fixing agent (the mordant) on cotton, chemists could make one dye produce a range of colors, from an intense dark red to pastel peach or from light orange to black. Even a glowing magenta could be toned down to baby pink.

Second, one dye-making process often led to others. Chemists learned to vary their recipes, as cooks do in kitchens. Treating magenta with other chemicals, for example, produced purples, blues, or greens. Accustomed to testing and analyzing compounds, chemists were now synthesizing them too.

Economics drove the industry as well. Dye molecules are complex, and they are synthesized in multistep, multi-ingredient processes. No single dye could pay for the enormous investment required. Moreover, since many dyes could be made in several different ways, competing companies drove prices down. To survive, chemical firms had to continually design new dyes. Soon color chemists, including Germans in English textile plants, earned high salaries and consulting fees.

The new colors fascinated the public and scientists alike. Perkin was only 24 years old when he was invited to lecture at the illustrious Chemical Society in London on May 16, 1861. The world's leading experimental physicist, Michael Faraday, came to hear the young man speak. A year later, when the International Exhibition was held in London, coal tar colors—mauve, aniline blue, yellow, and imperial purple—attracted excited crowds. In an area devoted to chemical products, the public gaped at glass cases filled with silks, cashmeres, ostrich plumes, and the like. They were dyed, as Professor Hofmann reported, "crimsons of the most gorgeous intensity, purples of more than Tyrian magnificence, and blues ranging from light azure to the deepest cobalt. . . . the most delicate roseate hues, shading by imperceptible gradations to the softest tints of violet and mauve." Next to them were samples of black coal tar and of the dyes themselves, some of them beautifully crystalline. In one case, Hofmann thought they resembled "the sparkling wings of a rose-beetle."

Hofmann himself made a fabulously brilliant violet that replaced Perkin's mauve, even though the professor's dye was not as fast as his student's. Dyers thought no one would want fleeting tints, but, no matter, the experts were wrong. Women craved raucous and dramatic hues; they dressed in plum purple trimmed with brilliant blue or in royal edged with scarlet. A color's fastness in light or laundries was immaterial; parasols shielded ladies' complexions *and* their gowns.

National market shares shifted as fast as fashion taste. Five years after the London exhibition, another international fair was held in Paris. By then, the dyes market had tripled in value, although French dye companies—like some of their colors—were fading. Their chemists were emigrating to Switzerland where future chemical giants, including Novartis' forerunners, Ciba and Geigy, would flourish.

Meanwhile, the fashion public's craze for sheer brilliancy was passing, and fastness was becoming important again. Aldehyde green was the first green that did not look blue in gas lighting; when the beautiful Empress Eugenie wore an aldehyde green silk dress to the gaslit Paris Opera, the audience was amazed when her gown looked green the entire evening. Manufacturers returned to the search for consistent color, ease and speed of application, and low price.

The relentless search for new and cheaper colors produced its own casualties. The Empress' aldehyde green was swept aside by iodine green, methyl green, malachite green, and so on. Natural dyes were also falling by the wayside. Canary Island farmers who raised cacti for tiny cochineal beetles were bankrupted; 70,000 of the dried beetles made only 1 pound of crimson dye, and the new synthetic colors were much cheaper.

With the public dazzled by color and companies desperate to survive, factors such as clean air, pure water, and workers' safety paled in importance. In a hasty pencil sketch of his family factory in England, Perkin drew one- or two-story buildings with tall brick chimneys and smoke blowing merrily out their tops. Water for the Perkins' factory came from an artesian well, and waste was, no doubt, dumped in the handy canal.

By this time, Perkin was just one of many competitors in the race he had started. After the death of his first wife, he remarried and had five more children. With a large family to support, he could hardly rest on his laurels. Like many other chemists, he began exploring the ramifications of the new structural organic chemistry. In 1859, the German chemist, Friedrich August Kekulé, showed how carbon atoms link together in long chains and rings to form organic compounds. Another German, Adolf Baeyer, demonstrated that heating complicated organic molecules with zinc breaks these molecules down into familiar, simpler compounds. Serendipitous discoveries such as Perkin's mauve would no longer suffice.

Using his new understanding of structural chemistry, Perkin studied one of the most important natural dyes known: madder red. Madder roots, native to Asia, had been grown for decades in southern Europe for their radiant and reasonably colorfast Turkey red dye. Depending on what chemicals were used with them, madder could also color fabric brown, violet, purple, or black. If Perkin could synthesize the active red agent in madder plants, he would achieve a major and highly profitable breakthrough.

Perkin's first project as a schoolboy in Hofmann's laboratory a decade before had been to analyze the coal tar product, anthracene. Thanks to those studies, Perkin could appreciate a French schoolmaster's discovery of the close relationship between anthracene and alizarin, the red dye in madder plants. Choosing a formidably stable relative of anthracene from among some chemicals left over from his student project, Perkin tried to break it apart into simpler compounds. Adapting Baeyer's method, he heated his compound almost to the boiling point with acid. Treating the products chemically, Perkin discovered that he had made alizarin. To manufacture it cheaply, however, Perkin would need ample supplies of anthracene. It was easy enough to make from tar but few tar distilleries even knew the compound existed. As a result, Perkin's brother visited almost every coal tar factory in Britain to teach manufacturers how to separate the anthracene from tar. In return, Perkin promised to buy all the anthracene that they could make.

It hardly seemed possible, but when Perkin applied for his alizarin red patent on June 26, 1869, he learned that a group of German chemists had beaten him to it—by one, heartbreaking day. Although Perkin lost the patent race, the Germans agreed to share his technology and create a cartel. The demand for alizarin's brilliant crimson red was huge. Perkin sold 1 ton the first year, 40 tons the second year, 220 tons the third year, and so on.

Economically and politically, artificial madder red was more important than Perkin's mauve and magenta. They were new, synthetic compounds, not imitations of natural compounds. Alizarin red was one of the first artificial copies of a natural chemical to be manufactured on a large scale. The price of natural madder collapsed, and large regions were bankrupted almost overnight. Synthetic alizarin ruined the French madder farmers of Provence and Languedoc who had to switch to growing potatoes and wine grapes. Even more critically, alizarin red moved the scientific dye industry en masse from England to Germany.

Surveying the situation realistically, Perkin retired from the fray. He was tired of litigation, fires, and explosions, and he could see that Britain was losing the chemical race to Germany. Even Professor Hofmann had left England and gone home. At the age of 35, Perkin was already a millionaire, so, in 1873, he renounced manufacturing to return to the scientific research he had loved in his youth.

Perkin was right about the decline of Britain's chemical industry. By 1880, Germany's chemical firms controlled half the world market in coal tar dyes. Great Britain had the world's largest textile industry, the biggest investment banks, lots of coal, and a heavy chemical industry, but it manufactured virtually no dyes. Critics blamed Britain's shrinking chemical industry on Perkin's retirement and Hofmann's return to Germany; on Britain's poor patent laws and its lack of import tariffs and financial support for chemistry education and research; on the separation between academic chemistry and industrial practice; on the lack of social status for English chemists, and on and on. There seemed to be plenty of blame to pass around. Twenty years after Perkin launched the international battle for synthetic dyes, the contest was effectively over. Britain and France had lost; Germany had won.

Prussia (in northern Germany) was industrializing and urbanizing so quickly that onlookers called it Europe's Wild West. Building on synthetic alizarin red, Germany institutionalized chemical research. Perkin and other English inventors had established companies to exploit a product, but German firms exploited the research process itself.

Corporations invested in laboratories, professional chemists, and systematic research programs based on scientific principles. When Hoechst hired its first chemist, the investment paid off within a year with a major discovery. The Bayer Company, founded to make dyes shortly after Perkin introduced his mauve, financed a laboratory during the 1890s with 122 chemists, a library that subscribed to 500 journals, a bureau that patented discoveries, and a department that did nothing but abstract articles from foreign journals. Unlike their British counterparts, many German factories hired chemists as managers and gave them a share in the profits.

Like the early Leblanc washing soda factories in Britain, the early German chemical industry caused social and environmental havoc as it met consumers' needs. The German dye industry settled in the Wupper Valley just south of the Ruhr. Natural madder red had dyed the Wupper River for decades, and as factory owners switched from madder red to synthetic alizarin red, the river simply changed its red tint too. Dye firms made magenta with arsenic acid, and factory owners dumped their arsenic wastes into the North Sea or, through secret pipes, into the Wupper River on its way to the Rhine. Bayer dumped so much arsenic waste on its grounds that sick neighbors lined up weekly for compensation checks, and Bayer eventually moved downstream.

Continuous exposure to aniline vapors and arsenic compounds ulcerated workers' noses, lips, and throats. Hoechst employees left work covered with red dye. When Hoechst discovered in 1873 a safer way to make magenta with nitrobenzene instead of arsenic, the new process became the industry standard. In turn, nitrobenzene contaminated nearby wells. The Wupper River became famous as one of the most ill-used rivers in the world. The adjacent Ruhr valley was treated as an industrial preserve that workers entered at their own risk. Scientists did not know how to investigate water quality. And until the cholera epidemics of the nineteenth century terrified the public (Chapter 4), air and water pollution seemed unimportant.

In the meantime, German companies geared up to attack the biggest dye problem of all: indigo, the "king of dyes." For centuries, farmers in India had grown a native bush, *Indigofera tinctoria*, for its dye-rich branches. Introduced to Europe in the sixteenth century, indigo dye bankrupted the German farmers who raised woad, the only source of blue known to medieval Europe. Indigo, a more potent source of blue dye, provided a wide range of hues from darkest navy through bright blues to the palest pastels. When the British took over India in the mid-eighteenth century, they expanded indigo farming. Indigo was the most important British colonial dye exported and the last important natural dyestuff sold.

The first salvo in the attack on indigo occurred when the great chemist Adolf Baeyer succeeded in synthesizing the color in 1880. His laboratory process was astronomically expensive, but the hunt for cheaper ingredients would be herculean. Such a project could bankrupt even the largest companies, so they protected themselves by forming price-fixing cartels. It took BASF 17 years, an enormous sum of money, and an accident to discover a factory-scale method for synthesizing indigo. The accident occurred when a laboratory worker broke a thermometer and its mercury spilled out, contaminating—and catalyzing—a key reaction.

Within three years, German firms were making as much synthetic indigo as a quarter of a million acres of Indian farmland could produce. By 1913, sales of natural indigo had dropped from 3.5 million to 60,000 pounds. Indian indigo growers were ruined, and, if Britain had not insisted on her colony's continuing to grow indigo for a while longer, one million acres of farmland could have become available immediately for food crops. By 1968, even before indigo blue jeans became fashionable, half of India's landmass would have been needed to meet world demand for indigo dyes.

Coupling large-scale science and technology to synthesize indigo, German dye companies branched out into pharmaceutical and photographic chemicals. Experimenting with dyes, the German chemist Paul Ehrlich had discovered that methylene blue dye has a special affinity for living nerve cells. Realizing that some dyes are absorbed only by particular kinds of cells, Ehrlich wondered whether other dyestuffs would selectively stain disease-causing organisms. If so, he thought he could use them to destroy pathogens without harming other human tissues.

Formalizing the give-and-take that had long characterized the dye industry's relationship with scientific research, Hoechst financed a research institute for Ehrlich. Hoechst offered him a percentage of the profits on his discoveries in return for the license to develop them. By 1892, Hoechst was making Ehrlich's great discovery, Salvaran, the first cure for syphilis. Through similar arrangements with other scientists, Hoechst made a wide variety of medical products: a diphtheria serum that saved 50,000 young-sters yearly in Germany alone; a tetanus antitoxin; Novocain, the first syn-thetic anesthetic; a tuberculosis diagnostic test; a serum against foot and mouth disease; an adrenaline substitute; and the first insulin manufactured in Germany. Bayer, which had made heroin to ease the coughs of TB patients and to satisfy the cravings of drug addicts, switched to marketing aspirin for headaches, pain, and fever.

Dye companies also expanded into explosives. Before about 1850, gun-powder was the only blasting powder for building railroads and for mining. Alfred Nobel's nitroglycerine made dynamite reasonably safe for construc-tion use. But some dyes are also unstable compounds that explode. For example, picric acid yellow, a flashy canary yellow tint, became a new explosive. A chemist at a major Manchester dye factory once carried a flask of this dangerously unstable coal tar dye in the passenger compartment of a Manchester-to-London train to an arsenal to be tested as a detonating com-pound. In 1887, some of the compound blew up and destroyed the Man-chester dye factory.

As the chemical industry expanded, Perkin continued his own scientific research in the peace of his private laboratory. He had not lost his touch. Among the synthetic methods he discovered is one now called the Perkin reaction. He used it to make a synthetic substitute for a vegetable substance called coumarin, which has a pleasant, vanillalike odor. Coumarin spawned the synthetic perfume business and made luxurious scents available to all. Once again, a Perkin chemical started a new industry, albeit a modest one in comparison with dyes and pharmaceuticals. Despite the worldwide impact of Perkins' discoveries, he was not knighted by the British monarchy until 1906, the fiftieth anniversary of his discovery of mauve. The world chem-istry community feted him lavishly that year, and he traveled to the United States collecting further honors. A year later, at the age of 69, he died peace-fully, at home.

Thus, Perkin did not live to see the German coal tar dye industry that he had launched dominate World War I. In the first great technological war in history, German dye factories switched easily from making dye chemicals to producing military explosives and war gases. With no dye industries of their own, Britain and France sent their soldiers to war in khaki, blue, and red uniforms dyed with Swiss chemicals. The French government had protected some of its madder farmers by giving them a monopoly on dyeing army uniforms, so French soldiers marched to the front lines in bright madder red pants, easy targets for German sharpshooters. Two German U-boats clandestinely delivered 800 tons of dyes and pharmaceuticals to New York and Baltimore in 1916 to pay for rubber and strategic metals. A Bayer executive joked that, without the dyes, a long war might convert Americans to all-white fashions. Bayer's fears, even if true, were quite unnecessary. By then, the lives of even ordinary people had been imbued with a fabulous rainbow of colors, and no one could imagine surviving without them. Perkin's mauve revolution had triumphed.

3

Sugar and Norbert Rillieux

March 17, 1806–October 8, 1894

Norbert Rillieux, the man who sweetened our lives with sugar, was a straight-talking, free African American in slave-holding Louisiana and a cousin of the French Impressionist painter Edgar Degas. Norbert Rillieux's triple-effect evaporator helped fill the world's sweet tooth with cakes and candies. His invention, used today wherever large amounts of liquid must be evaporated, fills our kitchen cupboards with powders and our medicine cabinets with pills and capsules. It condenses and powders milk and makes instant coffee, soup, meat extracts, gelatin, and glue. It also distills petroleum, makes seawater potable, and recovers wastes from dye factories, paper plants, distilleries, and nuclear reactors. All this from a sometimes testy man who would not—could not—sugarcoat his views. As a free man of color in pre-Civil War America, he knew his worth. He could be gracious with those who respected his talents, but he could be quite irritable, combative, and, as a friend put it, "excessively frank" with anyone he suspected of injustice or duplicity.

Norbert Rillieux was born on March 17, 1806, to a wealthy white man and his longtime mistress. Norbert's father, Vincent Rillieux, was a cotton merchant and engineer. His mother, Constance Vivant, was a free African American from a rich real estate family in New Orleans; she herself was the daughter of a white father and a black mother.

Vincent Rillieux freely acknowledged his family. Norbert was baptized by a Roman Catholic priest in St. Louis Cathedral, where blacks and whites knelt side by side to pray. The child's birth was registered in City Hall in a mixture of French and English as "Norbert Rillieux, quadroon libre, natural son of Vincent Rillieux and Constance Vivant." The words, *quadroon libre*, stipulated that Norbert was a free African American with more white ancestry than black.

Marital arrangements like the Rillieux's were common in New Orleans early in the nineteenth century. Reporting on his visit to New Orleans during the 1850s, Frederick Law Olmsted said, "Many . . . form so strong attachments that the arrangement is never discontinued, but becomes, indeed, that of marriage, except that it is not legalized or solemnized." Norbert's parents remained together for many years, had several more children, and Vincent Rillieux never married anyone else.

When Norbert was born, New Orleans was still a small town by modern standards. Its 8000 inhabitants included 4000 whites, 2700 slaves, and 1300 free African Americans, most of them of mixed racial heritage, like Norbert and his mother. Founded by the French 100 years earlier, the region had been under Spanish rule for 35 years before it was returned to France for sale to the United States in the Louisiana Purchase of 1803. New Orleans' French past graced the town with an opera house, cafés, cabarets, Parisian fashions, French-language signs, and gardens with orange and lemon trees, roses, myrtle, and jasmine.

Nowhere was New Orleans' Mediterranean heritage more apparent than in its race relations. In this most un-American of American cities, blacks and whites lived on the same streets, shared rooming houses, and danced, gambled, ate, drank, and made love in the same integrated places of public accommodation, despite abundant laws to the contrary. Upper-class whites hired free men of color to teach their daughters music, and black and white veterans of the Battle of New Orleans of 1812 wined and dined together at celebratory banquets.

According to oral tradition, white men courted women of mixed race at so-called quadroon balls and negotiated the terms of their relationships with the women's families. Some men settled large sums, up to $8000, on the woman of their choice. The man generally bought her a house and agreed to set aside a certain sum for their children. The connection typically lasted several years or more.

The practice, called plaçage, has become so larded with nostalgia that it is difficult to discern the heartaches it must have caused. A black mother is known to have killed her child to protect it from the white woman who owned them both; the owner hated the infant because it was her husband's child. A planter told Olmsted that he had sent his natural sons north to be educated because they could not be brought up "decently" at home.

The widespread miscegenation of a society that was formally dedicated to quasi-apartheid created some extraordinarily complex relationships and a special legal class of mixed-race African Americans, many of whom were light-skinned, educated, prosperous, and, like Norbert and his mother, free.

Louisiana's free people of color—known by the French term as *gens de couleur libre*—were legally betwixt and between. They could not vote or serve on juries, nor could they marry whites. But free African-American males could sue and testify in court and own slaves and real estate. They could also work in the building trades, an important consideration in a town with an exploding population. The ratio of skilled to unskilled workers in New Orleans was higher among free African Americans than among Irish and German immigrants.

As heirs to prime New Orleans real estate, a number of free African Americans became quite wealthy before the Civil War. Norbert Rillieux's cousins included members of some of New Orleans' richest families. A few of his cousins were so confident of their social status and their ability to "pass" as white that they signed their names without the required term *free man of color,* or *f.m.c.* Many free people of color also invested heavily in slaves. When Norbert Rillieux was in his twenties, more than 700 of New Orleans' free African Americans owned an average of three slaves apiece, often family members who were eventually freed. Each of the 23 richest free people of color in New Orleans owned between 10 and 20 slaves.

The relatively easy-going French-dominated culture of Norbert Rillieux's childhood was poised on the brink of enormous change. Louisiana's sugar cane plantations began operation a few years before Norbert Rillieux's birth, about the time that Eli Whitney's cotton gin was invented. Sugar cane, a giant perennial grass, *Saccharum genus*, originated in tropical southern Asia and was known in the Middle East and China between 8000 and 6000 B.C. Arabs used sugar as a medicine and brought it to the Mediterranean where, grown by peasants, it was an expensive luxury. The Age of Discovery was partly a search for sugar, and Christopher Columbus brought sugar cane to plant in the Caribbean islands on his second voyage in 1493.

The New World immediately established a new and intimate link between sugar and slavery. Spain, England, and France grew sugar with slave labor on their island colonies, and their product was far cheaper than European sugar cane grown with free labor. So great were the profits that Spanish colonies shipped sugar alongside silver and pearls under convoy to Europe. Sugar was a luxury well into the mid-eighteenth century. When the future queen of Hungary, Maria Theresa, was married, her wedding gifts included precious gems—and sugar.

Sugar soon became the cornerstone of the infamous triangular trade. New England sailing ships picked up molasses, a by-product of sugar refining, from the West Indies. Then they took it to New England to make rum, sold the rum to slave traders in Africa, and transported slaves back to the

West Indies sugar plantations for more molasses. As slave ownership expanded in the New World and the price of sugar dropped, sugar consumption soared in Europe and North America. In Britain, the average person consumed 15 times more sugar at the end of the eighteenth century than at the beginning. During Rillieux's lifetime in the nineteenth century, consumption would increase sevenfold.

Louisiana was the last part of the New World to adopt sugar cane. Its alluvial soil was deep and fertile, but the winters were cold, and the state lacked the technical expertise needed to adapt a tropical crop to a semitropical climate. Then, in 1791, a few years before Rillieux's birth, slaves and free blacks on the French Caribbean island of Santo Domingo revolted, and French sugar technicians fled to New Orleans. Within a few years, they opened 75 sugar mills along Louisiana's navigable waterways. With the Louisiana Purchase of 1803, Anglo-Americans and other non-French immigrants poured into New Orleans. Thus, Norbert Rillieux grew up in a boomtown: part rollicking seaport, part capital of the new sugar cane culture.

Southern Louisiana became a one-crop region during Rillieux's youth. Sugar cane was expensive to grow, and its refining consumed enormous amounts of firewood and slave labor. Each plantation needed an animal-powered mill to crush the heavy canes and release their juices and a sugarhouse to evaporate the syrup.

In the sugarhouse, the liquid from the canes was heated in open kettles, clarified with calcium oxide, skimmed of impurities, and evaporated. In a system called the Jamaica train, slaves ladled the boiling juice from one steaming pot to another around the clock for two or three months at a time. During the grinding and boiling season, men, women and children alike worked 18-hour days to keep the juices bubbling. When the concentrated syrup started to crystallize, it was cooled and further granulated. Then, the sugar was stored in a hogshead barrel with a perforated bottom that allowed the uncrystallizable molasses to drain out. The remaining sugar, called muscovado, or raw brown sugar, was shipped north for refining.

As sugar cane plantations expanded through southern Louisiana during the 1820s, Vincent Rillieux sent Norbert to Paris for his education. The most liberal and sophisticated city in Europe must have dazzled the young man from New Orleans. In cafés and coffeehouses, middle-class Parisians could read a wide range of viewpoints published in newspapers. They could travel the city in new horse-drawn municipal buses and dine publicly in the cafés and restaurants that were making French cuisine a new art form.

Most important as far as Rillieux was concerned, the French were passionately debating their laws about slavery and the slave trade. For brief periods, slavery had actually been banned in French colonies, and the slave trade had been abolished. Moreover, French artistic and scientific circles were open to mixed-race men from the sugar-producing New World. Alexandre Dumas, the popular French novelist who wrote *The Three Musketeers*, was the grandson of a French count and a black woman from Santo Domingo. Of Louisiana's free African Americans, 27 writers published poetry in French; 2 physicians trained in Paris; a composer conducted a Bordeaux orchestra; and a playwright had 21 productions staged by Parisian theaters. With many of the state's free people of color educated abroad, African Americans were often far more cosmopolitan than white Louisianans.

Norbert's father, however, surely did not send his son to France to enjoy its heady freedoms but to master its science and sugar technology. Vincent Rillieux, who had invented a steam-operated cotton-baling press, would have understood Louisiana's desperate need for modern technology.

In any case, the young Rillieux was hardworking, aggressive, and scientifically gifted, and France recognized his talents. By 1830, when Norbert was 24, he was already teaching applied mechanics at the École Centrale in Paris.

France was a center for the development of thermodynamics, the study of heat and its conversion to other forms of energy. A few years before Rillieux's arrival in Paris, the French physicist Sadi Carnot had published his studies of steam engines and described the principles that became the second law of thermodynamics, placing fundamental limits on how efficiently heat can be used. Within a few years, James Prescott Joule of England would lay the basis for the first law of thermodynamics stating the equivalence of heat and energy.

Rillieux specialized in latent heat, the extra heat energy that must be added to vaporize a liquid that is already at its boiling temperature. The extra heat is called latent because it does not raise the temperature of the liquid. The amount of latent heat needed to convert water to steam is quite large; almost seven times more heat is needed to vaporize water than to bring it from room temperature to the boiling point. When the steam condenses back to water, the latent heat reappears, making burns from steam much more serious than those from boiling water. During the 1840s, railroad boilers and steam engines made latent heat a hot scientific topic, so to speak, and Rillieux is said to have published several highly regarded articles about steam engines and power. Later he arranged the heating pipes in his sugar evaporator like the pipes in the railroad boilers that were powering the enormous expansion of Europe's railroads.

Besides heat and energy, France was also vitally interested in sugar. The French, however, were growing beets rather than sugar cane. Furthermore, they were studying the sugar-making process with a scientific passion utterly unknown in Louisiana. Scientists had known for roughly 75 years that many plants contain sucrose, and Napoleon had launched a crash program to make France independent of imported cane sugar. After Napoleon's defeat, French scientists continued their research, trying to make beet sugar grown by free farmers in France competitive with cane sugar grown by slaves in the New World. A Louisiana planter touring France reported back with wonder, "We can scarcely conceive, accustomed as we are to the routine of our sugar-houses, how ardent is the spirit of inquiry [in France] and how prompt the practical testing of any scientific discovery bearing upon this subject."

In particular, the French were trying to use the steam from sugar boilers to heat sugar juice in a vacuum and evaporate the solution at low temperatures. A vacuum lowers the atmospheric pressure on the water's surface; as a result, the water molecules can escape as steam at a lower temperature. The amount of latent heat needed to turn water into steam is nearly the same whether the water is in a vacuum or at atmospheric pressure. However, in the refining process, some heat escapes into the environment. Keeping water at a lower temperature reduces the amount of this lost heat and makes for a more efficient and potentially more profitable operation.

Well aware that the open kettles in Louisiana's Jamaica train method wasted a great deal of heat, Rillieux immediately appreciated French sugar research and soon developed his own theories about the best apparatus for sugar making. European sugar makers had been heating sugar syrup in steam-heated evaporators in a vacuum since 1812, and Rillieux envisioned using the latent heat of the steam from one kettle to reduce the syrup in other kettles. He hoped to set up a cycle in which the syrup evaporated and gave off steam, which would condense and give its latent heat for other cycles of evaporation in other kettles. According to a basic law of thermodynamics, heat will flow only to cooler bodies. To direct the latent heat through other evaporating chambers, Rillieux knew he had to lower the temperature at the same time that he kept the water at the boiling point. To do this, Rillieux thought he could build a linked series of three enclosed containers with progressively more efficient vacuums. Then the syrup in each successive pan would boil at a lower temperature, and the latent heat would flow from one to another.

Rillieux's idea was brilliant, but scaling up his laboratory experiment to a factory process would be difficult. He tried to interest French machinery manufacturers in implementing his ideas, but an agricultural depression in France made sales impossible. It would take Rillieux a decade of struggle before he had an operating system.

Rillieux's reputation as a young man with modern ideas must have reached Louisiana, however, because Edmund Forstall, a planter and banker in New Orleans, asked him to become the chief engineer of a sugar refinery under construction there. Forstall had already hired Norbert's cousin and brother, who were also young free men of color.

In what may have been an agonizing decision, Norbert Rillieux left Paris and returned to New Orleans in 1833. He was 27 years old, one of the best-educated men in Louisiana, and as up to date about physical and chemical science as anyone in the South. But he was reentering the legal limbo of a free man of color and returning to a state that was deeply committed to slavery. Although the international slave trade to the United States had been abolished in 1808, Louisiana whites continued to import slaves both illegally from Africa and legally from other slave states until Abraham Lincoln issued the Emancipation Proclamation during the Civil War.

New Orleans had changed dramatically since Rillieux's birth. Four hundred steamboats wheeled up and down the Mississippi River, and the city's population had multiplied six times. Crime was flourishing, and murders seemed to be everyday occurrences. In the golden age of New Orleans dueling, almost every white man in public life had fought at least one duel. Defending one's honor was a serious matter, and Rillieux's prickly pride may have reflected this part of his New Orleans' heritage.

New Orleans was also filthy, no different in this respect from Paris. Garbage and waste clogged the streets of both cities, and disease was epidemic. During Rillieux's last year in Paris, cholera killed 18,402 people, most of them desperately poor. The year Rillieux arrived home, yellow fever struck New Orleans; 8000 people, one-sixth of the town's population, died.

Rillieux, however, was not returning to New Orleans for amenities but for sugar cane. Sugar planters were expanding rapidly and making more money than ever before. On Rillieux's return, the owners of Louisiana's 700 sugar plantations controlled a total of 36,000 slaves, or roughly 52 slaves a plantation. In ten years, the average number of slaves per plantation would increase by almost 50 percent. With profits rolling in, a white man could buy whatever he wanted, whether at a slave auction by day or at a quadroon ball by night. Louisiana planters—and their slaves—were producing one-fifteenth of the world's sugar exports. In 20 years, they would grow one-fourth of the world's exportable sugar.

Great fortunes could be made, and Norbert Rillieux was an ambitious, energetic man. Louisiana sugar growers were wealthier than any other group of Southerners before the Civil War. John Burnside, who started his career as a peddler with a backpack, owned one of the biggest plantation operations on record. His 7600 acres were as flat as a billiard table and worth $1.5 million; his 937 slaves were valued at half a million more.

Despite their social pretensions, Louisiana sugar planters were growing sugar with centuries-old techniques. Pinning a man's social status to the number of slaves he owned did not encourage efficient management. Furthermore, sugar planters were not scientifically educated. Louisiana had no universities or technical schools, and innovations—which came from France—were adopted slowly and reluctantly. Many Louisiana planters chose their seed from their poorest, least productive canes and ignored the fertilization benefits of animal manure, legumes, field stubble, and Peruvian guano. Above all, the inefficient Jamaica train boiled the sugar syrup too fast to form fat sugar crystals. Overall, Louisiana sugar had a bad reputation. As a Baltimore newspaper complained the year of Rillieux's homecoming, "a large proportion of [Louisiana sugar] is exceedingly dark, heavy, and abounding with dirt."

Louisiana sugar growers survived financially only because rising federal tariffs protected them from foreign competition. As energy costs also rose, however, new difficulties appeared. Planters had already stripped nearby swamps of wood to keep their sugar kettles boiling, and Mississippi River steamboats were competing for firewood upriver. Thus, when Edmund Forstall summoned Rillieux back to New Orleans to run his sugar refinery, he must have hoped that the young man could help him make a higher-grade sugar crystal and, at the same time, reduce his fuel and labor costs.

Rillieux thought his system could solve all three problems, but he quit his job with Forstall almost as soon as it began. Forstall had had a disagreement with Norbert's father, and the younger Rillieux honored his family ties. Years later, when Rillieux wanted to engineer drainage and sewer systems for New Orleans, the plan would fall through in part because he and Forstall were "sworn enemies."

Rillieux began a desperate decade as he tried to engineer his laboratory design into a practical apparatus, find craftsmen sophisticated enough to build it, and secure adequate financing to test it. As he perfected his design, he filed new and increasingly complex patents. Steam passed through condensing coils, gave off its latent heat, and evaporated the syrup in three chambers. Increasingly effective vacuums lowered the temperature at which the syrup in each chamber boiled and evaporated.

Within a year of his return to Louisiana, Rillieux realized that he would have to finance his project himself or attract investors. During the next decade, he tried both. He convinced several planters to let him build and test his equipment in their sugarhouses, but each time his locally built machinery failed. He amassed an enormous fortune in land speculation and then lost it in a bank failure. At one point, he offered to spend $50,000 of his own money to build his system on the plantation of A. Durnford, a rich free man of color whose patron was the eccentric white founder of Liberia. Durnford refused the offer because he did not want to "give up control of his people," i.e., his 75 slaves.

During this difficult period, Rillieux met Judah P. Benjamin, a millionaire and one of the most prominent Jews in nineteenth-century America. Benjamin was the first openly Jewish senator in the United States and would become Jefferson Davis' secretary of war, secretary of state, and attorney general. Famous as "the brains of the Confederacy," Benjamin would try in vain to convince Davis to free slaves who joined the Confederate army. After the war, Benjamin escaped possible arrest as a war criminal by fleeing to England, where he became an extraordinarily successful lawyer. Thus, Benjamin and Rillieux were both intelligent, highly educated young men who stood slightly outside the rigid social structure of the South. The two apparently became close personal friends, for Rillieux was a frequent and long-term guest at Benjamin's home in New Orleans.

In 1843, when a short-lived federal tariff encouraged the production of high-quality sugar, Benjamin and a partner, Theodore Packwood, offered Rillieux the use of their sugarhouse on the lavish Bellechasse plantation. With adequate financing for the first time, Rillieux was able to arrange for a reputable metalworking firm in Philadelphia to build his apparatus and ship it to New Orleans. Rillieux also organized a double-barreled attack on energy costs. As fuel, he would burn dried cane from the previous year's crop, and the syrup, inside vacuum containers, would be heated entirely by steam and vapor. Benjamin and Packwood agreed to pay Rillieux $13,500, provided his sugar was as good and plentiful as their previous year's crop. Rillieux predicted that Packwood would save enough on fuel and slave time alone to make a profit the first year.

During weeks of intense labor and deep concentration, Rillieux assembled his equipment on the plantation. When it was up and running, the system worked even better than anticipated. It increased Packwood's profits by 70 percent, enough to pay for itself in a single year. "The apparatus is very easily managed, and my negroes [sic] became acquainted with it in a short time," Packwood enthused. It halved fuel costs and made a better grade of

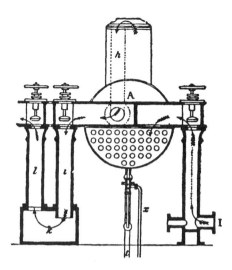

Norbert Rillieux's diagram accompanying his second U.S. patent. He built the equipment in 1844 at Theodore Packwood's plantation called "Scarsdale" in Louisiana. It was his first apparatus to operate successfully. (*From Noel Deerr, The History of Sugar, vol. 2, London: Chapman and Hall Ltd., 1950.*)

sugar. And wherever it was used, it eliminated the Jamaica train. Sugar growers needed fewer slaves, and no one tended dangerous kettles of boiling sugar syrup for weeks on end.

Judah P. Benjamin was thrilled at how the system turned a dark and impure fluid into snowy white, sparkling crystals as good as any refined in the North. He and Benjamin wrote articles for a local sugar journal describing the process. Their evaporated sugar took first prize in a local contest; the judges declared Rillieux's system "a complete revolution in the manufacture of our sugar. . . . Whiter and whiter, coarser and coarser will we grain our Sugar, and finally assume the first rank in every market of the world." Progressive planters hung on Rillieux's every word, and the African-American became the most sought after engineer in Louisiana.

Traveling around the state installing his machinery, Rillieux had to stay on slave-operated plantations. Like many free people of color, Rillieux may have regarded himself as the equal of the white ruling class, far above dark-skinned slaves. But in the antebellum South, Rillieux could not stay in the plantations' mansions. Rumor had it that he stayed in slave quarters, but a firsthand observer reported that on Benjamin's plantation Rillieux was given a special house and slaves to serve him.

Today, experts rank Rillieux's triple-effect evaporator "among the world's great inventions." Charles A. Browne, an eminent sugar chemist with the United States Department of Agriculture concluded that "Rillieux's invention is the greatest in the history of American chemical engineering, and I know of no other invention that has brought so great a saving to all branches of chemical engineering." It has been improved mainly by adding more stages.

Sadly, only about 13 of Rillieux's systems were installed before the Civil War. Most planters had no idea how his apparatus worked and remained suspicious. They were more accustomed to buying slaves than technology and did not adopt Rillieux's evaporator until the 1880s or 1890s. Only then did Rillieux's mechanization of the manually operated Jamaica train have an impact on Louisiana agriculture like that of Eli Whitney's cotton gin.

As Rillieux promoted his system during the 1840s, his position as a free African-American engineer became increasingly untenable. National tensions were mounting over slavery, and Southern whites tried to bolster the institution by restricting the legal rights of free blacks. By the time Rillieux was 50 years old, free people of color could no longer visit the city or walk its streets without the permission of a white man; the penalty was years of prison at hard labor.

Rillieux, for example, had trouble filing for U.S. patents. An official who returned one of his forms wrote, "It is required that the applicant shall make oath or affirmation of citizenship; and as the laws of the United States do not recognize slaves as citizens, it is impossible for the negro slave to bring his application before the office." Rillieux exploded furiously, "Now, I was the applicant for the patents and not the slave. I am a citizen of the United States and made oath of the facts in my affidavit. . . . How could the Commissioner arrive at such a monstrous conclusion against the express declaration to the contrary?"

Leaving Louisiana and its racial problems behind, Rillieux returned permanently to France around the time of the Civil War. Fearful of losing their federal subsidies, most Louisiana sugar planters initially opposed secession. Nonetheless, when their state seceded in January 1861, most supported the Confederacy. In the end, the war destroyed their sugar plantations and freed their slaves. According to some reports, Rillieux returned to France before the war, but his closest French associate wrote that Rillieux left the United States "after the war, exhausted and asking for nothing but rest."

Whatever happened, Rillieux was certainly not in New Orleans when a cousin, the Impressionist painter Edgar Degas, came to visit his mother's relatives for five months from 1872 to 1873. Norbert's father was Degas' great-uncle, and Norbert himself was a first cousin of Degas' mother. While in New Orleans, Degas painted several portraits of Rillieux's prosperous white connections, including *Portraits in an Office, Cotton Merchants, Woman with a Vase of Flowers, Woman on a Balcony,* and *Song Rehearsal.*

At the time of Degas' visit, the men in Rillieux's white family were briefly involved in the Unification Movement, an abortive attempt by pragmatic white and black businessmen to head off Reconstruction by radical Republicans and voluntarily integrate local governments and public schools. After the Unification Movement failed and Degas returned to France, Rillieux's relations moved on to support whites-only political movements. In a pitched street battle, an all-white militia fought an integrated city police force; 32 people died before federal troops restored order.

Safely back in Paris, Degas and Rillieux must have known each other. The engineer was the most prominent Louisianan in France, and Degas was greatly interested in industrial technology. The artist may not have appreciated having an African-American cousin, though. When the Degas family lost its fortune in 1873, the painter blamed Jewish bankers and became rabidly anti-Semitic. One can only imagine a conversation between the racist Degas and the blunt Rillieux.

Assessing the effect of Rillieux's equipment on slavery is not easy. Potentially, this apparatus could have saved large numbers of slaves from the arduous and dangerous work of handling boiling syrup. However, his apparatus was not adopted on a large scale until long after the Civil War, so it did not improve the working conditions of vast numbers of slaves. In fact, inasmuch as it made a few Louisiana plantations more profitable, it did not weaken the institution of slavery either. On the other hand, if the Civil War had never occurred, his invention might have eventually convinced sugar planters to abandon their reliance on slave labor.

Unlike Louisiana's planters, German farmers were interested in new technology and adopted Rillieux's equipment enthusiastically. In fact, Rillieux's triple-effect evaporators helped turn Germany's backward farms into industrialized models of scientific agriculture. By the time Rillieux had returned to Paris, Germany had already surpassed France in scientific research and sugar experimentation. Root crops—potatoes and especially sugar beets—were being grown with massive amounts of fertilizer. Sugar mills were buying huge tracts of land and installing Rillieux's apparatus, steam plows, and mechanical seed drills. By 1888, Rillieux systems were refining beet sugar in 30 German, 100 Austrian, and 20 Russian factories. As German peasants moved to western Germany for better-paying factory jobs, beet growers hired seasonal, immigrant labor, primarily Polish women.

They were not slaves but, as one German planter put it, "They were easy to acquire and then to dispose of, [and] they were not demanding in respect of board and lodging."

Unexpectedly, Rillieux-produced beet sugar added both sweets and meat to European diets. Sugar consumption more than doubled during the last 25 years of his life. At the same time, penned livestock could be fed molasses and the beet residue, tops, and pulp from sugar mills and distilleries. When the beet pulp was dried and sold as fodder, farmers could—for the first time in history—establish the size of their animal herds according to market prices instead of local fodder supplies. By 1900, Germany's scientific, industrialized agriculture was exporting farm machinery, fertilizers, and seed to the world.

Rillieux lived to see the enormous effect of his invention on American and European sugar making. Financially secure, Rillieux married Emily Cuckow, a French woman 21 years his junior. Abandoning sugar engineering for more than a decade, he studied Egyptology and hieroglyphics. He never returned to Louisiana, though he looked every inch the southern colonel: a trifle portly with the requisite white moustache and goatee and a softly tied silk bow at his neck. He hired a young Frenchman who became his secretary and, later, a prominent sugar engineer. Unlike those who tangled with Rillieux's pride, the devoted Frenchman fondly remembered Rillieux as a gracious and hospitable man and as a storyteller with a thousand tales to tell about his sugar-making past.

4

Clean Water and Edward Frankland

February 20, 1825–August 9, 1899

As six major epidemics of cholera swept the globe during the nineteenth century, fecally contaminated drinking water killed millions of people. For more than 30 of those terror-filled years, the resolute courage of one chemist, Edward Frankland, protected the public health. Edward Frankland believed that water was guilty until proven innocent, and he condemned tainted water with the righteous conviction of a law-and-order prosecutor. As the illegitimate son of a rich lawyer and a chambermaid, however, Frankland had to hide his origins. So he is almost unknown today, although during his lifetime he was one of Britain's most important chemists.

Frankland discovered the fundamental principle of valency—the combining power of atoms to form compounds. He gave the chemical "bond" its name and popularized the notation we use today for writing chemical formulas. He codiscovered helium, helped found synthetic organic and structural chemistry, and was the father of organometallic chemistry. He was also the first person to thoroughly analyze the gases from different types of coal and—dieters take note—the first to measure the calories in food.

As a result of Frankland's out-of-wedlock birth, he became a painfully shy man who shunned publicity. His courage arose from his convictions that the public deserved clean drinking water and that students deserved a sound scientific education. Thus, Frankland's life as a chemist is also the story of how a dedicated scientist overcame the stigma of illegitimacy in socially rigid Victorian England.

Frankland's mother Margaret was a country girl, the daughter of an itinerant calico printer. In 1824, she went to the nearby town of Preston to work as a maid for the Gorsts, a wealthy family of distinguished Lancashire lawyers and judges. The Gorsts' 20-year-old son Edward was living at home, and the two young people had a secret affair. When Margaret Frankland became pregnant, the Gorsts were horrified. Any hint of scandal would destroy the young man's prospects. His father functioned as the queen's chief legal officer in Lancashire County, and his family was expected to be an unblemished example for all. An illegitimate child disgraced both mother and father, and the latter was expected to support the child or face the consequences in court.

Edward Gorst set aside an annuity of £1200 for Margaret Frankland and her child—provided that his identity was never revealed. He paid Margaret the interest from the annuity, about £60 a year, a well-nigh princely sum, since raising a child cost about £8 a year. Eventually, the annuity seems to have been replaced by a one-time payment of £1500.

Gorst's secret remained safe for almost 150 years. Then, a modern historian, curious about the paucity of information about Frankland's life, discovered his parish baptismal records for February 20, 1825. They explained Frankland's reticence about his past: the records identify the infant Edward Frankland as the "son of Peggy Frankland . . . single woman."

The child's name combined his natural father's first name and his mother's maiden name. Thus the Gorsts were protected from publicity, but the child was not. To anyone who knew him, Edward Frankland's use of his mother's unmarried name was a blazing sign of "bastardy," a Victorian disgrace. Edward's tarnished birthright followed him throughout his life, affecting his education, his career, his marriage, and finally, his posthumous reputation. In the end, it almost obliterated his accomplishments and prevented us from paying our respects to a man whose dedication saved thousands upon thousands of lives.

When Margaret Frankland was banished from the Gorsts' household, she moved back to her family home outside Garstang to give birth and raise her son. Considering her lack of education, Margaret was a woman of remarkable intellect, energy, and character. In a country where 40 percent of the men were illiterate, she taught Edward the alphabet before he was two. As befitted England's infamous age of flogging, she gave him a strict and corporeal moral upbringing. Growing up meant being caned, and Frankland recalled that, "When I was about two years old, my great-uncle Robert, who was almost my godfather, made me a birthday present of a birch-rod, which I well remember to have proudly carried home, and which was frequently used by my mother with great benefit to myself."

Margaret later opened a small boarding house in the nearby town of Lancaster in northwest England and, when Edward was five years old, married one of her lodgers. At first, as Edward recalled, "Matters did not go quite so smoothly with me at home. My stepfather was rather severe with me, and, with a thin stick, gave me many a beating which I probably well deserved." Despite this, Edward remained close to his mother and stepfather as long as they lived.

As his stepfather worked his way up the social register from cabinetmaker to railway guard, tavern keeper, agent, and finally, gentleman, the family moved frequently. Once, while living in nearby Manchester, Edward and his mother had to flee for their lives to escape a cholera epidemic. Because of the family's many moves, Edward attended eight schools, which he described in vivid detail in an unfinished autobiography. One school was run by student monitors who blackmailed pupils for money and favors. In a classics-only school that overlooked the town's place of execution, Frankland and the other children watched almost 20 hangings. Elsewhere, the teacher beat the heads of students so hard with a thick hazel stick that it often broke. Edward's head was never free from swellings, many larger than a pigeon egg. Frankland, who as an adult was no friend of corporeal punishment, was surprised that his parents never complained.

Of Frankland's many teachers, only James Willasey taught science or encouraged Frankland's obvious abilities. Deeply grateful all his life, Frankland regarded Willasey as "a real educator" and raised an annuity to support him in old age. Willasey in turn willed all his possessions to Frankland, who proudly wore his teacher's seal on a watch fob.

Frankland's lifelong affection for his teacher stands in stark contrast to his opinion of his biological father. By the time Frankland was a teenager, he almost certainly knew his father's identity and his mother's need for total secrecy. The boy may even have met his father. But Frankland coolly distanced himself from the man and said tersely, "He took no interest whatever in my education or training and therefore directly exerted no influence over me."

Frankland wanted to become a doctor, but medical school was far beyond his mother's means or his biological father's inclination. So in 1840, when Frankland was 14, his mother apprenticed him to the next best profession, pharmacy. It was, Frankland complained rather unjustly in old age, "six years' continuous hard labour, from which I derived no advantage whatever, except the facility of tying up parcels neatly." Frankland grew to be tall and muscular with thick glasses, light brown hair, a ruddy complexion, and broad, extraordinarily dexterous hands. As an apprentice, he worked more than 70 hours a week, wheeling heavy casks of treacle through town and hauling 100-pound sacks up a steep and narrow staircase. To grind a pound of cocoa, he worked a 20-pound pestle continuously for a day. To make ointment, he spent more than 24 days grinding six pounds of mercury into 14 pounds of lard; the poisonous mercury vapors may have exacerbated some of his later anxiety and timidity. Frankland's master was the only pharmacist in town who closed his shop for the Sabbath, and Frankland used the day off to visit the local Mechanics Institute library, read Joseph Priestley's *History of Electricity*, and perform its experiments.

Despite his diffidence, Frankland seems to have had a remarkable capacity for making friends, and a surprising number of kindly people intervened to help the youth, perhaps to compensate for his clouded birthright. Three physicians, Christopher Johnson and his two sons, tutored him and other local apprentices in chemistry and medicine. The Johnsons loaned the young students books and converted a cottage into a simple laboratory for them. Thanks to the Johnsons, several Lancaster youths overcame the town's cultural and educational backwardness and became eminent scientists and engineers. The Johnsons also found Frankland a job in London at the Government Museum of Economic Geology where an assistant gave Frankland his first sophisticated instruction in chemical experimentation and processes. A young German friend, Hermann Kolbe, taught Frankland everything he had learned about analyzing gases from the chemist Robert Bunsen, of Bunsen burner fame.

Although Frankland had not yet studied even algebra, his analytical chemistry skills were advanced enough to land him teaching jobs at several short-lived schools. At one of them, he befriended a fellow teacher, John Tyndall, who later became a prominent British physicist. The two men made a mutual improvement pact to wake at 4 a.m. each day and study together. Frankland taught Tyndall chemistry, and Tyndall taught Frankland biology and mathematics. Then they left together to earn doctorates—in less than a year—from Bunsen in Germany. Bunsen taught Frankland how to analyze substances chemically, first burning them, then measuring the volumes of the resulting gases, and finally getting their proportions by weight. Not much, perhaps, but as Frankland said, "I had the advantage of direct instruction from the inventor of the process, who also taught me how to make . . . most of the other apparatus required."

Armed with a prestigious Ph.D. from Marburg, Germany, Frankland returned to England in 1849 to become a professional chemist. While teaching in a miserable engineering college crippled by faculty squabbles and financial problems, he made two landmark observations. First, Frankland discovered an extremely important series of organic compounds that contain metals. The first such compound had been discovered in 1827 by a German chemist, and during the 1840s Bunsen worked on organic compounds containing arsenic, which many at the time considered a metal. Elaborating on Bunsen's explorations, Frankland coined the term "organo-metallic" to describe the group.

Then he swiftly produced as many different varieties of the compounds as possible, including dimethylzinc, which convinced other scientists to accept Avogadro's theory, a foundation of atomic chemistry; and methyl-mercury iodide, the first of many organomercury compounds known to poison people who eat mercury-contaminated fish. Despite his skill at synthesis, Frankland did not discover tetraethyl lead, the gasoline additive that became one of the most important industrial compounds of the mid-twentieth century (Chapter 6).

While studying organometallic substances, Frankland gradually became aware of another basic regularity in nature that no one had noticed before: each element has a definite combining power. Organometallic substances are so highly reactive that the energy from sunlight is strong enough to transform one compound into another. Chemists were still almost a decade away from accepting Avogadro's distinction between atoms and molecules, but Frankland realized a stunning fact: valency determines the proportions of the elements in a compound.

As he described it, "When the formulae of inorganic chemical compounds are considered, even a superficial observer is struck with the general symmetry of their construction; the compounds of nitrogen, phosphorus, antimony and arsenic especially exhibit the tendency of the elements to form compounds containing 3 or 5 equivalents of other elements, and it is in these proportions that their affinities are best satisfied." As he noted, nitrogen forms NO_3, NH_3, NI_3, and NS_3, while phosphorus forms PO_3, PH_3, and PCl_3; antimony forms SbO_3 and $SbCl_3$; and arsenic makes AsO_3, AsH_3, and $AsCl_3$, etc. He observed that elements can also join with five atoms, as in NO_5, NH_4O, NH_4I, PO_5, PH_4I, etc. "Without offering any hypothesis regarding the cause of this symmetrical grouping of atoms," Frankland stressed, "it is sufficiently evident, from the examples just given, that such a tendency or law prevails."

Valency, as the principle is called today, is one of the fundamental concepts in chemistry. In more modern terms, the valence of an atom equals the number of bonds that an atom has for combining with other elements; hydrogen, for example, has one, while other elements have more.

As Frankland sent his report on valency to the Royal Society on May 10, 1850, fame and success seemed assured. Sadly, incompetence intervened; the society's secretary "inadvertently laid [Frankland's report] aside in his private drawer"—and forgot it for a year. The German chemist Friedrich

August Kekulé ignored Frankland's work and claimed the valence theory for himself. It was 20 years before scientists recognized that Frankland had founded the theory of valency, while Kekulé had contributed to it at a later date.

In contrast to the lack of recognition for his valency theory, Frankland's work in organometallic compounds attracted considerable attention. When the city of Manchester opened England's first provincial university, Frankland was appointed its chemistry professor. Frankland was a self-made man, and Manchester was a city of self-made men made rich by Britain's textile industry. Its university was a new kind of institution for Britain. It was wholly secular, and its professors were chosen by merit, rather than by the established Church of England. Furthermore, the students—all male, of course—were admitted without regard to religion, rank, or social status.

At 26, Frankland had attained a considerable degree of professional success and seemed outwardly secure. The need for total secrecy about his father's identity had left its mark, though. He was excruciatingly shy and was a poor speaker who later had to be dragged into accepting public office. Throughout his life, he sought social acceptance, financial security—and personal obscurity.

The secret of Frankland's birth endangered his marital prospects as well. While in Germany, Frankland had fallen in love with Sophie Fick, a German girl of impeccable ancestry. Frankland may have confided in Sophie, but betraying his mother's secret to Sophie's family would jeopardize his mother's financial security and his professional future. To marry Sophie, he would have to falsify his father's name on the marriage certificate, although lying would make him vulnerable to conviction as a perjurer—a serious charge indeed. Thus, Frankland was playing for high stakes on February 7, 1851, when he married Sophie Fick in St. Martin-in-the-Fields Parish Church in London. On the marriage certificate, he invented a fictitious name for his father, "Edward Frankland, solicitor." It was as close to the truth as he dared to go.

As Frankland scrambled to get an education, earn his livelihood, and find a way to marry, he must have often envied his natural father's legitimate son, John Eldon Gorst. Although Frankland served a six-year apprenticeship, his legitimate half-brother attended Cambridge University. From then on, the two half-brothers—the one unaware of the other's existence—advanced through life on separate, parallel, and profoundly unequal paths. While Frankland struggled to make ends meet, his Gorst sibling advanced smoothly from the law to become a member of Parliament for Cambridge borough and university, a solicitor general, an undersecretary of state for

India, and a knight of the realm. Frankland was understandably unfair when he said that none of his natural father's children "have particularly distinguished themselves."

After his marriage to Sophie, Frankland once again set about piecing together bits and pieces to make a secure life. Although it was now possible for a poor Englishman like Frankland to dream of becoming a professional chemist, Manchester's university paid only £150 a year for full-time teaching. As a result, Frankland and other British chemistry professors doubled as consultants to industry and government and as expert court witnesses, chemical analysts, writers and journalists, and inventors and entrepreneurs. Governments were replacing hereditary retainers with professional civil servants who consulted scientists as neutral experts to resolve conflicts; despite their growing authority, few consulting chemists earned much money.

Frankland tried his hand at anything he could find. He analyzed guano for estate owners; he advised Manchester University to boil and filter its water; he analyzed hard water for railroads concerned about minerals in the boilers of their steam locomotives; he detected lead contamination for water suppliers; and he served as an expert witness in court. With analytical chemistry still in its infancy, scientists could find enough contradictory evidence to support almost any side of an argument. Frankland, for example, once testified against a former client and used privileged information he had learned as the company's consultant. In another case, he told a polluting Leblanc washing soda factory to "make the surrounding neighbourhood believe you have [gotten rid of all the hydrogen chloride] for without this faith stupid farmers will detect muriatic acid in every diseased ear of wheat or decayed branch of quickthorn, and old fish women will be quite certain that their oysters and mussels are in the last agonies of death from the same cause." Discussing another pollutant, he suggested disingenuously, "Is it possible to take the waste in [boats] and throw it into the Severn [River]?"

As chemists learned how to analyze chemicals more accurately, it became harder to testify so cavalierly on behalf of polluters. Within a few years, Frankland had become one of Britain's leading chemical experts testifying *against* industrial emissions. In fact, when he decided in 1857 to move to London to improve his financial prospects, Manchester's polluting industrialists were delighted to see him go.

Even in London, Frankland had to combine three teaching positions for a while; he worked in a hospital, at a military academy, and at the Royal Institution. He often wished for a fourth job because the break between his 10 a.m. and 3 p.m. lectures was too short to do anything but teach. Subsequently, Frankland worked at the Royal Institution for six years where he enjoyed a light teaching schedule and could focus on research. Michael Faraday also worked at the Royal Institution, and today the research that Frankland conducted there is considered as important for chemists as Faraday's electromagnetism studies are for physicists.

In a burst of new syntheses during the 1860s, Frankland in London and Marcellin Berthelot in France transformed the chaotic state of organic chemistry, the study of carbon-containing compounds founded by Lavoisier. This new branch of chemistry was still unpopular in England; few chemists realized that William Perkin's discovery of the first synthetic dye in 1856 would make organic chemistry a colossal source of wealth. When Frankland began his studies of the lactic acids, organic chemistry was so confused that, for example, acetic acid had at least 19 different formulas.

Working feverishly, Frankland demonstrated that synthesis—combining simple ingredients to make more complicated compounds—could be a powerful source of new organic substances. He defined carboxyl (COOH) as the structural unit of organic acids. Frankland has been described as one of the great founders of synthetic organic chemistry, in which the properties of compounds depend on how atoms are arranged in the molecule. Frankland's work during the 1860s was thus an important step toward the development of structural organic chemistry.

Frankland's hard work paid off when, at the age of 40, he was appointed to a prestigious professorship to replace August Wilhelm Hofmann, who had taught William Perkin (Chapter 2) at the Royal College of Chemistry. Even this post was cobbled together with money from different sources. In addition to his regular teaching duties, Frankland had to administer examinations for up to 50,000 mechanics, clerks, apprentices, artisans, and other young adults studying chemistry in Britain's night classes and upper elementary schools. He was also responsible for analyzing London's water supply. Once more, Frankland was moonlighting. But this time, he could parlay two unprepossessing positions into powerful weapons for reform.

First, by indulging his passionate belief in science for the people, he gave students the kind of hands-on education in chemistry that he had wanted as a young man. Before Frankland, students everywhere learned science from books; most never even entered a laboratory. Working tirelessly over a period of 15 years, Frankland gradually changed that and dramatically improved the state of science education in Britain. He compiled a list of 109 experiments that students needed to understand firsthand in order to pass his examinations. He wrote a textbook that became a standard for chemistry instruction, in part because it incorporated his ideas on valency and organic structures and his newly developed notation system.

While Lavoisier had established a rational system for naming elements and compounds, Frankland developed the system that we use today for writing chemical formulas and for depicting the bonds between the atoms in molecules. As Frankland synthesized more and more isomers, compounds with the same formulas but different molecular structures, he found traditional formulas confusing; they showed the types and numbers of elements but provided no clue as to how the atoms were arranged inside the molecule. To remedy the problem, Frankland depicted the atoms in functional groups and drew lines between them to indicate the bonds between the elements.

$$H-O-\underset{\underset{O}{\overset{\|}{}}}{\overset{\overset{O}{\overset{\|}{}}}{S}}-O-H$$

Sulfuric acid, in Frankland's notation, from his textbook, *Lecture Notes for Chemical Students,* vol. 1, London, 1876.

Frankland's notation was a big step toward showing how atoms or groups of atoms are arranged in space and how molecules can combine and function. In addition, it reduced student learning time by two-thirds.

For teachers, Frankland wrote a training manual and ran summer workshops. Since the government paid instructors £4 for every student who passed a Frankland examination, teachers eagerly attended his programs. Foreign publications of his books and manuals spread his gospel of laboratory instruction for all. And, in the process of honing his writing and administrative skills, Frankland overcame his poor speaking ability.

No sooner had Frankland begun reforming science education, however, than London faced a life-threatening emergency: cholera. The disease causes vomiting, fever, and profuse, watery diarrhea. Half of all people with severe and untreated cholera die of dehydration and electrolyte imbalance. A total of six cholera pandemics—all now thought to have originated in Bangladesh—circled the world during the nineteenth century. For 50 years, there were never more than six years of relief between the end of one pandemic and the beginning of another. A seventh began in Indonesia in 1961 and continued on six continents into the twenty-first century.

The cholera epidemic that reached Europe and North America in the early 1830s killed more than 20,000 people in England. It was during this epidemic that Queen Victoria's personal physician, Dr. John Snow, removed the handle from the polluted Broad Street pump in London in the first recorded, appropriate measure to prevent waterborne disease.

Cholera is predominantly a disease of the poor. An official investigation of the 1832 cholera epidemic in Paris showed that up to 53 out of every 1000 inhabitants in the poorest neighborhoods died, compared to only 8 per 1000 in wealthy areas. The rich could flee, secure a supply of safe water, or, like the slave owners in New Orleans, drink claret even at breakfast. The poor drank from waterways that were their cesspools.

Cities were particularly easy prey for cholera, as urbanization and industrialization polluted water supplies. While London's water was the most notorious, it was probably not the worst. And although cities in the United States were late to industrialize, they too had problems as cities grew and the middle classes demanded more water for bathtubs, showers, and water closets. Chicago, for example, used Lake Michigan as both a water reservoir and a sewage dump. In 1862, the city fathers had the bright idea of dealing with wastewater by reversing the direction of the Chicago River; had the plan succeeded, Chicago could have polluted the Mississippi River basin.

Disease and contagion were already widely associated with decaying human and animal waste when Frankland took over as London's water consultant in 1865 and as virtually the only working member of the Rivers' Pollution Commission in 1868. Little was known about clean water. While some experts thought that decaying matter directly caused disease or indirectly nurtured disease-causing microbes, others regarded feces-rich water as no more than unacceptably disgusting. Until the German bacteriologist Robert Koch identified the cholera bacillus in 1883, no one knew how the disease spread from human feces to drinking water to human victim and back again. More than a century later, scientists led by Rita R. Colwell demonstrated that crustaceans infested with the cholera bacillus flourish in plankton blooms in warm, brackish coastal and inland waters fertilized with organic nutrients. During a plankton bloom, drinking one glass of untreated water can give a person cholera.

As the disease devastated cities, clean water issues threatened to tear British society apart. Arguing for "the greatest good for the greatest number," liberals demanded government action. In contrast, industrialists and Parliament argued that government should not interfere with business, even when the public health was at risk. No one objected to pollution in general or to uncontrolled urbanization and industrialization but, terrified of cholera, people demanded sanitary water.

For protection, they looked to chemistry. Although no one knew exactly how the disease was spread, it was clear that there was a relationship between cholera and unsanitary water, and chemists had decades of experience certifying the safety of mineral waters at elegant spas. Moreover, chemists had come to embody order, progress, and authority.

Frankland charged into his new job like a hanging judge. "My motto, unlike that in criminal cases, has always been assume water to be guilty until it is proved innocent," he declared. As a child, he had fled a cholera epidemic with his mother. In adulthood, he was an outdoorsman who loved to sail and fish in clear waters and hike in pure mountain air. In an expedition to the Alps, he and his fellow climbers were the first to spend the night at the summit of Mont Blanc, a feat previously thought to be beyond the limits of human endurance. For 30 years, Frankland was a strong voice—often the only voice—for clean water. Unfortunately, no one knew for sure what clean water was. Frankland staked out a radical position: whatever the deadly agents were, they were almost certainly introduced into water by sewage, so any trace of sewage raised a red flag. He became convinced later that some of the microscopic bacteria in water probably caused fatal diseases.

During his first two years as London's water analyst, Frankland devoted his superb manipulative skills to developing sensitive new techniques for determining the amount of organic nitrogen in water samples. As a working hypothesis, he assumed that the organic nitrogen originated in sewage or manure. Previous methods had underestimated the amount of ammonia and urea, the main nitrogen-rich components of raw sewage. Frankland's method was laborious and expensive, and it took other chemists six months to learn, but it was state-of-the-art science for the times, and it erred on the side of caution. In widely published, monthly reports to the government, Frankland ran horrifying tables that compared the pure well water sold by one of London's water companies with the nitrogen-tainted river water sold by seven other companies.

Soon Frankland was the world's leading authority on water issues. During the 1870s and 1880s, Frankland and his assistants conducted more than 11,000 analyses of water for clients from Asia, South America, India, and Europe. He worked for water companies, gas companies, brick works, breweries, copper mines, hospitals, asylums, schools, mansions of the landed gentry, and Buckingham Palace. The man who had begun his life as an impecunious pharmacist's apprentice was becoming, by today's standards, a millionaire several times over. Frankland's chemical analyses forced the closing of shallow wells and springs and the abandonment of hundreds of contaminated water sources, both at home and abroad. His recommendations, translated into French and German and published in North America, were widely adopted and used in court cases around the world.

As an expert witness, Frankland performed with an unbeatable combination of activism and authority. A poor lecturer in classrooms, he was nimble-witted on the witness stand, up-to-date on a multitude of facts, and, above all, able to explain clearly any relevant scientific principles.

He stressed that water's appearance should not be used as an indication of its safety. "I have now examined upwards of 1000 samples from all parts of the United Kingdom and have not yet met with a single case of clear analytical guilt which has not been sustained on further investigation. It is true that my verdict has repeatedly been met with vehement protestations of innocence, but further investigation always proved that these could not be sustained. The other day a gentleman brought to me two samples of well water for examination. I reported both as exhibiting great previous sewage contamination; he protested that it was impossible as the waters were bright and sparkling and possessed a high reputation; a week later he informed me that the source of contamination had been discovered. One of the wells was situated close to a large cesspool; the other received the drainage from a dog kennel."

One day in 1881, two bottles of holy water from Hagar's Well in Mecca arrived at his laboratory. After analyzing the liquid, Frankland said it was the worst drinking water he had ever seen. Thousands of Muslim pilgrims used it daily, but it was six times more polluted than the worst London sewage. Frankland notified authorities, but the well was not closed for 12 years, despite two cholera epidemics that killed thousands of people in Mecca. Similarly, communities everywhere disregarded Frankland's advice to treat sewage by spreading it on farmland. Because sewage treatment was expensive, communities concentrated—not on treating their sewage—but on transporting it elsewhere; in saving themselves, they contaminated water supplies downstream.

Unlike many of his competitors, Frankland relied on experiment rather than speculation. When an eminent analyst declared that sewage would be purified after it flowed seven miles downstream, Frankland countered with facts: "I find that percolation through 5 feet of gravelly soil removes much more organic impurity from sewage water than does a flow of 50 miles in a river at a rate of one mile per hour." Some water company chemists went so far as to claim that microscopic organisms actually purified water. As Frankland sarcastically described a competing water analyst: "You will always find him on the side of joint stock companies and against the public—companies pay well, the public does not pay.—*Voilà!*"

Frankland's relentless campaign for clean water made him many enemies. Sadly, a former student and assistant named James Alfred Wanklyn became a virulent opponent. For almost 15 years, Wanklyn's paranoid attacks on Frankland's character and science dominated Britain's water policy debates. Wanklyn had grown up in Frankland's hometown of Lancaster, so Frankland must have lived in dread that local gossip about his parentage would become public scandal. Luckily for Frankland, Wanklyn quarreled with so many other colleagues that the scientific community blackballed him. As one chemical journal complained, Wanklyn and his supporters suffer from "scientific afflatus," otherwise known as "hot air."

As before, friends rallied to Frankland's support. Frankland had joined the newly formed X-Club, whose eight members were united by a "devotion to science, pure and free, untrammeled by religious dogmas," as one of them explained. Most were close associates of Charles Darwin; they included John Tyndall, Thomas Henry Huxley, and Joseph Hooker.

Even at the pinnacle of success in Victorian England, Frankland had to contend with his origins. Shortly after the death of his first wife, Sophie, Frankland fell in love with a young woman named Ellen Frances Grenside. Once again, he had to decide how to identify his real father on a marriage certificate. By 1875, his natural father was long dead, and Frankland himself had become so prominent and controversial that he dared not lie. He risked the truth; on the marriage certificate, he identified his father as "Edward Gorst, Esquire." Luckily, few people saw the document.

Frankland's birth may have prevented him from attaining the highest professional honors. Frankland practically founded the Institute of Chemistry, the world's first professional association for scientists, but tellingly, he never became president of the prestigious Royal Society. Even Frankland's close friend Huxley wrote dismissively, "Frankland won't do."

The Society looked down on Frankland's money-earning projects as "grubby trade," but more than mercenary factors may have been at play. Another chemist, William Crookes, was elected president of the British Association for the Advancement of Science despite humble origins and his participation in at least one highly dubious commercial scheme. Perhaps some X-Club members knew about Frankland's birth, either from his old friend, John Tyndall, or more likely, through the machinations of his enemy, James Alfred Wanklyn. On the other hand, perhaps Crookes' background was simply deemed adequate enough for the British Association, which was far less elite than the Royal Society. In any case, governmental indifference to science probably explains why Frankland was not awarded a knighthood until 1897, a dozen years after his legitimate half-brother had received his.

After Koch's momentous discovery of the cholera bacillus in 1883, cheap and effective treatment of sewage became possible. The civil engineering of water and sewerage mains, reservoirs, sand filtration, and chlorination made waterborne diseases a thing of the past in much of North America and Western Europe.

Chlorine, introduced to London's water during a typhoid epidemic in 1905, was particularly important. Chlorine is not only cheap, but it also lasts long enough to destroy any pathogens that leak into the water through cracks in pipes. The use of chlorine to treat water saved countless lives. However, late in the twentieth century, after scientists learned how to identify tiny traces of chemicals in huge samples, it was found that chlorine bleach produces small amounts of chloroform, a suspected liver carcinogen in humans, and dioxin, a highly toxic hydrocarbon. Today, paper bleaching mills and many European water systems are replacing chlorine with other chemicals such as ozone and chlorine dioxide. Compared to chlorine, these compounds are more expensive, faster acting, and more rapidly decomposed.

Despite all these advances, the sewage-contaminated water that ravaged the nineteenth century is still a scourge of poor, developing countries at the beginning of the twenty-first century. Fully 25 percent of the population in third world countries still drink dilute sewage. It was not until the late 1990s that scientists discovered that simply filtering water through fabric—even cloth as cheap as sari cotton—removes most of the cyclops crustaceans that harbor deadly cholera.

Looking back over his life, Frankland must have been pleased. Fecally contaminated water was no longer a principal source of human disease. Chemistry students were conducting experiments in laboratories firsthand. He had published his collected *Experimental Researches* at great personal expense to document his scientific role for future generations. And he could be confident that he had probably foiled any immediate attempts to pry into his private life.

During his seventies, Frankland spent his summers in Norway, working on his memoirs with a young woman named Jane Lund. She was his secretary, close friend and companion, and possibly his mistress. While dictating his memoirs to Lund in 1899, Frankland collapsed. One of his daughters hastened from England to be with him. Whatever Jane Lund's relationship with Frankland had been, his daughter must have respected it, because, after his death, she left his room and gave Lund time to be alone with him.

Contrary to all custom, the Chemical Society which Frankland had served as president did not publish a memorial biography of him. A faithful protégé assigned to write the memoir stalled for years and finally refused outright because, he claimed, he held his "teacher's memory in very deep reverence." While researching his mentor's past, he may have stumbled on Frankland's parentage. The Chemical Society delayed its memorial oration for 35 years. Frankland's family published his unfinished memoirs in 1901 but destroyed the copies almost immediately. Frankland's tart comments about some of his colleagues bordered on the slanderous, and he had provided at least one embarrassing clue to his birth. A year later, his descendants published an expurgated version. In the end, Frankland's reticence about his birth almost prevented posterity from learning about his courageous life and his remarkable works.

5

Fertilizer, Poison Gas, and Fritz Haber

December 9, 1868–January 29, 1934

By discovering how to convert nitrogen from the air into ammonia for fertilizer, Fritz Haber saved millions of people from starvation. As Earth's population quadrupled during the twentieth century, our ability to turn air into bread prevented global catastrophe. Fritz Haber did not invent his nitrogen-fixation process to save humanity though; he organized its use for wartime munitions. Fritz Haber was an exuberant, buoyant, fast-thinking, fast-talking chemist with a boundless drive to succeed and belong. He believed that science must serve society, but he lived in an era of unquestioning nationalism. Thus, during and after World War I—The Chemists' War—Haber inaugurated and directed poison gas warfare. Ultimately vilified and rejected by the very country he had tried so desperately to help, Fritz Haber today epitomizes the conflict between duty to one's country and duty to a higher morality.

Haber was born in the city of Breslau, Silesia, then part of Germany, on December 9, 1868. As the gateway to German culture for many Eastern European Jews, Breslau bred many a superpatriot, Haber included. Fritz's mother died within days of his birth. His father, a civic leader and successful trader of dyes and chemicals, rejected the child and left his upbringing to various relatives. As a young man, Fritz wanted to become a chemist, but his father insisted that he join the family business. Only after Haber achieved worldwide fame did the two reconcile.

For someone who focused his adulthood on solving great scientific and social problems, Fritz Haber's youth was remarkably undirected. After graduating from an academic high school, he wandered restlessly for six years, attending six universities and working at three short-term industrial apprenticeships. Wherever he went, he found the chemistry either too boring or too hard, too routine or too authoritarian. Conflict stirred his young imagination more than routine chemical analysis. Once, in a student science club at the University of Heidelberg, his cheeky ebullience landed him in a student brawl and he acquired the facial scar that legend transformed into a fashionable dueling mark.

After earning a lackluster Ph.D. from the University of Berlin in 1891, Haber wrote a friend, "The thesis is miserable. One and a half years of new substances prepared like a baker's bread rolls. . . . One learns to be modest." In preparation for entering his father's business, he studied chemical technology in an alcohol distillery in Hungary, a Solvay soda factory in Austria, and a salt mine in Poland. His obligatory year in the Prussian army left him with a smart, military manner and a love of rank and discipline. His attempts to become a reserve officer failed, however, for this was a prestigious honor reserved for Christians, and Haber was Jewish.

Within six months of joining his father's firm, Fritz invested and lost a large amount of the company's money. At long last, his father acknowledged that his son might be more suited for scientific research than for commerce.

To succeed in a university, Haber would have to overcome two serious obstacles: his spotty chemistry education and anti-Semitism. German universities promoted few Jews to professorships. Prussia, the most powerful state in Germany, had earned the Jews' fervent gratitude by granting them civil liberties, but the passport to success remained a Christian baptism. Since Haber's family rarely attended synagogue, the 24-year-old pragmatically converted to Christianity in 1892. As with many other German researchers, science became Haber's religion. Germany's new dye and chemical industry was revolutionizing medicine and other fields, and the prospects for understanding and controlling nature seemed boundless.

Haber was soon attracted to the rigor and clarity of a glamorous new field, physical chemistry. Whereas traditional organic chemists described and ordered chemical compounds, physical chemists examined actual chemical reactions and proposed general, quantifiable laws to explain them. Finding an entrée to physical chemistry proved difficult, however. Germany's leading physical chemist, Wilhelm Ostwald, rejected three of Haber's applications for study. A few years later, Ostwald ignored another Jewish job applicant, Albert Einstein.

Haber found a place to study physical chemistry almost by chance. He had kept constant vigil at the bedside of a dying friend, whose grateful brother suggested that Haber apply to the Karlsruhe Institute of Technology, where an "influential relative" could help. The school, near the Rhine River in the center of German liberalism, maintained close ties with a large chemical and synthetic dye firm, the Badische Aniline und Soda Fabrik (BASF).

With his flair for the dramatic, Haber liked to tell how he arrived in Karlsruhe and discovered that the "influential relative" was barely more than a janitor. Whatever the truth of the tale may be, it is certain that Haber entered Karlsruhe as a lowly assistant and emerged, after many struggles, as a leading German scientist. His 17 years in Karlsruhe were the most brilliant of his career.

Karlsruhe was among a number of up-and-coming technical schools that were contesting the universities' monopoly on scientific research by solving Germany's industrial problems. Because of his scanty scientific qualifications, Haber taught dyes and textile printing while studying physics and physical chemistry with a friend. Within a few years, Haber was a wholly self-taught expert in physical chemistry and the author of influential books.

To master one scientific topic after another, Haber skipped dinners and studied until 2 a.m. With overflowing enthusiasm, he ignored the conventional boundaries between abstract and practical science; between chemistry, physics, and engineering; and between mechanics, technicians, and scientists. He solved industrial problems posed by the iron plates used to print banknotes and by Karlsruhe's corroded water and gas mains, and then made fundamental discoveries in electrochemistry. Conversely, he used the abstract theory of gas reactions in flames to explain to manufacturers why some reactions continue spontaneously while others stop. Soon he had contributed basic scientific insights to almost every area of physical chemistry.

One of Haber's few relaxations was dining with friends in a simple, local tavern. There he mixed fantasy and whimsy, told elaborate shaggy-dog stories, and composed nonsense verses on postcards to friends. As the sign posted over his regular table warned, "A little lying is permitted here." On a mountain hike one hot summer day, Haber would begin, he stuck his head into a well for a drink of water without noticing that an ox was doing the same thing. Simultaneously lifting their heads, they discovered to their mutual shock that they had exchanged heads. That is why, Haber would chortle, he had the head of a stubborn ox. As for his verses, they were products of sheer industry, and he attacked their rhymes, like his science, with total concentration.

Haber's talent for gaiety and laughter was enormously appealing. The Nobel Prize winning physicist Max Born, who later condemned Haber's wartime activities, "could not resist Haber's charm. . . . [He was a] fascinating personality, full of life and energy, with exemplary, though somewhat old-fashioned manners, a person with great mental clarity, who could think fast, was interested in all fields of science, and was an expert in many of them."

Pushing his prodigious capacity for work to the limit, Haber periodically collapsed. At the age of 25, he spent several weeks in a sanitarium for nervous illnesses. Five years later, in 1898, he rested at the Johannes spa; in 1900 he stayed at Wiesbaden, and so on. He suffered from sleeplessness, excitability, and nervous tension—symptoms then diagnosed as "neurasthenia." More than 500 European sanitariums treated neurasthenia, generally with quiet, quiet, and more quiet.

During the summer of 1901, Haber met Clara Immerwahr at a chemistry conference. Like Haber, Clara came from an assimilated Jewish family in Breslau. Her father was a well-to-do chemist who operated a beet sugar factory on his estate. As students, Clara and Fritz had met in a dancing class and fallen in love, but parental opposition had prevented the match. When they met again, Haber immediately proposed.

Clara Immerwahr was not sure she was suited for marriage. At 30, she had a teaching certificate and a doctorate, the first earned by a woman at the University of Breslau. Her degree was in chemistry, and she was eager for a research career. Nonetheless, after only three days, she accepted his proposal. Otherwise, she said, "one chord of my soul would lie fallow."

Haber, then 33, joyfully wrote to her uncle, "Fate has been kind to me. Your Niece, Dr. Clara Immerwahr, of whom I was fond as a student and then for ten years tried very hard but unsuccessfully to forget, has said 'yes' to me. We saw each other at the Congress in Freiburg, spoke to each other, and finally Clara allowed herself to be persuaded to try a life with me. . . . [We were] like a prince and princess in a fairy tale wrapped up in a dream." On August 3, 1901, three months after becoming engaged, Clara and Fritz were married.

At first, Clara tried to continue her work in chemistry. She attended chemistry seminars and events, translated two articles from English to German, and helped her husband with his 1906 book, *Thermodynamics of Technical Gas Reactions*. In an unusual move by a German scientist at the time, Haber dedicated the book to her: "To my loving wife Clara Haber, Ph.D., thanks for the quiet helping work."

But sustaining a fairy-tale dream with Fritz Haber was not easy. A month into their marriage, Clara became pregnant. She was frequently ill, but Haber often forgot dinner or brought guests home without warning. There were large groups to be entertained and houseguests hosted.

Three months after the Habers' son Hermann was born on June 1, 1902, Haber left for a five-month trip to the United States. The German

Electrochemical Society had asked him to make a fact-finding tour of American electrochemical industries and educational programs, and Haber seized the opportunity to distinguish himself. Even by the standards of the day, leaving his wife with a newborn infant was considered extreme.

Speaking after the trip, Haber discussed national stereotypes in chillingly prescient terms: "We are familiar with the distorted view of the American as someone who chases after dollars without a break, and who, because of his wish to become rich, loses his feeling for law and order as well as any interest in the world of culture. But is this any more accurate than the distorted view of the German that [I was] confronted with over there? . . . We are seen as a people who are good at parades and who write bad lyric poetry, who fawn on those above them and treat harshly those below them . . . who feel comfortable with a voluntary lack of independence in politics, who gladly accept the pressures imposed by the authorities and pass them on to their wives and daughters, whom they rob of freedom and the right to education both in marriage and in their lives generally."

Haber worried about his career. When he was passed over for a promotion, he suspected that his Jewish background was the reason. As a Jewish friend sardonically joked, "Before 35 I was too young for a professorship, after 45 I was too old, and in-between I was a Jew." Professional jealousy may have played a role as well. Haber's enthusiasm for interdisciplinary science often swept him into the bailiwicks of rival professors. Wilhelm Ostwald, the scientist who had refused Haber's applications for study, warned him, "Achievements generated at a greater than the customary rate raise instinctive opposition amongst one's colleagues." Privately, Ostwald complained that Haber emptied "a large pail of facts over our heads" far too fast.

In 1906, at the age of 38, Haber got his promotion and entered Germany's elite mandarin class of professors. As scientists flocked from abroad to study in his laboratory, Haber's position complicated his home life. German professors ran their departments like personal fiefdoms, and, as Frau Professor Haber, Clara was expected to entertain lavishly and burnish her husband's prestige. Instead, two weeks into his professorship, she entered a private sanitarium for a short stay which was attributed to migraine headaches and nervous problems. Back home, she tried to continue in chemistry. Despite her poor health and a sickly child, she managed in 1910 to give four lectures about chemistry in the home to an audience of 100; she earned a 100-mark honorarium, corresponding roughly to $500 today.

As Clara struggled, Haber gloried in his teaching responsibilities. He could be dictatorial, impatient, and outspoken, but with students he was often quite informal. When a young man ruined an experiment, Haber declared theatrically, "You robber and criminal, I will stab you in the belly with a rusty dagger." Then he helped the student with a lengthy tutorial. When another student fell asleep in the front row during a lecture, Haber protested, "Sir, when I was a student, I too slept in some lectures, but I was considerate enough not to sit in the front row to do it." Unlike other important professors, Haber could discuss science for hours on equal terms with a young physicist, as if the two were colleagues.

Verbally and action-oriented rather than contemplative, Haber talked his way through intellectual problems. Launching a monologue, he would pace the hallways with senior students for hours. Thinking was more important than succeeding, he declared. "Doing it was wonderful." Working in his laboratory, he smoked Virginia cigars, left them on mercury-saturated workbenches, and then chewed the butts, long before anyone recognized mercury's extraordinary toxicity. In seminars he bubbled over with ideas.

Inevitably, Haber became interested in applying his knowledge of physical chemistry to one of the leading scientific and social problems of the day: how to turn atmospheric nitrogen into desperately needed ammonia for fertilizer. Europe's population had tripled over the previous 200 years as public relief expanded, the severity of epidemics declined, and food crops were diversified. Yet despite a dramatic drop in mortality rates, Europe still feared that it would run out of food. Hydroelectric power plants and coal gas and coke factories produced small amounts of ammonia that could be used to make fertilizer for crops, but the quantities did not come close to meeting farmers' needs. Indeed, without North American and Ukrainian grain shipments and without nitrogen fertilizer from Peruvian guano, Europe in the early 1900s might have experienced another famine like the Irish disaster of the 1840s.

Europe looked to chemists—prestigious scientists who solved practical problems—to feed its growing population. As Sir William Crookes, president of the British Association for the Advancement of Science, said at the close of the nineteenth century, "It is the chemist who must come to the rescue of the threatened communities. It is through the laboratory that starvation may ultimately be turned to plenty." Haber was more interested in the science than in the politics of world hunger. Frustrated chemists understood the theoretical problem but did not have a solution. They knew they needed to turn the nitrogen in air into ammonia, for use directly as fertilizer or in other compounds such as ammonium nitrate. They called the process of combining nitrogen with other elements "nitrogen fixation." Berthollet, the eighteenth century French discoverer of bleach, had shown that ammonia consists of nitrogen and hydrogen, but he did not know the precise chemical formula or the molecular structure of ammonia.

For 125 years, chemists had been trying without success to make ammonia from nitrogen and hydrogen. The two nitrogen atoms that make up a molecule of nitrogen are held together by one of the strongest known chemical bonds, and no one could break the nitrogen molecules apart long enough to make large quantities of ammonia. Chemists could make nitrogen and hydrogen atoms combine briefly under heat, but the ammonia decomposed almost immediately back into nitrogen and hydrogen.

The problem was Germany's to solve. By the time Haber became a professor in 1902, Germany was fast becoming the world's leading industrial nation. Already its middle and working classes, though politically powerless, were richer than those in France or England. German scientists were breaking new ground in almost every field. German chemical firms were diversifying into drugs, agriculture, photographic chemicals, and explosives. The three largest chemical companies (BASF, Hoechst, and Bayer) employed almost twice as many chemists as German universities and technical schools.

The fact that Germany depended on imported fertilizer more than any other country gave it a special stake in the problem, too. The industrialization of Germany's sugar beet and potato farms was intimately linked to its use of natural fertilizer, especially nitrogen compounds from marine bird manure imported from Peru, Chile, and Bolivia. Yet experts predicted that Europe would exhaust South America's guano in 30 years.

Germany also had strong military incentives for developing a nitrogen-fixation process. Nitrogen compounds are used, not just in fertilizer, but also in explosives. As Europe moved into the twentieth century, scientists worked in what amounted to a cold war atmosphere. Science, no longer the international movement of Lavoisier's day, had become highly nationalistic. In 1900, when the Boer War broke out between German and English immigrants in South Africa, Anglo-German relations soured. Haber's critic, Ostwald, realized that, in the event of a European war, Britain's navy would block the import of guano Germany needed to make nitrates for explosives. Ostwald and Walther Nernst, the world's two leading physical chemists, worked on nitrogen fixation in their laboratories, but got nowhere.

Haber, the self-taught upstart in physical chemistry, entered the nitrogen-fixation race in 1903. He had certain strengths. Ever eager to overcome rejection and obstacles, he was a patient researcher who did not give up easily. He had put basic scientific principles to practical use and was intimately familiar with industrial chemistry. One of the keys to making ammonia commercially would be the ability to carry out gas reactions under pressure, and Haber understood gaseous reactions.

Finally, Haber knew how to blend the talents of skilled technicians, industrialists, and scientists from different disciplines. His English collaborator, Robert Le Rossignol, would develop the seals needed to maintain high pressures in an experimental chamber. A highly skilled mechanic, Friedrich Kirchenbauer, would build precision equipment needed for the reaction. Haber later thanked Le Rossignol and Kirchenbauer in his Nobel Prize speech and shared patents with Le Rossignol and prize money with both men.

With his team organized, Haber began looking at the problem in its simplest form—at normal atmospheric pressure. After publishing some preliminary results, Haber met Walther Nernst at a scientific conference in Hamburg. Nernst, who was only four years older than Haber, had a pugnacious personality that made him quarrel with almost everyone in academia. Worried that Haber's work cast doubt on the validity of his new law of thermodynamics, Nernst publicly ridiculed Haber's "highly erroneous data" and told him scornfully to do his "homework."

Haber was mortified and shaken by Nernst's dressing down. Afterward, he suffered from stomach, intestinal, and skin problems, and Clara worried about his health. Years later at a large conference, he and Nernst shared a rostrum but pretended not to notice each other.

Haber decided to rethink the entire problem. He decided to study nitrogen fixation, as Nernst had, under pressure. Because ammonia takes up less volume than its ingredients, he realized that squeezing nitrogen and hydrogen under pressure would promote their combination into ammonia. Responding to Nernst's challenge, Haber turned his laboratory into a world center for the analysis of high-pressure effects.

In an elegant study of thermodynamics, Haber and Le Rossignol discovered that hydrogen and nitrogen would stay combined only under extraordinarily harsh conditions: temperatures of 200°C (390°F) and atmospheric pressure 200 times stronger than normal. Such conditions were unheard of at the time, yet even they produced ammonia extremely slowly. To speed the process, Haber and Le Rossignol needed a catalyst, a metallic surface for the gases to combine on. By testing one metal after another, they discovered that osmium and uranium accelerated the process. To condense the ammonia gas into a liquid, they passed it from their apparatus into a glass flask surrounded by dry ice. The results were astounding. Haber raced joyfully through the chemistry building shouting, "You have to see how liquid ammonia is *pouring out*."

"Come down, there's ammonia," he called to Hermann Staudinger, whose office was upstairs. Sure enough, at the bottom of Haber's flask sat a little puddle of ammonia the size of a scant teaspoonful. It was not precisely "pouring out," but it was enough to amaze the chemists.

"I can see it still," Staudinger recalled years later. "It was fantastic." Haber had found a way to fix nitrogen in the laboratory.

Despite BASF's close ties with Haber and other Karlsruhe chemists, the chemical company was skeptical of his progress.

"How much pressure will be needed?" an executive asked Haber.

"Well, at least 100 atmospheres," Haber replied. One atmosphere corresponds to the normal pressure on Earth's surface.

"A hundred atmospheres!" the executive cried out in shock. "A hundred! Only yesterday an autoclave at 7 atmospheres exploded on us!" Haber appealed to BASF's chairman for support. The chairman asked the company's chief chemist Carl Bosch to render his opinion. Boldly, Bosch answered, "I think it can work. I know exactly what the steel industry can do. We should risk it."

On July 1, 1909, three BASF executives marched into Haber's laboratory to see his experiment for themselves. Naturally, with important people watching, one of Le Rossignol's seals immediately broke. Bosch walked out, leaving Haber and Le Rossignol discouraged and dejected. After the pair struggled for several hours to get the experiment working again, ammonia "flowed" once more. One of the remaining executives, Alwin Mittasch, was so impressed that, back at BASF, he convinced Bosch to support the project. BASF signed a contract with Haber that doubled his salary and offered tantalizing prospects for profit sharing, should his nitrogen-fixation process work industrially.

BASF set to work figuring out how to adapt Haber's laboratory experiment to a factory-sized operation. Haber's two catalysts, osmium and uranium, were scarce metals that were far too costly for large-scale production. In a crash program, Mittasch conducted 10,000 experiments to test 4000 catalysts—only to discover that some metallic oxides and cheap, easy-to-get iron worked best. Mittasch's testing process became a model for screening procedures in industrial laboratories. As Haber said tongue-in-cheek, "It is strange how new peculiarities are always revealed. Here iron, with which Ostwald first worked and which we then tested hundreds of times in its pure state, now is found to function when impure. I recognize again how one should follow every track to its end."

Five years after Haber patented his process, BASF opened its nitrogen-fixing ammonia factory in 1913. The Haber-Bosch process, as it is now called, remains the cheapest and most efficient method for turning atmospheric nitrogen into compounds that wheat, corn, and other plants can use. It became the model for twentieth-century industrial processes, most of which involved high-pressure synthesis. Without waste products or polluting odors, it became a model for clean industry as well. Above all, it ended Europe's fear of famine. When Haber invented the process, the world's population was 1.6 billion. The twentieth-century added 4.4 billion more people to the planet but, thanks in part to Haber's discovery, global starvation has been avoided.

By making "bread out of air," Haber freed Germany from its dependence on imported fertilizer. Chemistry soared to the peak of its prestige, and Haber became a national hero. A grateful empire made him a knight of the Iron Cross and a knight of the Kaiser House Order of Hohenzollern Swords, Order of the Crown Third Class. Prestigious German universities gave him honorary doctorates, and Kaiser Wilhelm II sent an autographed portrait.

Two months after announcing his discovery in 1910, Haber was offered a job in Berlin at a new Kaiser Wilhelm Institute. Several leading chemists, Ostwald, Nernst, and Emil Fischer, had been trying for several years to finance independent institutes to circumvent the opposition of German universities to modern reforms and industrial research. In the United States, millionaires such as Andrew Carnegie and John D. Rockefeller gained social prestige by donating money to public causes. Impressed by the practice, the German chemists decided to ask wealthy Jews to fund research institutes under the aegis of a newly formed Kaiser Wilhelm Society. Since Jews were often treated like social upstarts, many longed for public recognition.

Although the imperial government wanted scientists to help Germany become economically competitive, it did not want to finance institutes. In fact, a few days before the inauguration of the first Kaiser Wilhelm Society institute, it was still unfunded. At the last minute, Leopold Koppel, chair of the German Gaslight Company, offered to finance a Kaiser Wilhelm Institute of Physical Chemistry and Electrochemistry with two conditions: the Kaiser must thank him publicly, and Fritz Haber must be the institute's director.

Haber added a few conditions of his own. He must be a tenured state official with power to run the institute, earn 15,000 marks yearly (roughly $85,000 today), and live free in an institute villa.

Although Jews or former Jews accounted for only 1 percent of Germany's population, Jewish bankers were soon underwriting one-fifth of the Kaiser Wilhelm Society and its institutes. Jews gravitated to new fields and institutions where established barriers did not prevent them from getting jobs; in Haber's institute, one out of four staff members was Jewish. Later the Nazis criticized the Kaiser Wilhelm Society as a "Jews' Society."

Koppel financed Haber's institute lavishly with the best available laboratory equipment for state-of-the-art research and with five full-time scientific researchers who had no teaching duties. When Haber installed the only dining room and auditorium in the area, his institute became a lively hub of interdisciplinary activities.

The institutes were built on a royal farm in rural Dahlem, now an affluent suburb of Berlin. Rabbits and partridges nibbled at Haber's garden. The area was so isolated that, when his chemist friend Richard Willstätter moved next door, Haber advised him to buy a guard dog. The Habers lived next door to the institute; when he worked late, Clara brought him dinner on a tray.

After the Kaiser gave Haber the exalted title of "*Geheimrat*," or privy councilor, he behaved like "a Lion" who wanted to be "your best friend and God at the same time," or so thought physicist Lise Meitner. Haber's 1913 contract with BASF gave him 1.5 pfennigs for every kilogram of ammonia produced; by the mid-1920s, BASF had paid him enough to start rumors that the Habers dined on gold plates. Legends accumulated quickly: Geheimrat Haber conversed in couplets at parties, gave scientific lectures to his six-year-old son, and bowed low to the peasant women who scrubbed the institute's floors.

Berlin's scientific elite welcomed Haber warmly. He became close friends with Albert Einstein, Max von Laue, and Richard Willstätter, all future Nobel Prize winning scientists. During Einstein's divorce from his first wife, Mileva, Haber drew up Einstein's financial agreement with her, promised her the Nobel Prize money that Einstein was expected to win, and stood beside the physicist at the Berlin train station as he sobbed good-byes to his sons. For more than a decade, Haber mediated between Mileva and Einstein.

Yet as Haber's sun rose, his family life deteriorated. Rejecting their newfound wealth, Clara embraced a simple, semisocialistic lifestyle called the Reform Movement. She dressed in loose, uncorseted dresses, ate healthful food, drank coffee with her maids in the kitchen, and went to market instead of sending servants. Once, when she answered the front door herself, a visiting scientist assumed she was the cleaning woman. Haber's coworkers and students interpreted her dress as a protest against her husband, and other wives whispered that she did not know how to please a man. Dissatisfied with his marriage, Fritz blamed Clara. Outsiders wondered if the Habers could ever bridge their differences.

On July 28, 1914, Haber applied for a six-week summer holiday, provided war did not break out. A week later, Germany invaded neutral Belgium, and World War I began in earnest. In the first month, the German army took thousands of civilian Belgians as hostages, executed many of them, and torched Belgian villages and towns. A six-day rampage destroyed the center of Louvain and its 400-year-old university library, the repository of 750 medieval manuscripts and other treasures. The atrocities turned world opinion abruptly against Germany.

Germany's upper classes—which included academics like Haber—welcomed the war as an act of purification and a means of redemption. The widely respected physicist Max Planck felt that "all the moral and physical powers of the country are being fused into a single whole, bursting to heaven in a flame of sacred rage." Echoing the views of others, he asked a friend, "Could it really be such a terrible thing that has called forth so willing a sacrifice, so pious an enthusiasm? I cannot believe it."

Accepting without question the German government's version of events in Belgium, Haber and 92 other eminent intellectuals signed a manifesto, To the Civilized World: "It is not true that Germany is guilty of having caused this war . . . that we trespassed on neutral Belgium . . . that our troops treated Louvain brutally. . . . The German army and the German people are one." A counterproposal circulated by Albert Einstein collected only three signatures. Haber and many others gradually realized their mistake, but Haber refused to publicly repudiate the manifesto. After the war, his refusal cast deep shadows over his accomplishments.

Haber volunteered as a noncommissioned officer in the army. At first, military leaders told Haber that scientists were not needed so he busied himself finding a substitute for embargoed toluene to make antifreeze for the Russian front. Once the Allies and Germany dug themselves into trenches along either side of the Western Front, the line between them did not budge more than ten miles for the next three years despite the loss of millions of young lives. Berlin's high command had planned for a short war, much like Germany's victorious 1870 attack on France. Trench warfare used enormous amounts of explosives, and Britain's naval embargo blocked imports of nitrates. Germany had only enough explosives to fight for six months. Haber believed that on a large scale, the only practical way to make enough nitric acid for munitions was by oxidizing ammonia made by his process. Haber quickly turned his ammonia-making technology into a weapon.

World War I was the first war to involve science and technology on a grand scale. Until then, scientists had played no significant role in the German military. As Haber described it metaphorically, "The general lived, so to speak, on the second floor and greeted the academics who lived below, but a more profound connection did not exist." Haber spent the war running up and down "the staircase" mediating between the two communities. In a conflict of interest, he secured favored treatment for the chemical industry and his own process while collecting royalties on it. He convinced his old partners, Bosch and BASF, to make large amounts of nitric acid for explosives. He gave BASF insider information from government meetings and competitors and negotiated with other chemical firms to license his own process from BASF. By the end of the war, Haber's synthetic ammonia process furnished almost half of Germany's nitric acid for explosives. Haber had saved his country from early defeat. Without his discovery and leadership, Germany could have lost the war in six months, but at least seven million lives could have been saved.

Haber was not content with making nitric acid for his country. The military, desperate to end the stalemate and break through the trenches, asked Haber to find an *ersatz* weapon, a chemical substitute for traditional munitions. The chemical industry had manufactured metal canisters for storing liquefied gases under pressure since 1892, and Germany, France, and Britain were considering their use. France, for example, was contemplating tear gas, which is not fatal. Although the Hague Peace Conferences of 1899 and 1907 had banned the use of unusual, new weapons that might cause unnecessary suffering, Haber believed that poison gas would be more humane than high explosives and no worse than flying shrapnel. He argued that poison gas would save lives by shortening the war.

Some Americans agreed with him. The United States did not sign the Hague Convention; its delegate, Captain Alfred Thayer Mahan, saw no "logical difference between blowing up people in a ship, whence they could hardly escape, or choking them by gas on land." James B. Conant's chemical warfare work during the war did not prevent him from later becoming president of Harvard University.

Haber agreed to find a chemical weapon. He had already volunteered his services to the military; the Prussian ideal was duty and unconditional service to the state. Few statesmen anywhere argued that humanitarian concerns were more important than national interests; most Europeans believed that military orders must be obeyed even if they violated moral principles. Haber thought of himself as a latter-day Archimedes, the ancient Greek scientist who served mankind in peace and his fatherland in war. In service to his country, Haber invented a potentially fatal, offensive weapon—poison gas.

Living under fire at the front for weeks, Haber directed the burial of almost 6000 cylinders of liquid chlorine along a mile and a half line near the beautiful old city of Ypres, Belgium. On April 22, 1915, the prevailing winds shifted and blew west toward Franco-Algerian troops. The Germans opened all the canisters simultaneously, releasing within ten minutes 150 tons of chlorine. A white cloud turned yellow-green as it moved slowly across the ground and blanketed the French trenches. Vomiting and coughing in violent spasms, the soldiers retreated in panic. German army officers, who had not expected Haber's plan to work, were unprepared to attack the retreating French, however, and the Allies were able to regroup and retake the area.

Chlorine corrodes the eyes, nose, mouth, throat, and lungs and can asphyxiate its victims. Although many Allied soldiers recovered, others died within 24 hours, their lungs filled with fluid. According to the English General Staff, 7000 people at Ypres were poisoned and of those 350 died. In a break with convention, the Emperor personally promoted his 46-year-old Jewish noncommissioned officer to captain—without pay. The British treated Haber's counterpart in chemical warfare better; they made him a general, with salary.

Chlorine was the first weapon of mass extermination in history and the first full-scale, systematic use of scientifically developed chemicals, techniques, and protective devices in war. Although the pressure to break through the trenches was so great that another country might have tried poison gas too, the fact remains that it was Germany—led by Haber—that did so first. A German biographer, the son of one of Haber's poison gas colleagues, concluded that, "There is no question that Fritz Haber was the initiator and organizer of chemical warfare in Germany. He never denied this. Instead, even after the war, he continued to defend the use of chemical weapons as a feasible means of warfare and to support work in this area."

Haber's wartime institute expanded to include experimental animal houses and 2000 scientists, engineers, and technicians who worked surrounded by military guards on interdisciplinary projects for the government. Among the scientists who worked for Haber were future Nobel Prize winners Otto Hahn, James Franck, Gustav Hertz, and Richard Wilstätter. Synthetic dye factories manufactured most of Germany's chemical weapons. Practically speaking, Haber headed a division of the Prussian War Ministry. He certainly behaved like it. He enjoyed issuing orders and was good at it. His ideal was to obey and to be obeyed. He was obsessed with winning, and nothing else seemed to exist. Einstein was appalled that "this otherwise so splendid man has succumbed to personal vanity, and not even the most tasteful kind."

By the end of the war, poison gases filled one in four artillery shells used by both sides. In military terms, however, poison gas failed. Since masks provided quite effective protection, poison gas was never a decisive weapon on the Western Front; the fatality rate for firearms was ten times higher. Poison gas was not used in the next world war. In fact, if World War I had continued, chemical warfare would have backfired on the Germans. Prevailing winds blow eastward, and Germany had run out of mask material and had no fabric to reclothe soldiers blistered by corrosive gases.

Clara Haber reportedly pleaded with Haber to stop his poison gas work. She visited the training site for poison gas workers and was horrified by experiments conducted on animals. Early in the war, an experiment in the institute laboratory exploded moments after Haber left the room. One scientist lost his hand, and a young physicist, Otto Sackur, one of Clara's classmates at Breslau University, was killed. As Sackur lay dying, Haber stood speechless, unable to do anything but shake his head in shock. It was Clara who thought to try first aid and who ordered her friend's necktie cut away so he could breathe more easily. Haber later found a job at the institute for Sackur's daughter.

Sackur's death profoundly disturbed Clara Haber. She came from a family with a long history of severe depression. Relatives, including a sister, committed suicide. A few years before moving to Berlin, Clara Haber had written her thesis adviser a note of desperation on black-bordered mourning stationery: "What Fritz gained in these eight years (of marriage) is what I have lost—and even more—and what is left over of me fills me with the deepest dissatisfaction. It was always my view of life that it was only worth living if one developed all one's abilities to reach the heights and experienced as much as possible of what a human life can offer . . . [That is what made me decide to get married.] If my elation was short-lived . . . that is due mainly to Fritz's overpowering way in his home and marriage, besides which anyone perishes who doesn't assert herself more ruthlessly than he. . . . I ask myself if a superior intelligence really is sufficient to make a person more valuable than somebody else."

The week after the German poison gas attack at Ypres, the Habers hosted an evening party at home. Later that night, according to some accounts, Clara gave her husband an ultimatum: stop working with poison gas or she would commit suicide. There are also hints that Clara had learned that Fritz was seeing a young woman named Charlotte Nathan and that Clara may have found her husband with Charlotte at the party.

At dawn, Clara took Haber's army revolver, fired a test shot, and then shot herself in the heart. Her 13-year-old son, Hermann, found her still alive but dying. Although Clara left several letters and may have survived 20 minutes or more, little else is known.

The next morning, Haber escaped for the Eastern Front, leaving young Hermann alone at home. Whatever his reasons, Haber wrote a friend six weeks later that he had been so shaken that he had fled the scene for a place where bullets flew. Two and a half years later, Haber married Charlotte Nathan, a Jew roughly half his age. She was lighthearted and charming and managed the German Society, a club of leading Berlin personalities. Haber was passionately in love with her.

When Germany surrendered in November 1918, Haber plunged into severe depression. Friends said he seemed "75 percent dead." Until late in the war, he had expected Germany to win. When the Allies assembled a list of war criminals to be tried, Haber's name was reported to be on it. Growing a full beard, he dispatched his second wife, Charlotte, and their two small children to Switzerland. Haber stayed behind, apparently burning institute documents about chemical warfare. Two weeks later, he traveled to Switzerland under a false passport and tried to become a Swiss citizen. He did not return to Berlin for several months. Although interrogated for 17 hours by British authorities, he was not on the list of war criminals when it was published, and he eventually shaved off his disguise.

A year after Germany's surrender, the Nobel Prizes for the war years were announced. Most of the winners were German. Haber won the 1918 prize for turning nitrogen into ammonia for fertilizer; nothing was said about the use of ammonia in explosives or about Haber's work in poison gas. The prizes unleashed an international storm of protest, particularly in France and Belgium. Except for one Englishman, the non-German winners boycotted the ceremonies, primarily because of Haber. Press reaction to the prizes was extraordinarily hostile; many of the German winners had signed the manifesto of 1914 supporting the invasion of Belgium. Allied countries, especially the neutral states, singled out Haber because his ammonia process had lengthened the war by four years.

After the war, Kaiser Wilhelm abdicated and a republic was formed. Haber continued his poison gas research, although the Versailles Peace Treaty banned the manufacture and trade of poison gas, and the 1925 Geneva Protocol prohibited chemical and bacteriological weapons. Haber urged the creation of a new Kaiser Wilhelm Institute for chemical warfare and chemical pest control for agriculture and forestry. Fortunately, the proposal came to nothing. Haber never retracted his support for poison gas warfare, and during the 1920s he favored supplying Germany's small postwar army with chemical weapons. He also helped the German army build a poison gas plant in the Soviet Union and a mustard gas factory in Spain. A small group in his institute worked on chemical pest control, studies that would have particularly tragic consequences during World War II. In all, Haber participated actively in chemical warfare research until 1926 and was kept informed until 1929.

During the 1920s, Haber divorced Charlotte, an almost unheard of event for a high public official in Germany, and suffered financially from inflation and bad investments. At his request, BASF renegotiated his patent royalty arrangement when the pfennig became worthless. Friendships with fellow scientists sustained him during bouts of melancholy. Yet even with friends, he often had to apologize for angry outbursts. He wrote endearingly to Willstätter, "Oh, dear Richard! Have I so gravely erred that you are still angry? Your approval of me makes me very proud, but your affection means much more to me. Because essentially the psyche is incomparably more important to me than the intellectual and my psyche has simply attached itself to you excessively."

Haber gradually recovered much of his old dash and joie de vivre. He relaxed with chess and the newly fashionable detective novels and took friends on a boat trip up the Nile or invited them to his summer house near Lake Constance. Waiting with friends to be served in a busy restaurant, he grabbed a passing waiter by the coattails and begged with all the drama of his youth, "Could you bring me a coffin? How much is a cemetery plot?"

Haber was among the few German professors and scientists to actively support Germany's liberal Weimar Republic. Most academics disdained parliamentary democracy. As before the war, Haber worked to break down artificial barriers and restraints. He fought the chemical industry's attempts to control academic research, even though powerful industrialists blocked his appointment to chemistry's highest post, a professorship at the University of Berlin. He convinced Allied—and even some conservative German—scientists to work together again in international organizations. He organized an "Emergency Fund for German Science," which evolved into the science-funding agency, the German Research Foundation. And as a roving ambassador for the Weimar Republic, he took a trip around the world and established the first bilateral exchanges between Japan and Germany.

Trying to integrate the physical and biological sciences, Haber ran a famous colloquium series at his institute on everything "from helium to the flea." Even students were expected to ask questions. The sessions were high points of the Berlin science calendar. As Haber told a friend, "I am delighted with everything that exceeds my ability and am happy when I can admire."

Haber remained deeply disheartened by Germany's defeat. The Versailles Treaty had levied on the Weimar Republic a 132-million-mark indemnity, referred to by Haber as "50,000 tons of gold." In his last big gamble to save Germany single-handedly, Haber searched the seas for gold. Accepting contemporary estimates that seawater naturally contained six milligrams of gold per metric ton, he figured that the oceans must contain eight million tons of gold.

Disguised as paymasters and dishwashers to evade Allied scrutiny, Haber and his student assistants took a Hamburg-American Line ship to New York, sampling seawater as they went. Later Haber cruised to Buenos Aires and ordered samples from San Francisco Bay, Iceland, and Greenland. Five years later, he determined that contemporary estimates of seawater's gold content were a thousand times too high. He announced sadly in 1927, "I have given up looking for this dubious needle in a haystack."

Haber was slow to grasp the implications of the Nazis' rise to power. As Germans boycotted Jewish businesses and Hitler's brownshirts removed Jewish students from university libraries and laboratories, the Nazis passed a law on April 7, 1933, to "cleanse" the civil service and universities of Jews. By this time, Haber's Kaiser Wilhelm Institute was financed by the government and its employees were treated as civil functionaries subject to the new law. Haber himself was exempt because of war work and seniority. Eager for a chemical warfare center, Nazi authorities singled out Haber's institute and ordered him to fire its Jews. At the same time, the Kaiser Wilhelm Society told Haber to somehow keep his important senior scientists. He had until May 2 to act.

With breathtaking speed, Haber's life fell from a pinnacle of fame and glory to a state of catastrophe. As he wrote a friend, "I was one of the mightiest men in Germany. I was more than a great army commander, more than a captain of industry. I was the founder of industries; my work was essential for the economic and military expansion of Germany. All doors were open to me." But after April 1933, doors began to close, one by one, on the patriotic Jew.

Watching his friend agonize over the Nazis' demands, Max von Laue, an anti-Nazi Nobel Prize winner, recalled, "The spiritual suffering that this great man endured is unforgettable." Haber did not want to do poison gas research for the Nazis, and he wanted to protect young scientists who, without established scientific reputations, could not find jobs abroad. Einstein wrote Haber about Germany, "I can imagine your inner conflicts. It is similar to having to give up a theory that one has worked on all one's life."

Haber's world was disintegrating on other fronts, too. His health was deteriorating rapidly and, clutching a nitroglycerine bottle and silver spoon for angina pectoris, he moved in and out of sanitariums. The world thought he was still wealthy, but his support payments to Charlotte and their two children took his entire income. He used his savings, depleted by bad investments, to pay taxes and expenses. Tax officials hounded him, and a troublemaker complained to the Gestapo that Haber's passport should be revoked.

By now, Haber was cut off from all but a handful of friends and colleagues. Few academic associates visited or sent words of sympathy, although such gestures would have cost them nothing. The chemical industry, which owed Haber much of its success, had allied itself with the Nazis. Carl Bosch, Haber's old colleague in the nitrogen-fixation process, was the only industrialist who tried to help.

On April 30, under pressure from all sides, Haber acted. In a letter that enraged the Nazis, Haber resigned: "I have the right to remain in office, although I am descended from Jewish grandparents and parents. But I do not wish to make use of this dispensation. . . . My tradition requires that in a scientific post, when choosing coworkers, I consider only the professional and personal characteristics of an applicant, without considering their racial makeup. With a man in his sixty-fifth year, you will not expect any change in the thinking that has directed him in the past 39 years of his university life, and you will understand that the pride with which he served his German homeland all his life now requires this request for retirement."

German newspapers announced that Haber had resigned "for health reasons," but he quickly distributed copies of his letter to counteract the lie. Within two years, one in five German university scientists lost their jobs, 80 percent of them were Jews. Warned that he was destroying German science, the Führer fell into rages.

As Haber told a friend, "I have been German to an extent that I only now fully perceive." He wrote Einstein, "I was never in my life as Jewish as now."

After finding most of his workers jobs abroad, Haber left Germany on August 8 to give a scientific talk and never returned. "I have lived too long. . . . To me the lifework I have lost is irreplaceable," he mourned. Although his health was poor and his days of scientific research were over, his old enemies, chemical warfare officers in Britain, found their former adversary a temporary post at Cambridge University. The Zionist chemist, Chaim Weizmann, invited him to Israel. During World War I, Weizmann's acetone production process had kept the British in explosives just as Haber's ammonia process had supplied the Germans.

Bereft of family, fortune, position, institute, health, and home, Haber moved restlessly around Europe in a hideous *danse macabre*. In Basel, Switzerland, on January 29, 1934, he collapsed with severe heart pains in a hotel room. Later that same day, unable to speak for more than a few minutes, he suffered a heart attack. He died within hours.

Haber was buried in a Basel cemetery. At his request, the body of his first wife Clara Immerwahr was buried next to his, and his gravestone read, "He served his country in war and peace for as long as was granted to him."

After the Nazi takeover, Haber's second wife Charlotte moved to England where one of her sons, Ludwig Haber, became a prominent historian and wrote about chemical warfare, including his father's role in its development. Clara Haber's son Hermann moved to New York City where in 1946 he, like his mother before him, committed suicide.

By the time Haber died, Otto Hahn, acting as provisional director of his institute, had carried out the orders that Haber had resigned over. A Nazi Party member became the institute's director and, in the subsequent Nazi takeover, no other institute of the Kaiser Wilhelm Society suffered as severely as Haber's. The military planned to make the institute a center for poison gas research, and former staff members were not needed.

On January 29, 1935, the anniversary of Haber's death, the Kaiser Wilhelm Society held a memorial service. The Nazis forbade government and university employees from attending, so many officials sent their wives instead. In an audience of almost 500 women sat a few men, including Carl Bosch. It was the closest thing to a public protest that scientists as a group staged during the Third Reich.

In obituaries that infuriated the Nazis, von Laue compared Haber to a tragic Greek hero: a man with great nobility but fatal flaws, whose fate was foredoomed by an accident of birth that he had tried in vain to alter. "He was one of us," von Laue wrote. After the war, von Laue rebuilt Haber's institute, and in 1953, it was renamed the Fritz Haber Institute.

Haber's legacy, like his life, was a mix of high-minded science and nationalism gone tragically amiss. To obliterate Haber's achievements, the Nazis credited others with his nitrogen-fixation process and his chemical warfare work. Most horrifically, the Nazis used the pesticide Zyklon B—an offshoot of work begun in Haber's institute and supported by him—in concentration camp gas chambers. Among Haber's relatives, members of his stepsister's family lost their lives to Zyklon B cyanide at Auschwitz.

Yet Haber also left the world better able to feed its growing populations. By the time he died, the world was using annually 2.5 million tons of fertilizer made with his ammonia process. After World War II, fertilizer use skyrocketed 45 times. In terms of volume, ammonia made by the Haber-Bosch process is the sixth most important manufactured chemical in the United States. Thanks to nitrogen fertilizers, the Green Revolution could grow new strains of wheat and rice to feed Third World populations.

Not even Haber's nitrogen fertilizer is entirely innocuous, however. Today, excess nitrogen—half of it from fertilizer runoff—has deoxygenated vast bodies of water including the Gulf of Mexico, Chesapeake Bay, the Baltic Sea, the Black Sea, and the Adriatic Sea. With Earth's population expected to double to 12 billion by the year 2040, scientists are trying to devise ways to prevent more runoff pollution. Others hope to bioengineer nitrogen-fixing microorganisms directly into wheat and rice plants, so that Haber's ammonia will no longer be needed.

Were Fritz Haber here, he might well join them in their efforts. After all, Haber thought chemistry could solve almost any problem. And, as this complicated, tragic man told Philadelphia's Franklin Institute, "Nothing which man creates, either in pure or applied science, is of value for its own sake. Its advantage to mankind is the measure of its value."

6

Leaded Gasoline, Safe Refrigeration, and Thomas Midgley, Jr.

May 18, 1889–November 2, 1944

Without Thomas Midgley Jr., our modern American lifestyle is almost unthinkable. For 50 years our unprecedented personal mobility, our cheap gasoline, and our powerful cars depended on Thomas Midgley's leaded fuel. "Midge" air-conditioned our homes, offices, automobiles, and shopping malls and populated the Sun Belt. His safe refrigeration freed us from levels of food poisoning now known only in developing countries. Without Thomas Midgley, millions of infants would have died of diarrheal diseases, vaccinations would have been ineffective, and fresh food could not be shipped around the world. The discoveries of this one man fueled the enormous expansion of the automotive, aviation, refrigeration, air-conditioning, chemical, and petroleum industries.

At the age of 51, this convivial, whimsical man who liberated us from so many age-old burdens was paralyzed by polio. To maintain some small degree of independence, Midgley designed a system of ropes and pulleys to lift himself out of bed and into his wheelchair. Late one night in 1944, he strangled on the ropes.

For the next thirty years, Thomas Midgley was revered as a scientist who had made our lives healthier and happier. Only in the closing decades of the twentieth century could other scientists detect the far-reaching damage caused by our reliance on his leaded gasoline and chlorofluorocarbon refrigerants. Yet such was his creativity that many years ago he and his associates also invented some of today's substitutes for their destructive CFCs.

Midgley was born on May 18, 1889, into a family of successful inventors. His father held patents for automobile wheels, and his father-in-law patented inserted-tooth saws. According to a Midgley tradition, an English ancestor worked for James Watt, inventor of the steam engine. Young

Thomas Midgley began his inventing career on a high school baseball team in Columbus, Ohio, where he lived most of his life. Rubbing a ball with slippery elm-tree juice instead of spit, he and a friend pitched such reliable curves that professional pitchers adopted their trick.

When Midgley was sent to a Connecticut boarding school in 1905, he encountered the scientific tool that would help him make his most important discoveries. In his first chemistry class, the teacher cited the periodic table of the elements as evidence of God's existence. Midgley protested. As he described it, "We argued. I contended that it simply indicated that the atoms were made up of still smaller particles. The argument went on for days and weeks. A useless argument? Not in the least; for in the course of it I had occasion to learn much about the periodic table and to have it impressed upon my memory as a very useful tool in research work."

Planning to follow in his father's inventive footsteps, Midgley majored in mechanical engineering at Cornell University in northern New York State. Although Midgley would later become a self-taught chemist and the president of the American Chemical Society, he took only the general chemistry and elementary quantitative analysis classes required of all engineering students at Cornell. He was far from an A student; he worked as little as possible in most of his courses so that he could focus intensely on the few that did interest him. His plan worked; he was the only student hired by the recruiter from the National Cash Register (NCR) Company in 1911.

National Cash Register was located in Dayton, Ohio, a hotbed of invention in the early twentieth century. Wilbur and Orville Wright built the airplane in their Dayton bicycle shop. Charles Kettering, soon to become Midgley's close friend and mentor, electrified the cash register at NCR, revolutionizing business machines and retailing. Dayton itself pioneered the progressive city-manager form of municipal government.

Midgley's year at NCR convinced him that he too wanted to conduct experiments to discover new products, but industrial research was in its infancy in the United States. Midgley got sidetracked in his father's tire company for several years. By the time the family business collapsed in 1916, Midgley and his wife, Carrie M. Reynolds, had two children, Jane and Thomas III. As Midgley explained, "I suddenly found myself out of work with a wife and two children to support and very little money in the bank. I made a quick trip around the country contacting a variety of people in various industries, but without really finding a job to my liking. Upon my return home I arrived at the most important decision of my life. I decided to get a job working for Mr. Kettering, irrespective of the size of the salary, and let nature take its course." In the meantime, Kettering had started his own company.

Arriving for his first day at the old tobacco warehouse that housed Kettering's firm, Dayton Engineering Laboratories Company, Midgley recalled, "I was trying to open the door that looked like the front door of the building, but which was locked. As I strained and pulled at it, a rather lanky individual called out to me, 'Hey, bud, the architects just stuck that door on to look right to fool people. You get in on the side. Follow me.' "

The "lanky individual" turned out to be Kettering, and the door was a lesson in Kettering-style inventiveness: try a side route if the main one does not work. Soon Boss Kett and Midge, as they called each other, felt like father and son. Midgley said that his 15 years working with Kettering were as entrancing as the stories of the Arabian Nights.

When Midge and Boss Kett joined forces, the mass-produced automobile was ten years old. Horse-drawn carriages were still the primary mode of transportation, and cities were heavily polluted with dead horses and manure. Almost 74,000 horses lived in New York City in 1896, for example, and every day, each of those horses deposited approximately 20 pounds of manure in the city's streets. Even the best neighborhoods could have 20,000-ton manure heaps piled 30 feet high and 200 feet long. Annually, the carcasses of 8000 dead horses were abandoned in the streets, feeding clouds of flies, rats, and pigs owned by the poor. Cities could not be kept clean until horseless carriages replaced live animal power.

Kettering helped replace the horse by turning the horseless carriage into a vehicle that anyone could drive. The heavy iron crank that started early automobile engines kicked as brutally as a mule and broke many a strong man's arm. But Kettering's electrical self-starting ignition, still used today, was safe for both men and women. It doubled the market for automobiles and was an important step in the emancipation of women. Kettering also developed quick-drying automotive paints, four-wheel brakes, and diesel locomotives.

Despite all his successful inventions, Kettering contended that "the greatest discovery I ever made was Tom Midgley." Like Kettering, Midgley was an enthusiastic optimist about the future and about technology's ability to solve social problems. Midgley was also congenitally and consumingly curious. A friend said that Midgley had "ten ideas a minute, nine of them screwy, but the tenth a lulu." While chatting or golfing, Midgley often stopped a moment and then burst out, "I've just made an invention!" Over lunch one day, Midgley realized that the presence of an ice cube in each package of Clarence Birdseye's new quick-frozen food would prove that the food had never thawed. Midgley marched right down to a patent office to register his idea. By the end of his career, he held more than 100 patents.

Soon after Midgley began working at Dayton Engineering, Kettering gave him an assignment: knock. Everyone who drove a car before World War I knew what knock was. It was the metal-on-metal ping that occurred whenever the pistons in an internal combustion engine strained at peak efficiency. Driving up a hill made valves rattle, cylinder heads knock, the gearbox vibrate, and the engine suddenly lose power. When a vehicle pulled slowly out of an intersection, it was often trailed by a long "funeral procession" of other cars too underpowered to pass. If knocking continued long enough, it destroyed the engine. Knock cracked Army airplane pistons too and, as World War I combat and fuel shortages neared, it became an important military problem. Yet no one knew whether the engine or its fuel was at fault.

As a 27-year-old mechanical engineer, Midgley knew little about the chemistry of petroleum and internal combustion. But chemists didn't either. The world's leading chemists were German, and most of them studied coal products. As Kettering admitted, "We don't even know what makes an automobile run. It is so simple to explain it by saying, you take a charge of gasoline and air into the cylinder and compress it and ignite it with a spark, and it explodes and pushes the piston down, and that makes your car go. . . . If you stop right there, it is a logical explanation. But what does the spark do? What do you mean by combustion? . . . So I say, quite solemnly, that we haven't the slightest idea what really makes the contraption run."

Theoretically, the key to improving engine performance was squeezing the mixture of air and fuel inside the engine cylinder into a smaller volume to confine the detonation and make the pistons turn the drive shaft more efficiently. Engineers spoke of this as increasing an engine's compression ratio, but increasing the compression ratio caused even more knocking.

The amount of knock was also affected by the type of petroleum used. Fuels are given octane ratings based on their propensity to knock. High-octane fuels knocked less, and cars required fuel with a rating of 87 or better to run smoothly. California and Borneo, for example, produced a naturally high-octane fuel rich in aromatic hydrocarbons like benzene and toluene. These fuels, however, were in short supply and expensive; during the 1920s, even airplanes used gasoline with octane ratings as low as 50.

Kettering thought that the American auto industry was at a crossroads. Like Europe, it could develop small and efficient high-compression engines to use an expensive, high-octane gasoline. Several European cars for the rich—Rolls Royces, Isotta 8's, and Mercedes, for example—could already reach speeds of 70 and 80 miles per hour. But the American auto industry had another choice as well: it could try to make large, powerful engines that ran on cheap, low-octane fuel.

Kettering preferred the second approach. His client, General Motors (GM), was trying to overtake Ford's basic Model T, the number one selling car during the teens. Making automobile transportation for the masses—not just for the rich—demanded a low-cost fuel. But General Motors could not sell comfort, convenience, power, and style to the middle class with a pokey car that knocked while climbing hills.

As a mechanical engineer, Midgley knew where to start: he had to define knock before he could hope to cure it. Improvising a high-speed camera, he wrapped film around a tomato can and secured it with rubber bands. Then he spun the can on roofing nail pivots. Photographing the engine through a quartz window in the cylinder, he showed that part of the fuel inside the engine cylinder was exploding prematurely. As Midgley described it, "When a spark occurs in a cylinder, a wall of flame spreads out from this point. . . . [However,] when any gas is heated either it must expand or its pressure must rise. The layer of gas just in front of the flame is so intensely heated that it rises to a very high pressure, and in some cases . . . the gas in front of the flame wall is subjected to such a high pressure that it goes off with a bang—that is detonation." When the fuel detonated, knock occurred, dissipating much of the fuel's power to the engine block. No wonder cars could take advantage of only about 5 percent of the fuel's energy.

Midgley began searching for a way to prevent premature detonation and knock. It was a tough, uncompromising problem, and the tobacco warehouse laboratory where he worked did not even have running water. He worked whenever and wherever; disappearing from home for days at a time, he slept on a cot at the laboratory. He had a fabulous memory for technical details, but forgot where equipment was kept. He was personable, but he was "an aggressive kind of fellow" too, thought Kettering. Midgley could draw more valid conclusions from sketchier data than anyone else around.

Kettering told Midgley about his "trailing arbutus" theory of knock. The trailing arbutus plant can bloom under snow because its red-backed leaves absorb radiant heat from the sun. Perhaps a red dye would make fuel absorb radiant heat from the flame and vaporize sooner. Not a very scientific theory, but it was better than nothing. Midgley was an inventor with a penchant for trying out ideas. So without stopping to calculate the odds of the theory's working, he marched to the stock room for a dark, oil-soluble dye. None was available.

"What have you?" Midgley asked.

An attendant took down a bottle of dark-colored iodine. "Try this," he said.

Midgley added the iodine to the fuel of a knocking engine and, to his amazement, the knock disappeared. Buying up every oil-soluble dye in Dayton, he tested them all, only to find that none of them killed knock. Yet something had worked and Midgley was nimble-minded, so he tried a colorless iodine compound. Again, knock disappeared. It was the iodine—not the dye—that quieted knock. Iodine was impractical; it would add a dollar to each gallon of gasoline, it corroded and clogged the engine, and its exhaust reeked. Nevertheless, iodine showed Midgley that chemical reactions in fuel could solve the problem of knock and that chemistry was the key to finding other antiknock compounds. Midgley began staying up late at night to study chemistry. The engineer was becoming a chemist.

More curious than cautious, he found discovery far more exhilarating than safety. For chemists like Midgley, timidity was the enemy of invention. When Henry Ford visited, Midgley saturated a handkerchief with ethyl iodide and shoved it in his coat pocket. Then, with fumes wafting around, he made dramatic, abracadabra-like passes over a violently knocking test engine. When his suit pocket hovered over the engine's air inlet, some of the iodine found its way into the engine and stopped the noise. It looked most mysterious, and Midgley must have grinned.

During World War I, Midgley developed a benzene-based fuel that helped reduce some of the knock in Liberty fighter planes, and he helped design a flying robot torpedo called the "buzz bomb." One day a plug exploded and spattered metal particles into the cornea of Midgley's eye. His doctor could not remove them. Experimenting on himself, Midgley bathed his eye with liquid mercury until the mercury formed alloys with the metal bits and flushed them out. Neither the aviation fuel nor the buzz bomb was ready before the war's end, but they did turn Midgley into a fully-fledged, self-taught chemist. They also helped awaken the petroleum industry to the need for scientific research.

After World War I, Midgley resumed his all-consuming search for a cheap antiknock agent. Airplanes were still on his mind. The war and the growing importance of air travel highlighted aviation's needs for high-compression engines to improve the power-to-weight ratios of aircraft. Midgley's laboratory was stacked with airplane pistons cracked by knock. Almost hit or miss, he screened every chemical compound that came to Dayton, eventually 33,000 in all. At the same time, he developed a tool that gave fuels their octane ratings for the next 25 years.

The 1920s were the decade of the car as well as the airplane though. Americans were richer and more consumption-oriented than ever. Mass production techniques in cars, mining, timber, and even cigar making were bringing luxury goods to middle-class workers whose real earnings jumped 11 percent between 1923 and 1928. As the number of automobiles on

America's roads more than tripled, General Motors overtook Ford as the world's largest carmaker. And as engineers improved the efficiency of internal combustion engines, the need for more efficient fuel became even more pressing. Adding to the car industry's pressure for a solution to the fuel problem, the U.S. Geological Survey announced—mistakenly—that world petroleum deposits would be depleted in a few years.

The E. I. du Pont de Nemours & Company, Inc., which owned a large block of General Motors stock and manufactured paints, varnishes, artificial leather, and celluloid for GM, wanted to conduct the carmaker's chemical research and development work too. In particular, Du Pont pressed GM to spend $100,000 to study the fundamental science of fuel combustion in engine cylinders. Du Pont objected to Kettering's "cut and try, qualitative methods" and thought the fuel problem required more than "merely the discovery of some cure-all which can be added in small quantities." But Kettering wanted a cheap solution to sell more cars. Midgley talked with Du Pont executives, including Wallace Hume Carothers (Chapter 7), on and off for four years, but—tragically, as it turned out—nothing came of their discussions. Meanwhile, General Motors almost shut down the funding for Midgley's antiknock project several times. Once, in a critical test of his creativity, the company gave him only one more week. If he could not produce any new results by then, the project was finished.

"We thought we had worked hard up to this day," Midgley recalled, "but our work was mere idleness compared to the feverish activity that we crowded into the next seven days and before the time was up we had found another compound, aniline." A chemical building block of coal tar compounds, aniline is found in the natural blue dye, indigo, and is used in the manufacture of synthetic dyes (Chapter 2). Aniline was cheaper and more effective than iodine, but it was also toxic, corroded metal, and had a wretched, earthy smell. Midgley admitted, "I don't think humanity would put up with this smell, even if it meant twice as much gasoline mileage."

In the laboratory, Midgley was a businesslike, hard-driving boss who wanted work well done. Off-hours, he and Carrie blew off pressure partying Prohibition-style. He made excellent gin, and his family thinks he invented the screwdriver, an orange juice cocktail laced with vodka. Far from being an eccentric loner, Midgley was personable and jovial. Given a drink and a circle of friends, he gabbed science the night through in a hotel bar and put in a full day's work the next day. As he joked, "I have always had a fondness for intelligent people. And the more we drink, the smarter we get." One of his Valentines to Carrie was a telegram, "I've got whiskey, I've got wine, Won't you be my Valentine?"

Early in 1921, Midgley discovered several effective antiknock compounds. Once again, the compounds had a terrible stench, this time with a devilish garlic-and-onions odor. A highly perfumed Chevrolet test car dubbed "The Goat" surged up hills with a compression ratio of 7:1. This was far more powerful than the usual 4:1. The Goat's gas mileage was also 40 percent better.

But the smell of these selenium and tellurium compounds was so powerful and persistent that anyone who came near it was ostracized for days. Even after a bath and a change of clothes, Midgley still reeked. He joked, "When we went to the movies, I would look around until I found a man of Mediterranean extraction, and we would sit down beside him. Presently people would scowl at him from all directions as they got my perfume, but we were secure and comfortable." On trains, Midgley filled entire smoking cars with his smell. Carrie Midgley banished Tom to the basement for seven long months, and some members of Midgley's team openly discussed abandoning the search.

Although Midgley's compounds were clearly unmarketable for passenger cars, the Army was willing to ignore odors. In 1920, Major R. W. Schroeder used an early antiknock agent in one of the first turbosupercharger engines to set an altitude record of 36,020 feet, nearly seven miles. A few years later, Lieutenants J. A. Macready and Oakley Kelly used another Midgley antiknock agent to fly the first nonstop transcontinental airplane from New York City to San Diego.

Midgley's breakthrough occurred when a Massachusetts Institute of Technology chemist told him about a new version of the periodic table of the elements. The table was based on physicist Niels Bohr's 1913 model of the atom. It arranged the elements—not according to their atomic number, as traditional tables organized them—but according to the number of electrons and vacant spaces in their outermost electron shells. Thus, the table showed their valence, that is, their ability to combine with other elements. While Henry Ford's engineering department was still dominated by self-taught mechanics, Midgley carried Bohr's table in his pocket. It marked his transformation from an engineer to a research chemist.

Armed with the table, Midgley's group could focus its search on elements with atomic structures similar to those in their impractical antiknock compounds. Suddenly, Midgley's hit-or-miss search was transformed into a hunt guided by fundamental scientific principles. As Midgley explained, "What had seemed at times a hopeless quest, covering many years and costing a considerable amount of money, rapidly turned into a 'fox hunt.' Predictions began fulfilling themselves instead of fizzling."

Midgley noticed that almost every known antiknock substance was made of elements that sat bunched together in the lower right-hand corner of the table. Better yet, the lower elements with heavier atoms stopped knock rather effectively. The heaviest metal, lead, looked especially promising. "We thereupon predicted that tetraethyl lead would solve the problem," Midgley recalled.

Tetraethyl lead, $Pb(C_2H_5)_4$, a rare and poisonous compound that is soluble in oil, was discovered by a German chemist in 1852. Seventy-five years later, on December 9, 1921, Midgley's assistant Carroll Hochwalt succeeded in making a tiny amount of it in their laboratory. Midgley was in New York, so his second-in-command, T. A. "Tabby" Boyd, poured a teaspoonful of tetraethyl lead into a gallon of kerosene in a wildly knocking motor. The ear-splitting noise stopped instantly and was replaced by a purr. Testing smaller and smaller amounts of tetraethyl lead, they discovered that one-twentieth of 1 percent was enough to make fuel burn more slowly and smoothly and prevent knock. It was an automotive dream come true; lead made both the cheapest and the most effective antiknock compound. Midgley's three-year search was over and, at age 32, he was about to become an extremely wealthy man.

In early road tests, leaded gasoline gave greater power and better mileage and made automobile motors operate with a marvelous smoothness free from noise and vibration. Because the tetraethyl lead also clogged spark plugs and exhaust valves and corroded porcelain, Midgley spent the next two years ironing out difficulties with the compound and its manufacture. After discovering that ethyl bromide cured the clogging problem by releasing the lead into the atmosphere, he organized a process to capture bromine from the ocean. Since there are only 65 parts of bromine in a million parts of seawater, ten tons of water had to be treated to reclaim one single pound of bromine. When a joint subsidiary, Ethyl-Dow Chemical Company, was formed to produce the bromine for tetraethyl lead, Midgley became the firm's vice president.

In addition to solving production problems, Midgley wanted to understand how tetraethyl lead stopped engine knock, so Tabby Boyd worked on the problem through the early 1930s. It was the first GM-sponsored basic research that was not directly related to a corporate product. Boyd discovered that knock was related to fuel structure: compact hydrocarbons knock less than long, straight chains. Although chains predominate in natural petroleum, they burn too rapidly in the engine cylinder. Other scientists showed that tetraethyl lead does not stop knock directly; instead, tetraethyl lead decomposes in the engine cylinder and produces the actual antiknock agent.

With a reckless flair for drama, Midgley used an elaborate series of laboratory demonstrations to help sell the additive to executives and scientists. Holding a small, open bottle of tetraethyl lead up to the air inlet of a knocking engine, he liked to show how its fumes silenced knock's explosions. Midgley was versatile: he could invent, devise a practical manufacturing process, and even sell the invention.

As Midgley developed tetraethyl lead, health authorities grew alarmed about the potential for widespread lead poisoning. Lead is a neurotoxin and damages the central and peripheral nervous systems, the blood-forming organs, and the gastrointestinal tract and can cause convulsions, coma, insanity, and even death. Physicians have known for 2000 years about workers who were acutely poisoned by working around lead—the dropped wrist of the painter, for example. In the 1930s, health scientists understood that small amounts of lead accumulate in the body and can eventually reach dangerous amounts, but nothing was known about the long-term effects on the public health of low-level exposure to lead.

With a considerable degree of foresight, Kettering and Midgley realized that more than just workers' health might be involved. They wondered whether tetraethyl lead might endanger anyone who breathed air polluted by leaded exhaust. As lead built up in heavily traveled roads and tunnels, would it accumulate in the bodies of human beings who breathed the exhaust? At the time, no one knew that adults absorb about 40 percent of the lead they inhale or that children absorb up to half the lead in exhaust and suffer nervous system damage.

"From the outset it was appreciated that putting tetraethyl lead into gasoline might possibly introduce a health hazard," Tabby Boyd said years later. "The first opinions of the doctors who were consulted were full of such frightening phrases as 'grave fears,' 'distinct risk,' 'widespread lead poisoning,' and the like. The source of the possible hazard to health thought of at first was not so much that from the tetraethyl lead itself as that from *finely divided lead dust in engine exhaust* [author's italics]."

The American public still considered chemicals to be harmless unless proven otherwise. Federal law did not require testing new compounds for toxicity. Neither the Environmental Protection Agency nor the National Institute of Occupational Safety and Health (NIOSH) would be established for nearly half a century. Despite the lack of regulations requiring him to do so, Midgley considered negotiating with two eminent institutions, Harvard Medical School and Columbia University, for an objective study of tetraethyl lead's toxicity in automotive exhaust. Significantly, Midgley assumed that their research would be conducted free of corporate influence and published freely in scientific journals. Midgley wrote the dean of the Harvard Medical School, "We would of course render this assistance without any strings attached whatever . . . Freedom to publish all results and everything else would of course be quite the same as in other pieces of academic research work."

Midgley also asked the U.S. Bureau of Mines, the nation's authority on automobile exhaust fumes, to investigate the toxicity of exhaust emissions from automobiles using tetraethyl lead. The bureau planned "an exhaustive and impartial experimental investigation on the possibility of poisoning from the lead in automobile exhaust gases from gasoline containing tetraethyl lead, and to make the results public, regardless of what they might be." Although Midgley believed that health officials were alarmists—he called them "fanatical health cranks"—the focus of all these studies was to be the effect of lead-laden exhaust on the general public's well being. In the end, Midgley did not commission the two university studies, and industry exercised control over the Bureau of Mines study. In fact, the bureau's report was the last attempt at a large-scale, unbiased study of leaded exhaust and its effect on public health for 40 years. The U.S. Surgeon General was worried enough, however, to ask whether the public health had been considered. Midgley replied that it "had been given very serious consideration . . . although no actual experimental data has been taken." Midgley and his team assumed optimistically that the lead could be filtered out. "The average street will probably be so free from lead that it will be impossible to detect it or its absorption," Midgley reported.

Meanwhile, Midgley tried to find lead in the exhaust himself. He failed. With the confidence of the self-taught, he decided—not that his measurements might be wrong—but that the exhaust contained no lead. He reported, "There will not be enough lead used in the early stages of this development to present any health hazard whatever." Midgley was no toxicologist, and his results are not surprising. Only a handful of American corporations had toxicology laboratories, among them Du Pont, Dow, and Union Carbide. Scientists did not yet know how to build instruments capable of detecting minute traces of metal in air. And few studies of workers' health had been conducted in the United States.

German medical journals were full of articles about vocational health, however. In 1922, a German chemist warned Midgley that organic lead compounds such as tetraethyl lead "seem to possess, even in very reduced doses, the malicious and creeping poisonous effects which are possessed by inorganic lead compounds. . . . [They produce] a slow weakening and enfeebling of the whole body, which ultimately results in death. . . . I have used every possible means of precaution . . . Nevertheless, I think that I have severely damaged my health." Several of the chemist's coworkers were already dead. For whatever reason, Midgley ignored the warning.

After a year of working with concentrated lead compounds, Midgley and his assistant Carroll Hochwalt, acquired their own cases of lead poisoning. X rays of Hochwalt's bones revealed dark lead lines, and the smell of food made him nauseous; both lead lines and anorexia were known symptoms of acute lead poisoning. Midgley suspected, correctly, that tetraethyl lead could be absorbed through the skin, and he began wearing rubber gloves in the laboratory.

With his typical, light-hearted tone, Midgley told a colleague on January 19, 1923, "I contain a pair of lead-lined lungs. Symptoms being almost identical to the . . . second stage of tuberculosis except in one detail, subnormal temperature instead of abnormal temperature I find myself 2½ degrees shy at times, and if not for my health, simply out of self-respect, I feel that I must overcome this slight error or I shall soon be classified as a cold-blooded reptile. The cure . . . is. . . . to pack up, climb on a train, and search for a suitable golf course in the state named Florida. . . . In the course of 4 to 5 weeks my lungs should grow a new covering, my temperature should become normal," Midgley declared cheerily—and erroneously.

After six weeks of golfing in Florida, Midgley returned to work on March 15 with his temperature still below normal. Even so, he was confident that lead could be handled safely in the laboratory. After all, lead also appeared in house paint, water pipes, food cans, and many other common household products.

Tetraethyl lead went on sale to the motoring public on February 1, 1923. A Dayton service station sold leaded gasoline for 25 cents a gallon, 4 cents more than regular gas. When a customer asked for "Ethyl"—a trade name coined by Kettering to avoid the word "lead"—a gas station attendant turned a cock that dripped the additive into the fuel. Car owners noticed the difference immediately and spread the word: "Stops knocks!" "More power on hills," "Cooler engine," they told one another. In 1924, General Motors and Standard Oil of New Jersey formed the Ethyl Corporation and named Kettering president and Midgley vice president. In a complicated web of corporate relationships, Du Pont, a part owner of GM until 1957, manufactured the tetraethyl lead that Ethyl marketed.

During the spring of 1924, tragedy struck the Dayton plant where tetraethyl lead was blended. Two workers—men Midgley knew and socialized with—died of lead poisoning, and about 60 others became seriously ill with frightening symptoms of mania. The Ethyl Corporation announced that Midgley was "tremendously upset" and was considering abandoning the project. Four workers in a Du Pont plant in Delaware also died. The deaths were hushed up; no newspaper published the stories.

As the economic stakes and health perils of tetraethyl lead became more apparent, corporate pressure emasculated the government's study of leaded exhaust and the public health. General Motors was paying the U.S. Bureau of Mines in the Department of the Interior to conduct the study. Bowing to corporate demands, the Bureau agreed to refer only to the trade name "Ethyl" without using the scientific term that included "lead." The Ethyl Corporation also demanded and was given a veto over the study's content and publication. And, finally, the Bureau of Mines agreed to study— not the effect of exhaust fumes on the general public—but workers' exposure to the liquid and its vapors. Suddenly, tetraethyl lead had become an occupational, labor issue, not a broader, environmental one. Similar Bureau of Mine studies conducted with the American Petroleum Institute into oil-related air and water pollution met similar fates during the 1920s.

At the peak of the crisis, Kettering intervened. Tetraethyl lead was Midgley's baby, but it was Kettering's baby too. And General Motors' President Alfred P. Sloan, Jr., said he was ready to abandon the additive if its toxicity could not be controlled. General Motors had pinned all its antiknock research on a quick fix instead of studying the fundamental science of fuel combustion, as Du Pont had urged. Kettering and GM had no alternative to fall back on, so Kettering hired Dr. Robert A. Kehoe, a young and untried pathologist who knew little about lead poisoning, from the medical school of the nearby University of Cincinnati. The contrast between Kehoe and the Harvard and Columbia experts approached by Midgley is startling, but Kehoe would successfully protect tetraethyl lead for the next 40 years.

Winding up his classes that May, Kehoe moved to Dayton and spent the summer caring for "20-odd" men who had tetraethyl lead poisoning. Within a few weeks, Kehoe reported that the additive posed no danger for the general public and that strict safety regulations would eliminate the danger in factories. Kehoe instituted new factory procedures, and the number of new cases of tetraethyl lead poisoning fell to 18 percent of the Dayton staff, which Kehoe considered "almost complete disappearance."

Two months after Ethyl Corporation's formation, however, the infant company was threatened with extinction. One day Ernest Oelgert, a worker in a pilot tetraethyl lead factory in Elizabeth, New Jersey, became delirious and screamed that three figures were "coming at him." Later that day Standard Oil of New Jersey, which operated the factory, also sent home ill William McSweeney, a former general in the Irish Republican Army. The next morning McSweeney's sister-in-law had to summon a policeman, who needed three extra men to subdue McSweeney. Violently insane, the Irishman died in a local hospital three days later, bound in a straitjacket and clamped to an iron cot. This time, the newspapers paid attention. A company spokesman told reporters, "These men probably went insane because they worked too hard."

Over the next five days, four more tetraethyl lead workers died and dozens of others suffered severe neurological symptoms. Headlines called lead fumes "Looney Gas." In a processing plant, 80 percent of the workers became psychotic. Hallucinating workers brushed "insects" off their bodies in a Du Pont factory that employees called "The House of Butterflies." New York City, New Jersey, and Philadelphia banned the additive, and the Ethyl Corporation shut down production. In all, at least 15 tetraethyl lead workers died in Ohio, New Jersey, and Delaware.

Kettering was reportedly "very upset and worried." He could not understand how Standard Oil "allowed this matter to obtain such broad publicity," a colleague said. "The situation was just as at Dayton, and I do not see why it could not have been handled in the same way."

Five days after Ernest Oelgert died, Standard Oil held a press conference in its New York offices. Midgley was present. A reporter asked him if it was dangerous to spill the chemical on the hands. Midgley knew that it was, but called for tetraethyl lead. Pouring it into his palms, he washed his hands with it, and then held the bottle to his nostrils for more than a minute. Drying his hands on his handkerchief, he announced, "I'm not taking any chance whatever. . . . Nor would I take any chance doing that every day." Midgley did not mention his own lead poisoning or his trip to Florida the previous winter.

Referring to the euphoria that is a symptom of tetraethyl lead poisoning, Midgley told the *New York World:* "The essential thing necessary to safely handle TEL was careful discipline of our men . . . The minute a man shows signs of exhilaration he is laid off. If he spills the stuff on himself he is fired. Because he doesn't want to lose his job, he doesn't spill it." Apparently, Midgley's generosity and conviviality did not extend to his workers.

The day after the fifth worker died in a tetraethyl lead factory, the U.S. Bureau of Mines announced blandly that the additive posed no peril. Enraged scientists, public health experts, and activists attacked the study.

Under pressure from a frightened public, the U.S. Surgeon General convened a hearing in May 25, 1925. Industry, health, and labor representatives immediately split into two diametrically opposed camps. As the Yale physiologist, Yendell Henderson, observed, "The men engaged in industry, chemists, and engineers take it as a matter of course that a little thing like industrial poisoning should not be allowed to stand in the way of a great industrial advance. On the other hand, the sanitary experts take as matter of course that the first consideration is the health of the people."

Calling the 15 deaths "mishaps, so-called messes," industry representatives argued that tetraethyl lead was "a gift of God [that] at small cost adds fifty percent to gasoline mileage. . . . It must be not fears but facts that we are guided by." Public health and industrial hygiene experts countered that, by the time all the facts were in, powdered lead would have scattered everywhere. Several independent researchers attacked Kehoe and the Bureau of Mines for flawed methodology and sampling techniques.

The two camps even defined lead poisoning's symptoms differently: although recent evidence had shown that excess lead is stored in human bone, industry recognized only death or insanity as lead poisoning. Medical researchers recognized a wide range of effects, including the danger of long-term exposure to small amounts of lead.

The antilead forces were hopelessly outgunned. The prolead forces—the petrochemical and automobile industries—represented the corporate backbone of the United States, while the health researchers had taken a day off work and traveled at their own expense to Washington, D.C., for the hearing. The U.S. Public Health Service had no legal authority over industry and no money to investigate problems even when the public health was endangered. Labor was represented by two women, Grace Burnham and Harriet Silverman, and Ethyl had secretly hired one of the women's chief consultants to funnel their views to the company. The foremost lead poisoning expert was another woman, Alice Hamilton, the founder of occupational medicine and an MIT professor. Yandell Henderson, a member of the National Academy of Sciences who led the newspaper attacks on tetraethyl lead, had become a pacifist after working on poison gas for the Americans during World War I. And among those killed by tetraethyl lead were a radical Irish immigrant and an African-American janitor. Thus, workers' safety had "an unmistakable aura of Socialism or feminine sentimentality for the poor," as Hamilton put it. It was hardly a group to sway big business.

The Surgeon General formed a distinguished committee which called for a long-term, detailed study of tetraethyl lead, but conflict of interest plagued the committee from the start. As the Ethyl Corporation observed, it was "difficult to avoid involvement with the surgeon general's committee, especially when members of the investigating groups complained of inadequate funds and wanted advice from the Ethyl officials even in such matters as where to find room and board when visiting in the Midwest."

When the Surgeon General's committee completed its study, the nation's chief medical officer announced that tetraethyl lead would add less lead to the atmosphere than white house paint, and the Ethyl Corporation resumed production and distribution. Standard Oil gas station signs were jubilant: "Ethyl is Back." As a safety measure, tetraethyl lead was to be blended into gasoline in closely supervised factories instead of at service stations where attendants had been known to plunge their arms into the fluid and splash it up their noses. A billion-dollar-a-year industry was back in business. Even so, the medical adviser to Standard Oil of New Jersey strongly urged corporate president Walter C. Teagle to abandon the product; his advice was unheeded.

No broad study of tetraethyl lead was conducted. According to Kehoe, "It was thought that these necessarily extensive studies should not be repeated at present, at public expense, but that they should be continued at the expense of the industry most concerned." Kehoe proudly declared later, "The problem [of tetraethyl lead's toxicity] therefore was left to a very substantial extent in our hands, where it has remained ever since." Such cooperative arrangements were typical of the 1920s; in lieu of direct government regulation, industrial groups volunteered to collect technical information about the air and water pollution they caused.

In years to come, Kehoe conducted a series of elaborate and dangerous experiments to show that lead does not accumulate in the body. He fed and aerated young men with lead for up to five years while measuring the lead in their feces and urine (but not in their bones where lead is absorbed). Everyone he measured contained lead, whether they were Mexican peasants cooking in and eating off lead-glazed pottery or his controls, men who worked in tetraethyl lead plants. As a result, Kehoe decided that some lead pollution was natural and normal in everyone. Ethyl Corporation called Kehoe its "founding father." Midgley wrote, "The toxic hazards . . . have been controlled."

The reintroduction of tetraethyl lead guaranteed the early development of high-powered but cheap internal combustion engines and fueled the expansion of the automobile industry. Cars, tractors, trucks, and buses acquired peppy new personalities when redesigned with high-compression engines, better metals, and hundreds of minor changes. Suddenly, cars could power heating systems and radios. They could support heavy frames that did not sway on turns and steel bodies that did not crush when they rolled over in accidents. With Kettering's self-starting ignition and electrical system and with new high-compression engines running on Midgley's leaded fuel, the modern American automobile was essentially complete.

Within two decades of the introduction of tetraethyl lead, engine efficiency doubled, power per cylinder tripled, and the octane of regular gasoline rose from 55 to 75. Midgley's gasoline additive symbolized the technological wonders of industrial research and corporate America. Cheap fuel became an American entitlement. A 1950 Cadillac dramatically out-performed a 1921 Cadillac of equal weight and engine size and traveled far-ther on a gallon of gasoline.

The public loved leaded fuel for its pep, not its efficiency. Interest in fuel conservation faded when new oil deposits were discovered. Reassured about lead's dangers, Americans reveled in unprecedented personal mobil-ity and used tetraethyl lead to expand their reliance on automobiles. Sur-prisingly, Midgley did not think his discovery would increase passenger car ownership. Nevertheless, tetraethyl lead and the engine improvements it permitted helped form America's car-dependent society. Fuel-efficient cars and public transportation were no longer top priorities.

Ethyl Corporation swept the American market. By 1960, leaded gasoline accounted for nearly 90 percent of all automotive fuel sold and was one of the top 10 industrial chemical enterprises in the United States. Because Europe and Japan made smaller, more efficient engines, the United States used more than 80 percent of all leaded gasoline sold before 1970. Only Sun Oil Company, controlled by the Pew family, refused to "pay tribute" to Ethyl. Sun Oil bought naturally high-octane California petroleum and produced a "poison-free" fuel that was both knock-free and cheaper than leaded gasoline. Sun Oil used high-temperature cracking techniques and, during the 1930s, pioneered catalytic cracking, the technology that today transforms natural petroleum into high-octane fuel rich in aromatic hydrocarbons and branched hydrocarbon chains. During World War II, catalytic cracking produced huge volumes of high-octane fuel for long-distance bombers.

Catalysts were expensive, however, so the petroleum industry did not solve the problem of cheap, lead-free, knock-free gasoline until the 1970s, after General Motors adopted the catalytic converter. Lead compounds inactivate the catalysts, and sophisticated catalytic cracking techniques had to be developed to replace the fuel additive. Ironically, an even more diffi-cult job was finding a substitute for the protective coating that tetraethyl lead formed on exhaust valve seats; not even newly developed, extremely hard materials prevent wear and tear on them as well as tetraethyl lead did.

In 1925, General Motors and Kettering consolidated operations in Detroit, and Midgley rejected a lucrative offer to become a GM vice presi-dent. He was making more than enough money as a GM consultant, a vice president of the Ethyl Corporation, and a board member of the Ethyl-Dow Chemical Company. Midgley stayed behind in Ohio and worked on a new research project of his own: rubber, especially synthetic rubber. To keep him happy, General Motors reluctantly supported the endeavor. The Midgleys bought more than 50 acres in rural Worthington, Ohio, outside his old hometown of Columbus and planned an immense colonial-style mansion.

Columbus was conveniently located between Detroit and Dayton, and Midgley loved to drive. Leaving home at 5 a.m., he arrived at General Motors's Detroit laboratory at 9 a.m., worked until 9 p.m., and was home by 1 a.m. By 9:00 the next morning, he was back at work in the dining room of a Dayton mansion that he had converted into a small, private research laboratory.

By 1928, Kettering was in charge of the General Motors research department, and Frigidaire—the leading refrigeration company of the 1920s—was part of GM. At the tag end of a phone conversation with Midgley, Kettering announced, "The refrigeration industry needs a new refrigerant if they ever expect to get anywhere." A Frigidaire engineer would come to Dayton the next morning to discuss the problem with Midgley, Kettering added.

While Midgley had needed three years to find his antiknock compound, he solved the major public health problem of refrigeration in a few hours. That Saturday morning, Frigidaire's engineer outlined the problem to Midgley. Every refrigerant known was toxic, inflammable, or both. If refrigeration and air-conditioning were to become popular, a safe chemical refrigerant would have to be found.

The basic principles of refrigeration had been understood for 100 years. When a chemical expands into a gas, it absorbs heat and lowers the temperature of the surrounding space. Putting the gas under pressure compresses it back into a liquid so that it can be evaporated anew. This repeating cycle could be used to cool a refrigerator, a house, or even an automobile but no one had found a safe gas. Frigidaire was using sulfur dioxide, a remarkably toxic chemical. Even a tiny leak could wake someone from a deep sleep and send him racing—vomiting, coughing, and probably swearing—for fresh air. Similarly, ammonia, used by brewers, large-scale ice makers, butcher shops, and the like, was too dangerous for use by untrained personnel. Methyl chloride, another early refrigerant, proved lethal in some apartment houses during the 1920s when pipes connecting basement water-cooling equipment to refrigerators upstairs leaked. Highly publicized photographs of a dead family in 1925 prompted many municipalities to ban "death gas ice boxes." More than 100 people died from a refrigerant leak in a Cleveland hospital in 1929, and, because of the danger, most hospitals refused to use refrigerators at all. For the same reason, about 85 percent of U.S. families with electricity did not own a refrigerator and many of those who did kept the appliance on the back porch.

Frigidaire's primary interest, though, was not food refrigeration but air-conditioning. The company wanted a safe refrigerant to cool large public spaces such as movie theaters and railroad cars, where toxic or flammable chemical leaks could cause mass panic and fatal stampedes.

After meeting Frigidaire's engineer, Midgley talked over the problem at lunch with his assistants, Albert L. Henne, a hydrocarbon chloride and chlorine expert, and Robert R. MacNary. Midgley doubted that a single compound would solve the problem. He stressed that only a spectacular product would sell during the Depression. Intrigued, the three adjourned to the laboratory's library.

Midgley pulled his periodic table out of his pocket. While looking for an antiknock additive, he had searched for a particular compound with unknown properties. Now he was hunting for the opposite: an unknown compound with well-identified properties. He wanted something that had a boiling point between 0 and −40°C and that was stable, nontoxic, noninflammable, noncorrosive, and cheap. Today, he would have added two more prerequisites—zero ozone depletion and zero global warming potential—but no one could have imagined or detected those problems in the 1920s.

Volatility, the ability to evaporate at low temperatures, was the most important consideration. Midgley wondered whether volatility was related in some way to the periodic table. It took him only a fraction of a second to see that it is. The elements in every known refrigerant were clustered together on the right-hand side of the table.

Within this little group, the elements on the far right were the least inflammable, and the light elements at the top were the least toxic. Fluorine, located at the intersection between noninflammability and nontoxicity, was the only nearby element that had never been used as a commercial refrigerant. Fluorine is highly toxic, so no one had thought that some of its compounds might be harmless. It was, as Midgley admitted, a startling and exciting deduction.

"Plots of boiling points, hunts for data, corrections, slide rules, log paper, eraser dirt, pencil shavings, and all the rest of the paraphernalia that takes the place of tea leaves and crystal spheres in the life of the scientific clairvoyant, were brought into play," he joked.

Soon, as Midgley put it, "Everything looked right." Within a few hours, they had identified a whole new class of potential compounds: the chlorofluorocarbons, later nicknamed CFC's, and trademarked Freon by Du Pont.

With Midgley pacing up and down behind him, Henne prepared their first CFC compound, dichlorodifluoromethane, later called R-12 for "Refrigerant-12." The compound looked promising. Under pressure, it liquefied readily, an important property since the cyclical refrigeration process depended on the compound's continually condensing back into a liquid to

Thomas Midgley's periodic table was arranged to show the number of electrons and empty spaces in the electron shells surrounding atoms. Midgley found all his useful compounds on the far right-hand side of the lower table. He used tellurium (Te), iodine (I), and selenium (Se) for tetraethyl lead and chlorine (Cl) and fluorine (Fl) for refrigerants. *(From Thomas Midgley, Jr., "From the Periodic Table to Production"; reproduced from Industrial and Engineering Chemistry, vol. 29, February 1937, p. 243)* reevaporate. From library to laboratory, the entire discovery process had taken only a few hours. In later tests, R-12 was found to be noninflammable and nontoxic even though it combined highly inflammable methane gas and two of the most toxic gases known, chlorine and fluorine.

Although Midgley received the lion's share of the credit for the group's discoveries, Frigidaire executives did not want him in their factory; he seemed too disorganized for corporate life. If he had an idea, he might start work at 3:00 in the morning and finish the night on a cot in the laboratory. He got a plumber out of bed at 2:00 a.m. to look for valves and pipes, and he boggled up the company's requisition records. General Motors handled its "golden boy" gently, though; Kettering built him a separate laboratory outside Frigidaire's plant.

Over the next two years, Midgley and his group discovered and patented other chlorofluorocarbons and the halons, a class of bromofluoro-carbon compounds that are the world's best fire fighters. At the time, their remarkable stability seemed like an advantage. In the 1970s scientists were able to determine that CFCs and halons—which are so stable that they remain in the atmosphere for long periods of time—deplete the ozone layer 15 miles above Earth.

Midgley unveiled CFCs with characteristic panache at the annual meeting of the American Chemical Society in Atlanta in April 1930. After reporting that R-12 is nontoxic and noninflammable, he lit a candle on stage. Taking a deep breath, he inhaled the compound, held it in his lungs a moment, and then slowly exhaled, blowing the candle flame out. It was, literally, a breathtaking exhibition.

To develop the chemical, General Motors once again formed a partnership with a chemical company, in this case Du Pont. And again, Midgley became vice president of the firm, named Kinetic Chemicals, Inc. He was now 41 years old.

Within a few years, Midgley compounds were air-conditioning Pullman railway cars, deep gold mines in South Africa, a Detroit restaurant, a Dayton school, and textile plants in the American South, where the humidity distorted thread. During the 1930s, Greyhound experimented with air-conditioned buses, and more than 3000 cars were equipped with factory-installed cooling, primarily for the American Southwest. Automotive units were designed to lower temperatures by only 10°F (37.7°C), because cooler temperatures were thought to put riders into shock.

Home refrigeration got a slower start than did air-conditioning. But auto engineers, who were experienced with mass producing and advertising consumer products, finally convinced the refrigeration industry to switch to

CFCs. The impact was enormous. Safe refrigeration revolutionized medicine by making vaccinations effective and by reducing food poisoning and diarrheal diseases. It has saved millions of lives. Even today all vaccines must be refrigerated during storage and usually during shipment too. Important vaccines protect against polio, bacterial meningitis, diphtheria, tetanus, pertussis, measles, mumps, rubella, varicella, many types of influenza, hepatitis A and B, rabies, yellow fever, and typhoid. The introduction of each new vaccine has been a milestone in public health.

Before the spread of safe refrigeration, the failure rate of vaccines was high. Before 1931, despite widespread vaccination programs in the United States, 30,000 cases of smallpox were reported annually, and the actual number of American cases was probably closer to 300,000 to 600,000 yearly, according to Dr. Donald A. Henderson, who directed the World Health Organization's successful campaign to eradicate smallpox. Vaccines kept at room temperature were effective less than a week, so few were used before the 1940s, and only the smallpox vaccine was routine. Fortunately, the severe variola form of smallpox had disappeared by the twentieth century. Almost one-third of all deaths in the United States in 1900 were among children under the age of five; today, thanks in part to universal vaccination, young children make up less than 1.5 percent of all deaths.

Refrigeration also greatly reduced the incidence of food poisoning since many types of bacteria thrive in unrefrigerated food. Feeding young children safely was difficult, especially in summer; milk kept more than 12 hours had to be boiled. Even today, unrefrigerated food is a major cause of the diarrheal illnesses that can kill up to half the children under age 7 in poor countries. To imagine a world without refrigeration, one need only think of a poor village in a developing country.

Of course, safety was not the only benefit of refrigeration; convenience was another great advantage. With refrigeration, housewives no longer had to shop daily, and families did not have to eat produce as soon as it ripened. Fresh meat, dairy products, and produce stayed wholesome four to five times longer. Food could be bought in large quantities or on sale and served when it was wanted. Frigidaire advertisements boasted that families with an electric refrigerator saved $11 a month on their food bills. The appliances were cheaper than twice weekly deliveries of 100-pound ice blocks.

The biggest selling point wasn't health for the children or convenience for the women, however. It was ice cubes for the men, who, after all, controlled the family purse strings. Ad after ad praised the ease of making plentiful, sanitary ice cubes, free from sewage-tainted river water and from "faucet meltage," a dreaded phenomenon that wasted 10 percent of a washed ice chip. Soon refrigerators were cooling drinks, soda fountains, trucks, frozen food freezers, and hunters' game lockers. Grocers could even sell ice cream year-round.

Ironically, the two applications that Midgley developed CFCs for—refrigeration and air-conditioning in buildings—accounted for less than one-fifth of the CFCs used by the United States at their peak in 1985. More than half of all CFCs were in industrial solvents—uses that Midgley may never have imagined.

Had Midgley's CFCs been used only for their original purpose—refrigeration and building air-conditioning—Earth's ozone layer would not have been reduced as rapidly. The automotive refrigerant R-12, for example, proved to be a powerful greenhouse gas and contributed about one-half of a vehicle's total equivalent warming impact. When R-12 was replaced by Midgley's R-134a during the 1990s, the total equivalent warming impact of automotive air-conditioning dropped to 4.5 percent.

As Midgley wound down his refrigeration work for Frigidaire, he tackled domesticity as compulsively as he did chemistry. By the time the Midgleys began building their mansion outside Columbus, the stock market had crashed and the Depression was well under way. Midgley hired a crew of 50 to build a 10,000-square-foot house with eight bedrooms, each with a dressing room and bath, some with sleeping porches, and most with walk-in closets the size of normal bedrooms. The six-car garage, central air-conditioning, intercoms, and outdoor swimming pool were almost unheard of features in 1930. A paved driveway wound almost a mile past a 15-acre horse pasture and a 17-acre apple orchard to a glacial ravine visited regularly by geology classes.

Once the house and grounds were complete, Midgley burrowed underground. To keep his neighbors employed as the Depression worsened, he designed a subterranean fantasy: 500 feet of stone-lined underground tunnels seven feet in diameter, with a rathskeller attached for entertaining friends. Over the tunnel entrance he posted the words, *Quaff While Thou Canst*. Polished geodes almost a yard in diameter stood on either side of the basement fireplace. The underground tunnel was Midgley's way of sharing his wealth.

Midgley could do nothing by halves. Above ground, he planted an eight-acre lawn with putting-green grass that was highly susceptible to earthworms. Then he installed an automated sprinkling system to kill the worms that killed the grass. Under the spray, four gardeners in southwesters, goggles, and masks searched for worms. When drying night winds blew, a bedside alarm wakened Midgley to dial a telephone code that restarted the sprinklers. Midgley returned from a European tour satisfied that he had the world's finest lawn. The Scotts Seed Company agreed and adopted the Midgleys' white house and emerald lawn as its logo.

But Midgley was not at home much. He was enjoying life. He traveled widely, and not always for work. By this time, the Midgley marriage was having difficulties. The children were away in boarding schools, and Carrie was often alone. After arguments, Midgley put on his hat, went to the railroad station, and disappeared for days at a time. When his son asked where he went when he did his "hat trick," Midgley took Thomas III to a Greenwich Village bar in New York. Midgley was "on a toot" to blow off steam.

He developed hobbies with a passion: he produced metal castings of ant tunnels in the Mohave Desert to study their social organization; he made professional-level, 78-rpm recordings of his favorite poems as Christmas cards; and he published volumes of his own light verse. He wrote short stories too and at least one play. Convivial and humorous, Midgley became a much sought-after dinner speaker. In a typically optimistic talk, Midgley asked his audience to "join with me and with chemistry. . . . to see that . . . man-made molecules are applied exclusively to the pursuit of happiness. Thus may we comply with God's edict in Genesis that Man shall be in his likeness and have dominion over all the Earth."

Kettering and General Motors were finding it increasingly difficult to get Midgley to concentrate on commercial problems. He was having fun studying rubber at Ohio State University in Columbus. When General Motors stopping financing the work, Midgley outfitted a laboratory at his own expense on the third floor of the university chemistry building. Although he never established a formal relationship with the department, he paid the salaries of chemists Albert L. Henne, Alvin Shepherd, and Mary W. Renoll, who worked with him.

This time, Midgley was doing the kind of basic chemical research for rubber that had not been done for tetraethyl lead or CFCs. He discovered the distinction between two rubber components and laid the foundation for wartime synthetic rubber research. Most of his 15 rubber papers were published in scientific journals of the American Chemical Society. Midgley was proud of the work; given a major award for tetraethyl lead and CFCs, he talked only about rubber. In their interests, Midgley and Kettering had grown far apart.

In September 1940, while attending an American Chemical Society meeting in Detroit, Midgley began to feel feverish and weak. As his legs progressively weakened, he drove back to Worthington where he was shocked to learn that he had a severe attack of poliomyelitis. With characteristic grace, Midgley wrote the chemistry community a letter published in *Industrial and Engineering Chemistry* on October 31: "I have been spending my spare moments in bed figuring out the statistical probabilities of a 51-year-old male catching poliomyelitis, as I have, and this comes out to be substantially equal to the chances of drawing a certain individual card from a stack of playing cards as high as the Empire State Building. It was my tough luck to draw it."

Midgley's symptoms were particularly severe, aggravated by his age and perhaps also by the lead in his system. After months in the Columbus Children's Hospital, where the city's only therapeutic pool was located, he recovered enough to go home. He was paralyzed from the waist down but determined to maintain his independence. He designed intricate systems of bars, pulleys, and ropes to get in and out of bed, wheelchair, and swimming pool unaided. He could sit up only for short periods of time and found travel difficult, but he remained active in scientific affairs, primarily by phone and letters. As World War II neared, Midgley organized the National Inventors Council to advise the Defense Department. He used an elaborate setup of microphones and loudspeakers to confer with high army and navy officials and with scientists. Government officials were accustomed to consulting with polio victims; President Franklin Delano Roosevelt was one also.

During World War II, Midgley was regarded as a national hero. Within a week of Pearl Harbor, the U.S. military began adding extra tetraethyl lead to make 100-octane fuel for vehicles and long-distance warplanes. Britain's petroleum secretary Geoffrey Lloyd said later, "We wouldn't have won the Battle of Britain without 100-octane." The extra 13 octane points gave American and British planes one-third more power than German and Japanese planes. Allied pilots took off in one-fifth the space; climbed 40 percent faster out of antiaircraft fire; flew higher; and could carry 20 to 30 percent more bombs, or fly 20 to 30 percent farther. In the tropics, Allied troops rid their quarters of malarial mosquitoes with aerosol spray bombs containing CFC propellants, DDT, and vegetable-based insecticides. Soldiers extinguished fires in tanks and armored personnel carriers with bromine-containing halons without being overcome by toxic fumes.

As Midgley's health worsened, a cascade of awards rained down on him. To a dying man, they must have seemed bittersweet, like eulogies for the dead. In 1944, after 10 years as chairman of the board of the American Chemical Society, Midgley was also elected its president. No one else in the twentieth century, much less a mechanical engineer, has held both posts simultaneously. The National Academy of Sciences made him an honorary member, a rare distinction for an industrial chemist. By 1944, he was the most decorated chemist in the United States.

Midgley began saying his good-byes. Two months before his death, he introduced his old mentor, Kettering, with the chilling words, "From 1916, he has been my boss. He will be throughout eternity." In his last speech, telephoned from his bed, he urged his profession to fund basic research. "We are the only species of living creatures that even conceives of exerting any control over the environment thrust upon it. Admittedly, this control is far from complete. Its extension is greatly to be desired." At some point, he asked his country lawyer and friend what he wanted from "The Farm." The friend chose two singularly personal items: Midgley's writing desk and bookcase. Midgley added a pile of his beloved classical music records.

A few days later, Midgley's farewell to friends in the chemistry community appeared in *Chemical and Engineering News*. Citing U.S. patent records, he said that inventiveness peaks at age 35. Thus, "every executive who has lived beyond the age of 40 is guilty, to some slight extent, of not getting out of the way of young men." What did Midgley, who had discovered tetraethyl lead and fluorine-containing refrigerants before he was 40, intend to do about it?

He answered the question with the last verse of one of his 1927 Christmas poems, titled, "Lots of Living:"

"When I feel old age approaching and it isn't any sport,
And my nerves are growing rotten, and my breath is growing
    short,
And my eyes are growing dimmer, and my hair is turning white,
And I lack the old ambitions when I wander out at night,
Then, though many men my senior may remain when I am gone,
I'll have no regrets to offer just because I'm passing on.
Let this epitaph be graven on my tomb in simple style,
'This one did a lot of living in a mighty little while.' "

A few weeks later, on the morning of November 2, 1944, Carrie Midgley entered her husband's room and found him dead. At the age of 55, he had strangled on the overhead ropes and pulleys that he had designed for getting in and out of bed. His friends spread the story that he had become accidentally entangled, and the story stuck for 50 years. Death and cemetery certificates, however, reveal what must have been obvious to his friends: a mechanical engineer of Midgley's prowess would not have accidentally strangled on his own invention. In despair, Midgley had carefully planned his death.

At the funeral, the minister intoned, "We bring nothing into this world, and it is certain we can carry nothing out." Kettering, leaving the funeral, shook his head and grumbled, "In Midge's case, it seems appropriate to add, 'We can at least leave a lot behind for the good of the world.' "

Midgley's fantastic farm was sold within a year. In the mid-1960s, the State of Ohio razed it to build what became a 12-lane highway so that powerful cars fueled by tetraethyl lead could race through the glacial ravine. In 1973, four decades after Midgley discovered CFCs, a British scientist James Lovelock was surprised to discover that the atmosphere contained almost as much of one of Midgley's compounds, R-11, as the total produced since 1933. A year later, two Americans, F. Sherwood Rowland and Mario J. Molina, linked CFCs to the destruction of the stratospheric ozone layer that protects Earth from ultraviolet rays. In the atmosphere, each chlorine atom in a CFC cycles on and off, catalyzing the removal of about 100,000 ozone molecules at a time. And in 1987, a NASA expedition to the South Pole revealed that CFCs had pierced a hole in the ozone layer over Antarctica. Within months, an international agreement was reached to phase out the use of CFCs. Rowland and Molina shared a Nobel Prize for chemistry in 1995.

By the one hundredth anniversary of Midgley's birth, his reputation was embroiled in controversy. He had been a hero during his lifetime, but a 1989 headline asked, "Midgley: Saint or Serpent?" Nevertheless, the remarkable fact is that industry spent the 1990s converting from Midgley's ozone-depleting CFCs to less dangerous CFCs and to ozone-safe chlorine-free compounds that do not deplete the ozone layer—all substitutes discovered by Midgley and his colleagues. During the same period, attempts to eradicate the polio virus from Earth were delayed because many parts of the world did not have the refrigeration needed to keep the antipolio vaccine frozen at all times.

If Midgley were active today, what would he think of his discoveries? Would he agree with his mentor, Kettering, who used to say, "The price of progress is trouble, and I don't think the price is too high"? Certainly at first, Midgley would have defended his inventions heart and soul. But Midgley was a curious, compulsive, and creative problem-solver who strongly believed that science could make the future better than the present. And perhaps, when forced to concede the dangers posed by lead and CFCs, Midgley would have plunged headlong into the search for safe substitutes.

7

Nylon and
Wallace Hume Carothers

April 27, 1896–April 29, 1937

Amid what he called "storms of despair," Wallace Hume Carothers performed one of the great technological feats of the twentieth century, building huge molecules from small ones to make synthetic rubber, polyesters, and the first commercially successful synthetic fiber, nylon.

Carothers spent much of his short life struggling to get an education, and his meteoric career lasted less than a decade. Nonetheless, by manipulating the structure of molecules to produce specialized properties on demand, he inaugurated our modern era of plastics and synthetic materials.

Despite all these successes, Wallace Hume Carothers was a reluctant inventor. Tormented by depression and other health problems, he found solace in fundamental scientific studies of giant biological molecules. Until Carothers fathered the science of organic polymers, no one knew that the building blocks of living matter are extraordinarily long but otherwise normal molecules held together by ordinary chemical bonds. Carothers' discoveries about polymers paved the way for molecular biology and for the studies of proteins and DNA that have revolutionized modern science and medicine. Yet despite his monumental achievements, Carothers' story was, for 50 years, little known outside the company he helped to build.

Like many American chemists of his generation, Carothers was a product of the Midwest. Born on April 27, 1896, he grew up in Des Moines, Iowa, attended college in Missouri, and earned a doctorate in chemistry in Illinois. He was the oldest of four children, and, by all accounts, his upbringing was deeply religious, straitlaced, and narrow in outlook.

Carothers' parents viewed their gifted child through radically different lenses. His mother, Mary Evalina McMullin, who taught him to love music, recognized that, "He was deeply emotional and affectionate—& generous—

he hated his shyness—& the dark moods that assailed & engulfed him. I suffered too—realizing how alone he was—& seeing the struggle that was going on in his mind much of the time." In contrast, Wallace's father, Ira Hume Carothers, considered his son a poor learner. "He used to take more time at his studies than any of the other three children," Ira said. "When he mastered a subject he remembered it but he was very slow." Blind to his son's deep-thinking originality, Ira declared, "No doubt [the] quality of painstaking thoroughness can account for his later success." Unlike his wife, Ira said he had no inkling of Wallace's mental condition until after his death.

As a child, Wallace regarded his father as "incredibly remote, wise and exalted . . . on an inaccessible plane and . . . to be feared." As an adult, Wallace found it exasperating and sometimes sickening to be in the same room with him. When a friend described a pleasant afternoon spent with his own father, Wallace said he felt like "a fellow who has spent his life in the penitentiary . . . on reading a story of the great outdoors."

Wallace graduated from high school in 1914 determined to get an education and become a chemist. It would take him almost a decade of desperate struggle. His first step was to enroll in—of all places—his father's secretarial school. Ira Carothers was a teacher and vice president at the Capital City Commercial College. For almost a year, Wallace attended classes— no speaking allowed—from 9:00 a.m. to 4:30 p.m., with an hour for lunch and ten days off at Christmas. Several decades after the introduction of the typewriter, school administrators still devoted an hour each day to penmanship. Thus Wallace studied "muscular movement writing," including the development of movement, the theory of shade, blackboard writing, and the teaching of penmanship. He also practiced typing an hour a day; the use of carbon paper was carefully taught.

Reflecting the views of Wallace's father, the school refused admittance to "drones or victims of depravity" who indulged in such "vicious habits" as cigarettes or liquor. "We are not running a reformatory," the school manual declared. Anyone like Wallace who had college aspirations was forewarned: "When a businessman wants a bookkeeper, he isn't looking for a college graduate." It was a circumscribed environment that Wallace rebelled against almost immediately.

When Wallace was finally ready to enter college at the age of 19, he made another unexpected choice. Instead of the well-established University of Iowa, he went to Tarkio College, an obscure and tiny Presbyterian college in Missouri. The Midwest was dotted with small church-affiliated, liberal arts colleges early in the twentieth century. Those with German backgrounds often had strong chemistry programs, reflecting the home country's enthusiasm for the science. The United Presbyterian Church that ran Tarkio was of British origin, however, and when Carothers arrived in the fall of 1915 determined to study chemistry, Tarkio had 114 students but no permanent chemistry teacher.

Carothers' first one and a half years at Tarkio were probably the happiest of his life. In a photograph taken at the town railroad station, he wears a goofy, joyful grin. At Tarkio, Carothers loved singing anything from German lieder and church hymns to his old high school song. A college yearbook described him as "frantically popular." Close friends found him jovial, modest, and charming.

They also considered him wild and dissipated. Carothers sprinkled his conversation with "damn's" and "hell's" and smoked cigarettes and cigars until his tongue was raw. Despite signing a pledge in return for $50 from his father, he stopped chewing tobacco only when he realized that he could not lecture effectively with a wad in his mouth. He gambled for money at pool and poker. He saw *Inspiration*, his first film featuring a woman without a strip of clothes on. He also attended an "interpretative dance . . . [where] the garments of the Vestal virgins could have been drawn through the eye of the needle. But they were so darned graceful and beautiful that one forgot the audacity of their accouterments." Eventually Carothers took up alcohol and—in the final rejection of his childhood religious training—called himself an agnostic, one who simply did not know.

Carothers roomed with Wilko G. Machetanz, who became his lifelong confidant. Paraphrasing the psychologist William James, Carothers told Machetanz that he was "the only emergent peak to which I cling when all the rest of the world has sunk beneath the wave." Machetanz suffered from hyperthyroidism and was extraordinarily nervous. When winter temperatures dropped to 25° below 0 and the college ran out of coal, Carothers donned a heavy shawl-collar sweater and, night after night, read Mach to sleep with poetry. Caressing each word as he spoke in a quasi-theatrical air, Carothers rolled his head back and roared verse after verse in his beautiful baritone.

Carothers had a poem for every Tarkio occasion. As he pulled on his turtleneck, he quoted the poet Keats: "Ah, bitter the chill it was! . . . and silent was the flock in woolly cold." When a hair fell out, he quoted Swinburne: "The leaves of life keep falling one by one." On double dates, Carothers, Machetanz, and their steady girlfriends took turns sticking a knife at random into a poetry book and reading the poems that they found.

"Poetry, I think would scarcely ever relieve a man of depression, but it can paint a man's melancholy with beautiful colors, and give him a rather sombre joy in his own sorrow," Carothers wrote. Poems about death appealed to him; Swinburne's "Garden of Proserpine" was a favorite:

> ". . . she stands
> Who gathers all things mortal, in cold immortal hands."

After Machetanz became ill and left Tarkio, the two spent years scrambling for enough time and money to meet again. They seldom managed it, but they corresponded until Carothers' death. In more than 100 letters to Machetanz, Carothers described his hardscrabble struggles to continue his education, an ordeal that helped define the freethinking, driven man that he became.

Carothers spent five years at Tarkio worrying constantly about his desperate financial condition. Although he was an excellent student, he never knew from one year to the next whether he could remain in school. At first, he financed his studies by teaching bookkeeping in Tarkio's commercial business department, an experience so unpleasant that he vowed, "I'll be damned if I will spend another year in that eternally double damned Com'l Dept." He switched to a teaching assistantship in Tarkio's English Department and spent summers keeping accounts for an ice company and selling Wear Ever aluminum pans to the housewives of Iowa County. When jobs were scarce, Carothers spent two lonely summers hammering a typewriter as private secretary to Tarkio's chronically disorganized president. "Ten cents a day though don't pay many board bills," Carothers noted. "If I don't get out of debt now, the Lord only knows when I will, and at present rate I am not even holding my own. . . . Cash assets total up to about $31, and liabilities are legion."

Women—especially the brilliant but volatile Frances Gelvin and "The Divine Jesse"—preoccupied Carothers almost as much as his finances. Frances was one of Tarkio's rich girls; she dressed exquisitely and drove a Cadillac coupe. Jesse was Tarkio's music professor, and Carothers was haunted by "the warm influence of her presence and the touch of her lips." Both women longed to marry him, but Carothers was convinced that, until his thirties at least, a man without an independent income or a profession could not afford a wife.

He was also never entirely sure that he was in love. Asking Machetanz about Jesse, he wrote, "A man can't gush about emotions he doesn't feel, can he? . . . I once actually thot myself in love there, and even yet, there are times when she appears supernaturally beautiful and desirable—but the feeling is so damned intermittent, and I ask myself is this the way with love?"

As for Frances Gelvin, he finally decided that marriage with such a temperamental woman would have been "one continual civil war. . . . Fran has several qualities that I detest; and I have several which she detests with equal or better grounds. The war might have been interesting; and life would never probably have sunk to the level of common boredom, but I have a feeling that things would have ended up in a big crash one way or another."

As Carothers worked his way through college, his thyroid gland malfunctioned. It became enlarged, his pulse raced, exercise was a torment, and he remained rail thin despite an appetite that was sometimes a "fierce, uncontrollable, overmastering passion . . . [For dinner I] ate a steak, bread and butter, milk, pie, sundae, 15¢ worth of candy & topped it all off with six cinnamon rolls." Today, these symptoms suggest hyperactivity, probably caused by Graves' disease, an autoimmune condition of the thyroid. Carothers finally had part of his thyroid removed in a Chicago hospital in 1924. It was "rather an unpleasant affair," he reported. "Believe me, this business of having an extended operation while you look on is not much fun in spite of all the morphine."

Thyroid-level monitoring was crude throughout Carothers' lifetime, and the remaining portion of his thyroid probably continued to overproduce for some time. With too much thyroid hormone, he would have continued to have a high pulse rate, feel nervous and jittery, and sweat profusely. Stress worsened his symptoms. Hyperthyroidism can also unmask the symptoms of any latent mental condition, in effect worsening psychiatric disease; some patients experiencing the onset of hyperthyroidism appear acutely psychotic. Thus, the extent to which hyperthyroidism affected Carothers' mental health is unknown but may have been considerable. In any case, Carothers' thyroid problem was only one of several biochemical disorders that plagued him throughout his life.

Even more worrisome were Carothers' puzzling spells of melancholy or pessimism. As he told Machetanz, "I have the *Weltschmerz*," literally "world-weariness" in German. During one of these moods, he found that "science is beginning to lose its glamour for me." Chemistry, he thought, had become so specialized that few people would ever read, much less understand, his articles. On other occasions, he plunged deep into "the slime of self-disgust." Trying to understand his swings of emotion, he could not decide "whether the dejection is the cause of the failure of the work or vice versa. . . . The two seem to go together." Diagnosing the problem as physical and nervous depression, Carothers concluded that a little exercise was indicated.

During Carothers' second and third years at Tarkio, an inspiring teacher radically altered the course of his life. Arthur Pardee, movie-star handsome with a Valentino haircut, was only three years older than Carothers but had already worked his way through graduate school by teaching chemistry, physics, economics, and government at Tarkio. During Carothers' freshman year, Pardee took a leave of absence to finish his Ph.D. at Johns Hopkins University, then the nation's leading institution for chemistry. Even armed with a degree, Pardee had little choice but to return to Tarkio; job opportunities for chemists were extremely limited in the United States before World War I. Dyes and drugs were imported from Germany, so the typical American research chemist studied soils for the U.S. Department of Agriculture. Chemistry was one of the lower paid professions in the country.

Pardee's gift was spotting and nurturing talent; he would later teach Ernest O. Lawrence, the Nobel Prize winning inventor of the cyclotron. At Tarkio, young Pardee quickly recognized Carothers' natural ability and challenged him to get a world-class education.

Carothers took every science class that Pardee taught. Short of studying with a German-trained chemist, a Hopkins-trained Ph.D. was the best possible teacher for an eager student. With Pardee's strong encouragement, Carothers began thinking seriously about a career in chemistry. Carothers' father, who never sensed the professional possibilities offered by science, objected strongly. Pardee concluded that Carothers' parents were "nice, responsible people . . . [but] his family had really very little educational background." Privately, Pardee told Carothers that, if he pursued chemistry, the sky was the limit. As Carothers continued his struggle to get an education in science, Pardee became a bulwark of practical strength.

When World War I began, the Army rejected Carothers because his enlarged thyroid made his hands shake. As a result of the wartime manpower shortage, Pardee found a better job and Tarkio offered his position to Carothers. Although Carothers had been a student for only three years, Tarkio asked him to teach chemistry and take classes half time toward his bachelor's degree. Pardee urged him not to take such a grueling job and promised to find him a fellowship at a better institution. In what Carothers later decided was the biggest mistake of his young life, he turned Pardee down. Later he admitted, "There is a tide in the affairs of men, and I let it slip." Experiencing "melancholy approaching on despair," he moaned, "Oh, the unutterable folly of those years in Tarkio." It would not be the last time that Carothers clung to a familiar post rather than risk an unsettling move to a promising new place.

To prepare for teaching, Carothers was ordered to enroll at his own expense in summer school at the University of Chicago. The experience was an eye-opener and contributed to Carothers' disenchantment with Tarkio.

"Believe me," he wrote Machetanz, "the university methods of ingesting knowledge into the student are somewhat different from little old Tarkio. They expect a man to absorb a whole science in one large gulp, and to get it down too . . . I have decided that I don't know *any* chemistry."

In recognition of his special status, Tarkio students nicknamed Carothers "Prof" that fall. At first glance, he looked like the stereotypical, absent-minded professor; he squinted slightly through glasses and, when he was puzzled, the hair on one side of his part drooped down over his forehead. But when he thought of the answer he was searching for, his eyebrows popped up. He was slightly stooped, and standing erect required noticeable effort. His physique irked him. About six feet tall, he had such broad shoulders and narrow hips that ready-made suits did not fit.

Tarkio almost overwhelmed Carothers with work. From 7:00 a.m. to midnight, with time off only for meals, Prof scrubbed the chemistry laboratory; stocked student supplies; prepared solutions; washed, sorted, and labeled dozens of reagent bottles; and taught classes. Despite stage fright before lecturing, he inspired four Tarkio students to earn Ph.D.'s in chemistry. As a student, Carothers also shouldered his usual heavy load of courses. As he confided to Machetanz, "The veil of weariness . . . [is] completely shrouding me of late. There is something physiological about it, I guess—the weariness—battered nerves or something. At any rate, I am eternally tired even on arising to greet a glorious spring morning . . . [May] be it's the smoking. And maybe it's the symptoms of hyperthyroidism, but anyway, it's darned unpleasant."

In 1920, after five years at Tarkio, Carothers earned a bachelor's degree and, at age 24, began applying to graduate schools. He chose the University of Illinois on purely financial grounds, but it was a fortunate choice for both educational and personal reasons. American universities were building chemistry faculties, journals, and research laboratories, and Illinois was fast becoming the nation's leading center for organic chemistry. Roger Adams, the department chair, was developing a congenial faculty devoted to nurturing graduate students, the first generation of American chemists who did not go to Germany for their postgraduate studies. Adams, who would succeed Thomas Midgley, Jr. as president of the American Chemical Society, would train more than 200 chemists and place many of them in industry.

Carothers spent six years in Illinois' warm and convivial atmosphere. For the first time, he was surrounded by passionately enthusiastic scientists, several of whom became staunch pillars of support in times of difficulty. Carl "Speed" Marvel, two years older than Carothers but already Adams' right-hand man, took the new student under his wing. Marvel found

Carothers hard-driving and intense, yet also quiet and warm. When Carothers was in good humor, no one was funnier, cleverer, or wittier. But when he was depressed, his mood affected everyone around him. "And when he was low," Marvel said, he was "lower than a snake's belly." Marvel later learned polymer chemistry from his student and became the first academic polymer researcher in the United States.

Carothers was regarded as Illinois' best organic chemistry student, equally good at physical chemistry, mathematics, physics, and laboratory techniques. Moreover, as Adams put it, Carothers was a lovable man. Despite his obvious talents, he was without artifice or pretense. Nevertheless, when Carothers' savings ran out after a year, he had to leave Illinois to earn money teaching at the University of South Dakota, where the everfaithful Pardee had arranged a position.

Carothers had already discovered that scientific research filled an emotional void in his life. "A place in which to work, and work for my hands and mind to do," he wrote, "this has become for me an overpowering necessity . . . *not* rational, but arising spontaneously from the profoundest depths of being." Therefore, while his mentors kept busy synthesizing new organic compounds, Carothers delved into deeper problems: Why and how do chemical reactions take place? In 1866, Edward Frankland had introduced the term "bond" with respect to the atom's combining power or valence. By Carothers' time, scientists knew that bonds were electrical in nature and were associated with electrons. Carothers wanted to understand the behavior of the electrons around atoms as they form molecules. Trying to test the emerging theory of valence, he spent all his free time in South Dakota comparing two compounds that have almost identical properties but different structures.

Carothers' first scientific article, written at South Dakota, was published in 1923 by the prestigious *Journal of the American Chemical Society*. While most beginners publish in partnership with a more experienced mentor, Carothers was its sole author. When he left South Dakota at the end of the school year, he was not only solvent, but also a small step closer to building a scientific reputation. He had learned an important lesson as well: he had enough ideas to keep several people busy.

Carothers returned to Illinois' chemistry department that fall to concentrate for two more years on organic chemistry with minors in physical chemistry and mathematics. His thesis topic was related to Adams' signature discovery, a catalyst used to hydrogenate unsaturated fats for the shortening and soap industries. Carothers and 11 other collaborators produced 18 papers about the catalyst with Adams. At the same time, Carothers passed his French and German language requirements and helped Adams edit manuscripts. "He expresses himself in writing as well as any scientific man I know regardless of field," Adams wrote. Later chemists recognized Carothers' articles by their clarity, precision, and liveliness.

Carothers liked organic chemistry—the study of carbon-containing compounds—because it describes living things. Its fundamental theories suggested that the structure of organic molecules could be determined by analysis, synthesis, and the carbon atom's role in chemical reactions. To Carothers, these principles seemed simpler and more adequate than those of any other science. The nature of chemical bonding and molecular structure intrigued Carothers far more than Adams' more routine laboratory syntheses. Carothers read scientific literature more broadly and deeply than his professors too, remembered what he read, and made vital connections between far-flung facts.

He became interested in a new theory of chemical bonds based on Niels Bohr's 1913 model of the atom, which Thomas Midgley also used to discover tetraethyl lead and CFCs (Chapter 6). Scientists already knew that atoms could form molecules by transferring electrons, but the new theory suggested that chemical bonds could also be formed when atoms share electrons.

Carothers wrote an innovative article that was one of the first to apply the new theories to organic chemistry. Adams was skeptical but, even as a student, Carothers exercised his own scientific judgment and, in January 1924, he mailed his second article to the *Journal of the American Chemical Society.* The article was controversial, and six reviewers for the journal deadlocked 3-3 over whether to print it. The journal's editor gave Carothers the choice of withdrawing or publishing his article. Courageously, the young man chose to publish it. Years later, Carl Marvel regarded "The Double Bond" as "a landmark . . . one of the fundamental papers in organic chemistry." Its publication transformed the shy and self-deprecating Carothers into a mythic hero on campus, where he was called "Doc" long before he had a Ph.D.

Science, politics, labor relations, philosophy, music, literature, and sports—it seemed that everything interested Carothers. Soon after Sinclair Lewis' novel *Babbitt* was published in 1920, he praised it as a literal depiction of Midwestern conformity and provincialism. When Marvel introduced him to fly-fishing in the Wisconsin woods, Carothers loved it. Although friends often found it difficult to tell when Carothers was pleased and happy, he was so excited trying to land a muskie from a rowboat that he almost jumped in after the fish.

Despite his academic and social successes, Carothers regarded graduate school as "a form of slavery . . . with all the elements of adventure and enterprise which a nut screwer in a Ford factory must feel in setting out for work each morning." As always, he enrolled in extra classes, even though his teaching load as a graduate assistant was far heavier than he had expected. When Roger Adams asked him to teach organic chemistry, Carothers had to attend another summer session at Chicago and once again pay for his own supplies, including $25 for chemicals. As usual, he was losing money; his income was $70 a month, but his expenditures were $90 and rising. The University of Illinois did not permit smoking on campus, and he and his friends had developed a passion for off-campus billiards and afternoon coffee.

One day, as Carothers worked in the laboratory, poisonous bromine spilled on his face and legs, and bromine gas filled his lungs. It could have been far worse; the young man working beside Carothers lost most of his penis. Hospitalized for a week as chunks of flesh fell from his leg, Carothers wondered whether chemistry was worth the struggle. He taught at a major university but had no accident insurance, and his bank balance stood at $1.00. He longed for someone to talk to about literature and philosophy, but his classmates read only science. Laboratory air caused an unpleasant dermatitis on various parts of his body.

By the time Carothers was released from the hospital, his health problems included hyperthyroidism, dermatitis from chemical fumes, bromine poisoning, and bewildering bouts of depression. He sometimes dreamed of escaping to a laboratory to work on "ideas of vast commercial importance" in New York, Paris, Vienna, or Berlin. At one point, he fell into a paralysis of indecision and depression, known in the 1920s as an "abulia." Friends whispered that Carothers carried a vial of potassium cyanide in his pocket and that he had threatened to commit suicide. Adams sent Carothers home to rest for a summer, quietly giving him full credit for the missing weeks. Far from hiding his mood swings, Carothers read books on depression and discussed them with friends. Only Carl Marvel, his graduate school friend John L. "Jack" Johnson, and letters from Machetanz could lift Carothers out of his depressions; it was a job they would perform often over the coming years.

Carothers claimed that he kept going only because he finally received one of Illinois' few scholarships, $750 "embellished with esteem." But he must also have persevered because he loved chemistry. As he admitted, even the smell of his laboratory coat, "saturated with the inexpressibly pungent and complicated odors of lab no. 219 [filled him] with a nostalgia to return to the atmosphere of sweetly blended sulfur dioxide, bromine, chlorine, ammonia, hydrogen chloride, phosgene, chloroacetone, etc., etc., etc."

Carothers reached a milestone in his career on May 19, 1924, when he defended his thesis and received his Ph.D. At the age of 28, he was older than most recent Ph.D.'s, but the chemistry faculty considered him one of the most brilliant students ever to be awarded a doctoral degree at Illinois.

Adams hired Carothers to stay on as an instructor, the lowest rung on the academic ladder, for $1800 a year. Carothers' class lectures were low-key and conversational, like his written articles, but his students worked overtime. When one climbed through a laboratory window on Thanksgiving Day, he found the rest of his classmates already there. Carothers, Carl Marvel, Jack Johnson, and several graduate students formed an informal seminar group to talk chemistry over bootleg beer.

During his second year of teaching at Illinois, Harvard University offered Carothers a job. Harvard's chemistry chair, James B. Conant, had worked with Roger Adams on the United States's poison gas projects during World War I. Conant promised Carothers a substantial raise: $2250 for the 1926 to 1927 school year, and Carothers accepted.

During the summer between the two jobs, Carothers traveled to Europe with Jack Johnson, ostensibly to attend a scientific congress in England, but actually to vacation in Paris. Carothers found third-class on a French ocean liner "a little boring at times . . . mostly miscellaneous foreigners—Italians, Poles, of the partly Americanized class." He enjoyed Paris during its heyday as an American literary outpost, though. On the Left Bank, he bought a 100-page, illustrated book that the French writer and artist Bruller Vercors had published a few months before. Its title was *21 Practical Recipes to Commit Suicide*. Despite its name, it was humorous, some even thought charming, the kind of book almost anybody could have bought. At the time, Johnson attached no significance to it. While in Paris, Carothers met a young French chemist, Gerard Berchet, who later played an important role in the discovery of nylon. Returning to New York, Carothers smuggled James Joyce's banned novel, *Ullyses*, through customs.

As a fledgling faculty member at Harvard that fall, Carothers was somewhat surprised by its working conditions. In a cheery letter to Jack Johnson, Carothers related how a chemistry assistant pried ten thumbtacks out of the Harvard administration. The assistant "was permitted to put in a requisition for thumb tacks to the number of ten (10), said thumb tacks to be purchased by the University and given to the assistant for use in connection with Chemistry 5, and the cost (purchase price + expenses incurred in their purchase) to be pro rated among the students of the course & charged to their individual accounts."

On a more serious note, Harvard's chemists were divided among several small, isolated buildings, and Carothers missed the warmth and collegiality of the University of Illinois. Nevertheless, for teaching, Harvard was an "academic paradise" because his class assignments were confined to one semester a year. Carothers' diffidence seemed to disappear in a classroom, and he taught a large class of elementary organic chemistry with distinction.

At the same time, Carothers suspected that he was trying to work on too many research projects. He published just one article while at Harvard. And despite his raise, he had enough money for only one pair of trousers, which were redolent of the laboratory and darned in two places where chemicals had eaten through. He concluded that saving money was a gift he did not have.

When asked to give talks, Carothers became nervous and sweated profusely; he nearly collapsed from stage fright several times. He consulted psychiatrists but confided in none. During the 1920s, the public viewed psychiatry as something akin to a mystic cult, quackery, or an excuse to wallow in sexual fantasies. Psychiatrists were among medicine's lowest-paid specialists. It would be many years before the biochemistry of depression and anxiety disorders was understood; scientists did not accumulate conclusive evidence linking depression with organic causes until the 1960s. Thus, Carothers' reluctance to confide fully in a psychiatrist was neither unusual nor unwarranted. In fact, his deep interest in modern psychiatry and his frank acknowledgment of his mental problems set him apart from most of the population.

In 1927, during Carothers' second year at Harvard, he received an extraordinary job offer to direct basic research in organic chemistry for the E. I. du Pont de Nemours & Company, Inc., of Wilmington, Delaware. The man behind the offer was Charles M. A. Stine, a visionary organic chemist who wanted Du Pont to explore the scientific principles underlying its different products and technologies. It was Stine who had urged General Motors Corporation and Midgley to investigate the science of the internal combustion machine (Chapter 6). Stine was convinced that corporate-sponsored fundamental research would add to Du Pont's prestige among scientists when company employees published and presented papers. Until then, universities pursued and published almost all the basic scientific research conducted in the United States. Stine regarded the possibility that pure science might yield practical results as quite secondary.

Du Pont was no longer the small factory that Eleuthère Irénée du Pont had established after learning to make gunpowder from Antoine Lavoisier in prerevolutionary France. The Du Pont corporation had supplied the

Allies with 40 percent of their explosives during World War I, and, by the 1920s, the company controlled one of the world's biggest industrial empires. Du Pont family members were celebrities who lived like royalty in magnificent palaces. With noblesse oblige, they renovated 100 Delaware schools, paid old-age pensions to all qualified Delaware residents, and built a highway for the state.

Over the previous 15 years, Du Pont had transformed itself into a diversified chemical company by acquiring technology from GM, French interests, and German dye chemists and by developing other processes in-house. Du Pont had learned to turn a variety of chemicals—including cellulose and nitrocellulose, the key ingredient in one of its explosives—into sophisticated products. Brightly colored nitrocellulose lacquers developed by Du Pont were replacing basic black for automobiles. Products packaged in moisture-proof cellophane manufactured from cellulose were attracting customer attention in the new self-service stores that were revolutionizing retailing. Rayon, also produced from natural cellulose, made inexpensive, though baggy, women's hosiery; and, when Paris couturiers designed rayon dresses in the late 1930s, middle-class women dressed as fashionably in "artificial silk" as rich women did in natural silk.

Profit margins were excellent; cellulose, the structural material in plants, was cheap. In addition, Du Pont was beginning to reap huge profits by making the tetraethyl lead that Midgley had discovered for General Motors. Despite Du Pont's new product lines, a U.S. Senate committee labeled the firm "the Merchant of Death" because of its activities during World War I. In retaliation, Du Pont inaugurated its famous public relations campaign, "Better Things for Better Living Through Chemistry."

Research had helped Du Pont convert from explosives to consumer goods. The company opened the first modern research laboratory in the American chemical industry in 1902. By 1921, the United States had more than 500 industrial research laboratories eager to duplicate goods previously imported from Germany. Most American industrial laboratories applied known scientific facts to practical problems, however. Thus, Du Pont's offer to Carothers embodied the first attempt by an American chemical manufacturer to discover new fundamental scientific explanations for natural phenomena. If Carothers was willing to work for industry, Du Pont was an attractive choice.

Few chemists interested in fundamental research, though, were willing to work for industrial laboratories. In fact, several university professors approached by Stine had already turned him down. Shifting tactics, Stine began hunting for "young men of exceptional scientific promise but no established reputation." Carothers qualified. At 31, he had published eight articles in organic chemistry, including the innovative "Double Bond," and Adams and Marvel at Illinois and Pardee's friends at Hopkins recommended Carothers as "one in a million."

That September, Carothers took a train from Boston to Wilmington to visit Du Pont's laboratories for the day. Within 24 hours, Du Pont officially offered him the job. Over the next month, Carothers pondered and probed, trying to understand just how committed Du Pont was to basic research and how much freedom he would have to pursue problems of his own choice. Thanks to the postal service's next-day delivery, their correspondence has much of the immediacy of today's e-mail.

Over and over again, Carothers emphasized that he was not interested in—or good at—research directed toward making a financial profit. As he put it later, he wanted to do pure research to increase scientific knowledge, and "any financial profit that might accrue would be so much gravy." He was frank: "I don't want to make the change unless it appears that there will be some real gain in making it. My present position is not altogether ideal, but it promises to develop into something which will be very nearly that providing I stay with it for two or three years and make good."

Stine reassured him, "We are interested in you because we believe you will not only do work of a high order, but also that you will select worth while problems. . . . I mean worth while from a scientific point of view and not from the point of view of direct financial returns." Tempting Carothers with a supply of skilled assistants, Stine promised that, if Du Pont considered his research topics interesting, his research team would grow.

Nevertheless, on October 9, 1927, Carothers flatly rejected Du Pont's offer. Harvard was building a new chemistry laboratory to attract graduate students, and Carothers enjoyed teaching. Four days later, he wrote Du Pont to explain further. "I had considerable difficulty in adjusting myself to the change from [Illinois] to Cambridge, and now that the adjustment has been pretty well made do not like to make another change unless there is a clear cut and indubitable advantage to be gained in so doing." He was also honest about his health: "I suffer from neurotic spells of diminished capacity which might constitute a much more serious handicap there than here." Far more important than his worries about adapting to Du Pont's corporate culture were his remaining concerns about the freedom to do research and publish in an industrial laboratory. "The real freedom and independence and relative stability of a university position are sufficient to compensate for the difference [in pay]." Carothers knew his own mind, and he never wavered from it. He was interested in studying natural phenomena, not in practical engineering or invention.

Stine refused to take no for an answer. That very week, he sent his second-in-command to Harvard with orders to stay until Carothers took the job. Why was Du Pont so very interested in Carothers? Of course, Carothers' exceptional scientific talent and outstanding recommendations were significant, but Du Pont had another reason as well. During Carothers' visit to Wilmington, he had expressed interest in the theory of polymers—and polymers were Du Pont's bread and butter.

As Carothers later explained in a talk, the bulk of living things is made of large, long-chained molecules called polymers. They are the only organic materials with strength, elasticity, toughness, pliability, and hardness. Polymers provide structure for both plants and animals, and they perform intricate regulatory and reproductive functions in living cells. The foods we eat—cellulose, starch, and protein—are made of polymers. Timber and clothing—whether made from leather or fur, or from fibrous cotton, linen, silk, and wool—are also composed of polymers. Weight for weight, cellulose and silk are stronger than steel, and rubber exhibits a combined strength and elasticity that is not even remotely approached by any other organic material. Today, we know that polymers also make enzymes, deoxyribonucleic acid (DNA), and ribonucleic acid (RNA).

Despite the importance of natural polymers, few scientists in the 1920s studied their complicated structures. Academic chemists investigated ordinary organic compounds such as soap, sugar, alcohol, and gasoline with low molecular weights between 50 and 500 atomic mass units. Most organic chemists knew that the molecules of natural substances such as starch, protein, cellulose, and rubber were exceedingly large with molecular weights over 50,000. Their size gave them puzzling properties, including high viscosity in solution, high melting points, low solubility, and mechanical flexibility. No one knew how to purify, isolate, synthesize, or identify their huge and immensely complicated structures. German chemists condescendingly referred to organic chemistry as "Schmierchemie," or grease chemistry, and no large university in the United States devoted a department to large polymers.

Industrial chemists, unlike academics, had studied natural polymers empirically for years. But each industry worked in isolation with its own textbooks, handbooks, conferences, journals, and societies. Wood chemists had little to do with leather, wool, or rubber chemists, and none of them investigated the scientific principles underlying all their specialties.

Nevertheless, these trial-and-error industrial chemists had been turning cellulose and other natural polymers into plastics for several decades. After 1870, celluloid—nitrocellulose plasticized with camphor—replaced amber and costly animal hooves, horns, bones, ivory, and tortoise-shell in knife handles, billiard balls, hairbrushes, toothbrushes, mirrors, and the like. Celluloid film made motion pictures possible. In 1910, Leo H. Baekeland, a Belgian chemist who immigrated to New York, used phenol and formaldehyde to make Bakelite plastic for electrical insulation and telephones; manufactured under pressure, Bakelite became the familiar kitchen countertop. The new plastics filled a vital need. Wild rubber trees, for example, are natural polymers but, with soaring human populations and rising standards of living, they and many other natural polymers were becoming scarce and expensive. In addition, natural polymers could not provide the precise properties and consistent standards demanded by modern industry. Soon plastics were used for small items such as radios, scales, barometers, telephone indexes, iron handles, mimeographs, and soda-fountain dispensers. Leading artists and industrial designers of the 1930s liked plastic because it is strong, lightweight, and can be mass-produced in a rainbow of colors by molding machines.

Carothers shrewdly recognized that the relationship between the structure and the properties of polymers should intrigue university scientists and Du Pont alike. Carothers' interests and those of his would-be employer were beginning to converge. Exactly when all the pieces fell together is unclear. As Carothers later recalled, "Dates of some events that, in retrospect, seem important cannot be established with certainty. As a matter of fact many of these events had no very clearly defined dates; they were simply ideas first grasped as possibilities, which, by slow growth became firm convictions." When he learned more about polymers during his job interview at Wilmington, he returned to Harvard and reviewed the scientific literature. It was clear to him that most published statements about polymers were wrong.

In the meantime, Du Pont upped its salary offer by 20 percent to $6000 a year and continued to reassure Carothers that he could work on theoretical problems in an industrial setting. Carothers was changing his mind. Finally, on October 31, 1927, Carothers told Du Pont, "I have decided to accept your offer if it still holds." He could start work in three months.

Writing Machetanz about Du Pont's "kingly" job offer, he said, "It is a fairly heavy gamble. I may not like it, but it looks alluring . . . I expect to have nearly the same freedom in the selection of problems as at Harvard, and to have really trained assistants. To speak really hyperbolically of the job I shall be directing research in pure organic chemistry for the largest chemical corporation in the world. And since so far as I know no other corporation is doing research in pure organic chemistry, the job will be unique." For several years, Carothers' job was all that he had been promised.

Carothers was reading about a fierce controversy raging among European chemists. After the German Emil Fischer determined the three-dimensional structures of sugars and proteins, most scientists recognized that they were quite large polymers, that is, molecular chains with many links or parts. But most organic chemists could imagine only the kind of compounds that they could create in their laboratories: substances composed of small, identical molecules. They reconciled the paradox by assuming that large polymers had to be aggregations of many small molecules held together—not by ordinary forces—but by unique and mysterious forces.

Hermann Staudinger, a professor at the Zurich Polytechnique School, ignited the argument in 1920. Staudinger had witnessed the first teaspoonful of ammonia made by Fritz Haber and, after becoming a pacifist, argued with Haber over poison gas during World War I. Later as a Swiss professor, Staudinger developed a hypothesis that large organic molecules are true molecules, practically endless chains held together by ordinary chemical bonds. He called these long chains "macromolecules" but had little data to prove his theory. After hearing Staudinger speak, another eminent Swiss professor scoffed haughtily, "Such a thing does not exist." Staudinger, as arrogant and dogmatic as he was charismatic, ended his talk with Martin Luther's words, "Here I stand. I cannot do otherwise!"

The climax to the debate came at a tumultuous 1926 conference organized by Fritz Haber, the discoverer of nitrogen fixation (Chapter 5), and his friend, Richard Willstätter, a Nobel Prize winning organic chemist. Out of several hundred organic chemists at the Düsseldorf meeting, only Staudinger defended his long-chained molecules against attack. Shaking his finger furiously at his opponents, Staudinger was led back to his seat several times. As one chemist explained, "We are as shocked as zoologists might be if they were told that somewhere in Africa an elephant was found who was 1500 feet long and 300 feet high." Most European scientists did not accept Staudinger's macromolecules for many years, and he did not win a Nobel Prize until 1953.

In summarizing the session, however, Willstätter admitted that Staudinger might be right. "For me, as an organic chemist, the concept that a molecule can have a molecular weight of 100,000 is somewhat terrifying," Willstätter said. "But, on the basis of what we have heard today, it seems that I shall have to slowly adjust to this thought."

Carothers was among the few Americans to accept Staudinger's argument, but he did more than that. On November 9, 1927, within ten days of accepting Du Pont's job offer, Carothers outlined a plan of action for settling the European debate. It was also—unknown to him—the blueprint that would lead him to nylon seven years later. The plan guided his work at Du Pont for the next several years.

To answer Staudinger's critics, Carothers knew he had to resolve three issues. First, he would have to build one of Staudinger's macromolecules. Next, he would have to confirm that they were indeed long-chained molecules, not merely aggregates of smaller molecules, as others claimed. Finally, he would have to prove that the forces holding the chains together were ordinary valence bonds, rather than a mysterious weak force.

He planned to use such familiar chemical reactions to link smaller molecules together that no one could doubt the identity of the resulting macromolecules or their bonds. If Carothers succeeded in building a macromolecule, he could then examine its properties. If they were similar to those of rubber, for example, scientists would have to agree that rubber was a long-chained molecule held together by normal bonds. As Carothers noted modestly, "This idea is no doubt a little fantastic and one might run up against insuperable difficulties."

Within weeks of moving to Du Pont in February 1928, Carothers further refined and developed his strategy for making long-chained molecules. He decided to use one of the simplest and best-understood reactions in chemistry: combining alcohols and acids to make esters. To that he added a twist: he would use only molecules that have alcohol or acid groups at both ends. A molecule that can undergo chemical reactions at one end can join another atom or molecule only once, but with a reaction site at each end, he could keep adding molecules one at a time, like links in a chain, until he had assembled a long molecule. "And unless my ideas are badly swollen we should be able during the next year to open up what is practically an untouched field in organic chemistry and a rather big one," he wrote Machetanz.

Commenting from Illinois, Adams agreed that a general study of large molecules sounded enticing, but atrociously difficult. Today a molecule's structure can be determined in minutes, but infrared spectroscopy, sophisticated X-ray crystallography, and nuclear magnetic resonance imaging were far in the future. Carothers was relying on a state-of-the-art device invented in 1925 by a Swede named The Svedberg. The high-speed apparatus separated molecules in solution according to their molecular weight. Du Pont was the first industrial laboratory to own an ultracentrifuge; although it produced meager and unreliable results, it won its inventor a Nobel Prize in 1926. Carothers planned to use it to calculate the molecular weight of his polymer chains.

Despite Adams' worry, Carothers fairly licked his chops. Emil Fischer had synthesized the world's largest known protein with a molecular weight of 4021. "It would seem quite possible to beat Fischer's record . . . It would be a satisfaction to do this," Carothers declared.

To start his unique new job—the post that in nine years would make his fame and fortune—Carothers took a train to Wilmington in February 1928. He had no trouble finding his way; he joked that anyone could recognize the station "by the imposing majesty of its architectural conception and execution, the giant porphyry columns with golden architraves, etc." Carothers often used a high-flown formal style in humorous letters; in contrast, his scientific papers and serious correspondence are precise and conversational without pomposity. Anyway, he added matter-of-factly, Wilmington's first train station was the only one in town.

After moving into a room in a boarding house where he could take his meals, Carothers started work in Stine's small new building for basic research. Its mission was so unusual that local wags called it "Purity Hall," and its researchers, "The Virgins." Du Pont's Experimental Station was an informal, congenial place to work, though. Employees used first names, and anyone with a question simply walked over and asked the resident expert.

Reporting to a friend, Carothers wrote cheerily: "A week of industrial slavery has already elapsed without breaking my proud spirit. Already I am so accustomed to the shackles that I scarcely notice them. Like the child laborers in the spinning factories and the coal mines, I arise before dawn and prepare myself a meagre breakfast. Then off to the terrific grind arriving at 8 just as the birds are beginning to wake up. Harvard was never like this. From then on I occupy myself by thinking, smoking, reading and talking until five o'clock. . . . Regarding funds, the sky is the limit. I can spend as much as I please. Nobody asks any questions as to how I am spending my time or what my plans are for the future. Apparently it is all up to me. So even though it was somewhat of a wrench to leave Harvard when the time finally came, the new job looks just as good from this side as it did from the other. According to any orthodox standards, making the move was certainly the correct thing."

At first, Carothers worked alone, experimenting with 75 pounds of elemental mercury. Breathing the vapor from elemental mercury was known to cause neurological problems, including agitation and depression. In many laboratories in the 1920s, however, safety was still a matter of personal discretion, and ventilation hoods were far from perfect. Chemists regarded themselves as daring scientists and regularly went home in clothes reeking of chemicals. Mercury was not the only poisonous substance Carothers worked with. Two years later, he tried to fireproof wood with tetraethyl lead. When he heated the additive in a flask, it burst into flames and poisonous fumes escaped into the air. Lead can damage the central nervous system and, in the most severe cases, lead to insanity or death. Mercury vapor and tetraethyl lead may have contributed to Carothers' baffling mixture of hyperthyroidism and mood swings.

Carothers had no control over hiring, and his team of recent Ph.D.'s expanded slowly. A company executive interviewed prospective candidates, and he deliberately did not pick the cream of the crop. Refugees from the world's leading chemical centers in Germany were available for the asking, but he refused to hire a Jew. During nine years at Du Pont, Carothers worked with a total of 20 young assistants, generally 10 at a time. Most were male Protestant Ph.D.'s of British and German descent, and more than half came from the Midwest.

Carothers forged unusual bonds with two of his young assistants. The first was a physical chemist, Paul J. Flory, who later won a Nobel Prize. When he began working for Carothers at the age of 24, Flory barely knew what a polymer was. He knew only that many chemists thought polymers were of dubious scientific value. Then one day, Carothers came into Flory's laboratory and sat down to chat. Flory thought that Carothers was "a very cultured person, very refined, and privately charming" and "a scientist of extraordinary breadth and originality." Carothers used diagrams rather than mathematics to think about molecular structure, but he was the only Du Pont scientist who understood Flory's physical chemistry; Carothers' boundless curiosity was unfettered by superficial boundaries between specialties.

Speaking to young Flory that day, Carothers said in his slow and measured way, "You know, the polymer field is an area where it is my belief [that] mathematics could be applied." Flory spent the rest of his life doing just that and dominated the field of polymers for two decades after World War II. So gentle was Carothers' leadership, however, that it was only after his death that Flory "realized how much of a shield he had been, and how much of an influence. . . . It was an extraordinary opportunity, I realize now in retrospect."

Significantly, when Carothers picked his own laboratory assistant, he chose, not a Protestant Midwesterner, but a young Russian Jewish immigrant. Carothers secured a Du Pont college scholarship for Joseph Labovsky and, when the young man graduated and was digging ditches during the worst of the 1930s Great Depression, Carothers rehired him. After spotting Labovsky one evening at a concert, Carothers often asked his young assistant to work late, ostensibly to set up experiments, but actually to chat about Russian music and literature. Carothers especially admired Tchaikovsky's romantic Pathétique Sonata and Dostoevsky's *Crime and Punishment* and carefully imitated Labovsky's pronunciation of Russian names.

If they talked past midnight and Carothers was in a high and happy mood, he drove Labovsky home. Concentrating on their conversation instead of his driving, Carothers almost got a traffic ticket once. A policeman stopped him at a stop sign to say that he had not made a full stop, but Carothers talked his way out of the ticket.

"I stopped," Carothers told the officer.

"Yeah," replied the cop. "But it wasn't a full stop."

"I stopped," Carothers repeated with his usual precision. "What could be more than a stop?"

Other evenings, Labovsky watched Carothers slip into depression. His speech would become strained and slow, with long spaces between comments. Then he might drift back into his office, have a drink perhaps, and sleep overnight on a cot in an adjacent walk-in closet. "When he was depressed, he was a very sad human being," Labovsky said. "He was just pathetic to look at."

During regular laboratory hours, Carothers maintained a harmonious, quiet, albeit formal atmosphere. He dressed summer or winter, like most white-collar men, in a dark wool three-piece suit. Smoking heavily, he spoke slowly and economically, in what seemed to be carefully thought-out formulations. Politely, he came right to the point: "Joe, will you please do this or that?" Despite his unassuming modesty, there was never any doubt who drove the operation. His touch was light, though. On Martin Cupery's second day at work, Carothers told him, "Now remember, Cupery, you're not working for me. You're working with me." Reviewing his assistants' work regularly, he prevented them from going off on tangents. In four years, Cupery never heard a cross word from Carothers. Crawford Greenewalt, a future Du Pont president, found Carothers "kind, unprepossessing, gentle."

Although Carothers was considered a brilliant experimentalist, he rarely conducted experiments at Du Pont. His job was to think and write. "Ninety-five percent of experiments can be proven with pencil and paper and don't require demonstration," he often said. Carothers spent more hours reading scientific literature in Du Pont's third-floor library than any other Du Pont scientist. He liked to sit at a long table overlooking oak and tulip poplar trees. Taking notes, he held a hard pencil between his first and second fingers in an awkward position that belied the long hours he had spent in penmanship classes in his father's secretarial school. Carothers had the rare ability to recognize the significant points of a problem and, in a simple, Du Pont-issued notebook, he designed experiments for his assistants to conduct. When the experiments were finished, the group analyzed the data together. They were answering important questions about the chemical reactions that form polymers.

Despite his laboratory's outward calm, Carothers was poised on the brink of an almost superhuman outpouring of scientific achievement. Over the next three years, between 1929 and 1931, he would transform the chaos of organic polymer chemistry with a clarity of focus and definition. He would settle the argument between Staudinger and the rest of Europe's chemists. As a leading polymer scientist later commented, Carothers' work was "a volcanic eruption, the reverberations of which are still being felt."

Guided by his strategic blueprint and aided by his team of young assistants, Carothers began to attack the central puzzle: Were polymers long but otherwise normal molecules? The first step was to break Emil Fischer's record by building an even longer polymer chain. To do that, Carothers and his team began by making compounds with alcohol groups on each end. That accomplished, they worked throughout 1929 on adding slowly and cautiously, one acid at a time to the alcohol groups. A compound made of an alcohol and an acid is an ester; and by reacting alcohol groups with acids over and over again, Carothers made the first polyesters—literally, molecules composed of many esters. Carothers' early polyesters are not used in today's textiles, but they opened the door to the modern world of synthetic fibers.

As the polymer chains began to grow, Carothers worried that their ends might double back and join to form rings. Fortunately, he discovered that, beyond a certain size, the two ends of his polymers were so far apart that they were unlikely to join together. Carothers and his team determined the molecular weight of each new product in Du Pont's ultracentrifuge. When the molecular weights finally hovered around 5000 or 6000, they knew they had surpassed Fischer's record-breaking molecule.

At this point, suddenly and unaccountably, they seemed to hit the proverbial stone wall. No matter what they did, they could not produce a chain with a molecular weight beyond 5000 or 6000. Their morale was so high, though, that they felt annoyed rather than discouraged. As Carothers' friend and chief assistant Julian Hill explained later, "We operated on defying things that we thought were affronts."

Puzzling over the problem, Carothers concluded that water might be the culprit. It might be creating an equilibrium in which some of his carefully made polyester chains were transformed back into smaller acids and alcohols. If true, he had think of a way to get rid of the water. At a conference several years before, he had seen a piece of equipment called a molecular still. It looked much like a hot plate with a vacuum for removing volatile reaction products such as water. Although he improved its design, the contraption was cantankerous and hard to use. Nevertheless, Hill tried heating the polymers in the still. And sure enough, as water slowly escaped, his compound became tough, horny, and elastic. And when it melted, it was much more viscous than originally—clear evidence of its increased molecular weight.

Carothers had already settled the controversy between Staudinger and his opponents. He had built Staudinger's macromolecules, and the properties of his macromolecules were identical to those of natural polymers. Even more, his path-breaking technique of condensation polymerization had demonstrated that his macromolecules consisted of long chains held together by ordinary valence bonds.

Carothers published a massively documented, landmark paper on polymerization in *Chemical Reviews* in 1931. In it, he created a new science. He showed logically that polymers are long but ordinary molecules and that there is no theoretical limit to the length of a polymer's chain. He described how to make polyesters by adding compounds to long chains and by using condensation to eliminate the water that formed. He invented a new terminology, defining terms such as recurring unit, end group, copolymer, addition polymer, and condensation polymer. He called polymers with molecular weights over 10,000 "superpolymers." For example, Carothers termed rubber an addition polymer, formed by adding compounds to chains, but he suspected—rightly—that cellulose and silk are superpolymers formed by condensation polymerization. In addition to resolving the chemical nature of polymers, Carothers' work laid the foundation for the industrial development of polymers for textile fibers and plastics of many kinds.

Written in his clear and supple prose, his report and the series that followed it inspired a generation of American scientists to study macromolecules. While many European chemists still doubted that polymers could be true molecules, Carl Marvel believed that in the United States, "After that article, the mystery of polymer chemistry was pretty well cleared up and it was possible for less talented people to make good contributions in the field."

On a deeper level, Carothers explained all those mysterious properties of large polymers that had so baffled early organic "grease chemists." Writing in surprisingly physical terms that reflected his deep understanding of natural phenomena, he explained that the special attributes of polymers are caused—not by any unusual kind of chemical bond—but by their linear shapes. "The physical behavior of a molecule whose length is 100 times as great as its other dimensions must be profoundly different from that of a small compact molecule. Enormously long, flexible, and clumsy molecules must be very sluggish in their kinetic behavior, and it is not surprising that high polymers cannot be distilled or that they are never obtained in the form of thin mobile liquids. Very large molecules . . . are not capable of adjusting themselves instantly to any changes in physical environment."

Carothers' fabulous creativity and deep insights occurred, however, amid a growing maelstrom of emotional upheaval. He missed the intellectual stimulus of a university and its lengthy vacation rest periods. As usual, he was saving just "slightly more money than nothing at all." He still suffered from stage fright. When asked to speak at a scientific meeting in St. Louis, he got "such a bad case of cold feet and such acute brain fever over the matter that it was necessary for me to repudiate my promises [to speak] or abandon all attempt to do any work."

Most disturbingly, he developed a distorted perception of the value of his own work. Within a year of his arrival in Wilmington, a tragic chasm began to grow between his estimation of his accomplishments and the reality of the scientific revolution he was creating. Looking back on 1929, the year when he planned and began his studies of polymers, Carothers considered its "most striking feature would be the sharp increase in liquor consumption . . . Nervous fears and depressions were fairly frequent and intense but probably no worse than in previous years . . . The last day of the year was marked by an address to a group of organic chemists, delivered in a state of slightly stupid indifference induced by restricting the luncheon to 1 qt of Port wine and a few passages of Milton. . . . It is planned to make a strong effort to struggle through with the year 1930."

Carothers may have been shy and depressed, but he amassed a surprising number of friends in Wilmington. He loved racquet games and played tennis with his friend and assistant, Julian Hill, at the Du Pont Country Club. He joined the University and Whist Club, a men's social organization. And when the Wilmington YMCA opened squash courts, he wrote a Harvard colleague for his racket: "I don't want to put you to a lot of trouble in this matter. I think it would come through all right if you would just attach a shipping label to it with my name." He played squash as violently as possible, moving fast and "like a cobra," as one onlooker put it. Sports temporarily brightened him; his athletic style was the opposite of his slow-moving, slow-talking, listening mode at work.

Omnivorous reading made Carothers a brilliant and witty conversationalist in small groups of friends. Hill thought that, after a drink or two, Carothers became the funniest man alive. His humor was understated. When referring to a transmission box labeled "positively infinitely variable," Carothers always added dryly, "Within finite limits." At parties, he charmed guests by pulling from his pants pockets wooden blocks assembled into molecules. Stereochemical approaches to complicated compounds were becoming important in chemistry, he emphasized.

Although Carothers was transparent and innocently open about his insecurities and mental health, many of his young colleagues stood in awe of him. Thus, when Carothers showed Julian Hill his capsule of cyanide, Hill interpreted it as bravado. More ominously, Carothers could list the famous scientists who had committed suicide.

As Carothers' international reputation grew, Du Pont doubled his research budget, invitations to speak at scientific meetings poured in, and he was named an associate editor of the *Journal of the American Chemical Society*. He devoted many hours to editing and reviewing other scientists' articles before publication. He usually wrote brief and businesslike remarks, such as, "This sentence does not convey any meaning to me and I should think it might well be omitted." But occasionally, he let loose with a literary flourish: "This is one of the feeblest efforts that has come to my attention in a long time. As the set essay of a college senior it might, by the exercise of some indulgence, be allowed a passing mark, but as a contribution to a scientific journal of any kind it has no claim to consideration."

Even as Carothers was explaining the fundamental nature of large biological molecules, he orchestrated a miraculous two weeks in the history of industrial research. During April 1930, he and his team invented not only Neoprene, the first high-grade synthetic rubber, but also polyester, the first synthetic fiber that closely resembled silk. It was a dazzling accomplishment that can still make industrial chemists starry-eyed.

Neoprene, Carothers' first practical invention, was made reluctantly, as "a kind of side issue" to his scientific investigation of polymers. Synthetic rubber was of great commercial interest. The car-happy United States used half the world's natural rubber, and demand had outstripped the supply from wild rubber trees in the Amazon. Price fluctuations on British rubber plantations in Southeast Asia provided further incentive for the development of synthetic substitutes. Du Pont had been trying without success to make synthetic rubber from divinylacetylene (DVA), which had been discovered by a chemistry professor at Notre Dame University, Father Julius A. Nieuwland. After several explosions and serious accidents, Du Pont asked Carothers to find out what was wrong.

Carothers was interested in rubber, but his reasons were scientific rather than commercial. He thought of natural rubber as a relatively simple example of a highly polymerized substance. So in 1930, without any immediate commercial goal in mind, Carothers gave Arnold M. Collins, a 31-year-old chemist familiar with DVA, the job of exploring its chemistry. Carothers wanted Collins to purify their samples of DVA and identify its impurities. Carothers suspected that impurities had caused the explosions in Du Pont's laboratories.

After distilling one of the impurities from crude DVA, Collins let the new substance sit over a weekend. When he returned to work on Monday, April 17, 1930, it had solidified into a tiny, cauliflower-type mass. Collins stuck a wire into the glass vessel and fished a few cubic centimeters of the substance out. It felt strong, resilient, and elastic, much like vulcanized rubber. Almost without thinking, Collins threw the mass against his laboratory bench. It bounced like a golf ball. Collins had made chloroprene in his test tube, and over the weekend it had spontaneously polymerized into the high-grade synthetic rubber that Du Pont would market as Neoprene.

Surprisingly, the idea that Collins' new compound might form the basis for a synthetic rubber took several weeks to evolve. And it was not Carothers, but Stine's successor, Elmer K. Bolton, who first realized that the molecular structure of Collins' mass was similar to that of isoprene, the main constituent of natural rubber. Bolton had studied in Germany and was familiar with its World War I efforts to develop an ersatz rubber for tires.

Collins had every right to be thrilled with Neoprene's discovery; Carothers had told his French chemist, Gerard Berchet, to try the same reaction, but Berchet had not emptied his test tube. Carothers, however, got little personal satisfaction from his unsought invention. He regarded Neoprene somewhat disdainfully because it involved no new chemical principles or techniques. He also considered his 23 Neoprene articles "abundant in quantity but a little disappointing in quality." Even worse, he feared that if Du Pont lost money on the laboratory curiosity, the company might lose its enthusiasm for his scientific research.

Neoprene, announced November 3, 1931, made Carothers well known, if not exactly famous. More than 400 newspapers published articles "composed almost entirely of hot air in the wrong key," observed Carothers. He thought that Collins should have gotten more credit than Father Nieuwland. Carothers even refused a medal because he said that he had been "a collaborator in a cooperative development involving a large number of persons." As Carothers told a college journalist, "You will understand that it represents a cooperative rather than a personal achievement." Public recognition meant little to Carothers. On another occasion, when his friend Jack Johnson accused Carothers of stealing an idea, Carothers immediately offered to withdraw his own work or publish it jointly with Johnson, even though the latter realized just as quickly that the idea had been Carothers' alone.

Carothers' fears about the profitability of Neoprene were groundless. Du Pont marketed it cleverly as a specialty rubber, more durable than natural rubber and more resistant to oil, gasoline, solvents, sunlight, and heat. Throughout the Depression, Neoprene sold at several times the price of natural rubber, and Du Pont paid Carothers a bonus of at least $10,000. Neoprene was used for telephone insulation, gasoline hoses, gas tank linings, gaskets, printing rollers, shoes, and heels. However, Neoprene did not make good tires. When the Japanese blocked exports of Asian natural rubber to the Allies during World War II, the Americans made tires from a German compound, styrene butadiene. In turn, the Germans used Du Pont's DVA catalytic technology to make their synthetic rubber.

Less than two weeks after Collins found Neoprene in his test tube, Carothers' laboratory made an even more promising discovery: the first synthetic fiber. On April 28, 1930, Julian Hill was back at his molecular still, boiling the water off a rather odd, long polyester with a molecular weight of about 3300. No one was thinking of making a fiber; Hill and Carothers were still trying to make the largest possible molecule. After 12 days in the still, the polymer had become highly viscous, the tip-off that it had gained a great deal of molecular weight and was thus an extremely long superpolyester. Touching the molten mass with a glass rod, Hill was surprised to see a single, fine filament form. In a process now known as "cold drawing," Hill pulled it out into an even stronger, pliable filament.

Carothers was working in downtown Wilmington at the time, so Hill organized a joyful cadre of helpers who drew cold filaments like taffy from the little ball of soft superpolyester. As the men ran laughing and whooping through the hallways, they increased the tensile strength of the material. Later tests revealed that the filaments had an unprecedented molecular weight over 12,000. With typical modesty, Carothers reported to Du Pont, "It should be noted that although I had formulated the general theory of condensation polymers and suggested a possible means of getting superpolymers, the first fibers were made as a discovery by Hill."

Although Carothers was rather bored by Neoprene, the discovery that polyesters could make long fibers intrigued him. Pulling the filaments under tension made them transparent, lustrous, very strong, and so pliable that they could be tied into hard knots. The properties and crystalline status of the filaments changed according to the amount of tension applied. Cold drawing oriented the polymer's chains along the axis of the filament and made the threads tough and pliable; the process is still used today to make nylon fibers. It was a "spectacular phenomenon," Carothers thought.

The new fibers were scientifically interesting—and they eventually laid the foundation for the synthetic textile industry—but at the time they seemed practically worthless. The first polyester fibers resembled those produced by the lowly silk worm, but Carothers did not think that the discovery would be commercially valuable. The polymer chains made in Hill's molecular still were still not long enough to make robust fibers. The filaments melted at such a low temperature and were so soluble that they could not be ironed or washed in dry cleaning fluid or hot water. Carothers knew he would have to make longer polymers if he hoped to make a marketable fiber. Instead, Carothers dramatized the romance of Hill's discovery by quoting the seventeenth-century microscopist, Robert Hooke, who had dreamed of making synthetic silk even "better than that Excrement" made by silk worms.

Carothers wanted to publish an article about the synthetic fibers, but a Du Pont executive told him to wait until patent applications had been filed. This was explicitly contrary to the agreement reached when Carothers was hired. But then, who had expected him to produce something that was potentially an industrial extravaganza? Displaying considerable skill at bureaucratic in-fighting, Carothers pointed to the terms of his hiring and compromised by waiting a year to publish the article. In the meantime, Du Pont filed a patent application trying to cover all synthetic fibers. Although the patent became an important part of Du Pont's portfolio of nylon patents, it was too broad to protect every synthetic.

Only after the patents had been filed were Carothers and Hill permitted to speak about the synthetic fiber at an American Chemical Society meeting in Buffalo, New York, on September 1, 1931. There they announced publicly, that, for the first time, it might be possible to make useful fibers from strictly synthetic material. As he cheerily wrote his former college girlfriend, now Frances Gelvin Spencer, "We have been enormously lucky in our research so far. We have not only a synthetic rubber, but something theoretically more original—a synthetic silk. If these two things can be nailed down, that will be enough for one lifetime."

The next step in the search for a marketable fiber seemed obvious. Instead of combining acids with alcohols to make ester fibers that disappeared in the wash, they would try combining acids with amines to make amides. Amide compounds are chemically similar to polyesters, but amide bonds, which are present in proteins, are stronger; amide compounds generally have higher melting points. Amide-based fibers would not disappear in hot water. If they could be spun at high temperatures—a big *if*—they might be ideal.

By July 21, 1930, Hill was back at work heating a superpolyamide in the molecular still. To his great frustration, he could not make any fibers. Only much later was it discovered that it would indeed have produced fibers, if only he had known the proper technique to use.

Amazingly, while Carothers' group explored related amide compounds, they discovered nylon's precursor, the amide compound that would eventually make nylon. No one recognized its importance at the time, however. In fact, in a completely rational and understandable move, Carothers put the amides on a back burner. In retrospect, he said, the decision seemed rather foolish, but he had his reasons. He was working at temperatures around 300° C (572°F) "where organic compounds begin to cease to exist," that is, decompose. His basic tool, the molecular still, was unreliable. Nor could he imagine any laboratory process that could mimic the way silkworms simultaneously synthesize and spin fibers with a high melting point and low solubility. Above all, the development of fibers was not basic research. So Carothers put the forerunner of nylon aside and continued working on polyester compounds.

Abandoning the hunt for linear, fiber-forming molecules, he turned to polymer ring compounds. Before Carothers, cyclic compounds were so difficult to make that no one studied them, but his group had tasted scientific blood and was happily publishing papers. When they discovered a series of ring compounds that produce synthetic scents, Du Pont sold the compounds to the perfume industry. The cyclic compounds were the last of Carothers' fundamental scientific studies. After completing them, he drifted for a while, unclear as to what direction his research should take.

Carothers' life was not all science, however. Carothers had met and fallen in love with a 23-year-old married woman. Sylvia Chalfant Windle Moore was a brilliant and beautiful young Quaker activist. She had graduated from Swarthmore College in 1929 before taking a job at the Du Pont Experimental Station. As a volunteer, she lobbied for the Women's International League for Peace and Freedom in support of the Geneva Disarmament Conference and restricting or eliminating offensive weapons. In 1935, the league would be a prime mover behind Senator Gerald K. Nye's investigation of the munitions industry when Du Pont was labeled a "merchant of death." Carothers' love for a league lobbyist says a great deal about his tolerance for dissent and maybe even about his own rebelliousness.

Some of Carothers' friends thought Sylvia was "terrific, bright, sexy, good-looking;" others thought she enjoyed wrapping Carothers around her finger. Carothers himself, who was 36 years old, described her as "23, tall, slender, pretty, intelligent (though married) and she has the largest capacity for friendship of anyone I ever met. . . . At the start it was like an unspoken and indisputable act of God . . . perhaps like an undergraduate's dream of perfect sympathy (springtime and sun rise) and now it seems to be angry sea salt and indignant clover."

To quiet his nerves, Carothers was resorting to increasing quantities of alcohol. With three other bachelors, he shared a house in an area called Whiskey Acres on fashionable Kennett Pike and bought bootleg liquor from a nearby mushroom farmer. On Christmas Eve, in 1931, after his three housemates left for the evening in formal attire—tails, white ties, and high hats—Carothers drove home through streets strung with gaily colored lights. Whiskey Acres had no lights or Christmas tree, and Carothers sat "alone with the moronic comments emanating from the radio, and (sadly enough) not quite sober either." He was giving a talk about rubber at Yale University on December 28, and, as he told a friend, "You can imagine the state of my nerves and the necessity of some soothing influences or other."

Scientifically, 1931 had been a stupendous year for Carothers; he had published his classic *Chemical Reviews* article on polymers. Yet he realized, "My nervousness, moroseness, and vacillation get worse as time goes on, and the frequent resort to drinking doesn't bring about any permanent improvement. 1932 looks pretty bleak to me just now."

When Carothers went to Yale, however, his talk was well received, and he went on to spend a weekend in New York with Sylvia Moore. He kept "fairly tight" as they went to bohemian restaurants, Broadway shows, and a "quite gaudy speakeasy which has fairly potable and very potent liquid refreshments and the most demoralizingly smooth and expert niger [*sic*] orchestra that I ever heard. For the first time in my life I had a really tremendous yearning to dance, and of course the girl I was with refused to dance with me because of my clumsiness." As he dated Mrs. Moore, Du Pont executives fretted about potential scandal. Carothers' position was that "social opinion means nothing to me."

As Carothers lost his scientific focus and drifted from one research project to another, financial and personnel changes at Du Pont were forcing him toward applied, commercial research—the very kind that Du Pont and Stine had promised him he would never have to do. Financially, the Depression was taking its toll. Du Pont was affected less than other U.S. companies; over the course of the 1930s its profits rose 50 percent thanks to profitable new products such as cellophane, titanium pigments, Cordura rayon tire cord, Lucite plastic, and Midgley's tetraethyl lead and Freon. Nevertheless, at the beginning of the Depression, even Du Pont slashed its work force and reduced wages and hours.

Even more than the Depression, personnel changes at Du Pont radically altered Carothers' ability to do basic research. The visionary Charles Stine had been promoted, and his successor was Elmer K. Bolton, the chemist who had recognized the importance of Neoprene. Bolton, a former postdoctoral student of Richard Willstätter in Germany, had helped establish Du Pont's successful synthetic dyestuff division and had participated in the decision to manufacture Midgley's tetraethyl lead. Bolton believed fervently in applied research and had opposed Stine's original proposal for a basic research program at Du Pont. Bolton quickly ended Purity Hall's special status.

Torn between pure science and Bolton's pressure for profits, Carothers felt betrayed. Deeply distressed, Carothers reminded their superiors of Du Pont's promise that he could do basic research, free of commercial concerns. The purpose of pure research is to increase scientific knowledge but now, Carothers anguished, "it is expected to pay its own way." As he said, his laboratory had "the rather desperate feeling" that its work must make money.

Confiding in Machetanz, Carothers wrote that as an "industrial slave . . . I still struggle along as a Group Leader, which is to say a kind of a Clerk. I never had any talent for clerical matters, and haven't developed along those lines to speak of. Research lately has been rather foul on account of the depression." Given an offer from a really good university like Harvard, he told Machetanz that he would leave Du Pont. Others experienced similar conflicts during the Depression, of course. Discouraged with short-term industrial projects, Thomas Midgley, Jr., stopped working for General Motors and financed his own research laboratory at Ohio State University. Unlike Midgley, however, Carothers thought his negotiating position was weak. Neoprene was not yet profitable, and nylon's precursor chemical was sitting on his back burner, waiting to be discovered.

In his defense, Carothers was performing a multitude of jobs that today would be divided among a variety of experts. By 1934, he was spending about a quarter of his time on applied problems for other Du Pont departments. He met with Thomas Midgley's assistants to try to get General

Motors' support for a long-range scientific study of the poisonous gasoline additive, tetraethyl lead. Besides trouble-shooting for various Du Pont departments, Carothers published 60 papers and was listed as the inventor or coinventor of 69 U.S. patent applications during his nine years at Du Pont. Research and development were so new to American corporations that Carothers' assistants drafted and he edited patent applications for Du Pont lawyers. "You were supposed to be so on top of the literature that you knew whether this was something new or not. . . . Those patents are really classical scientific papers," Hill explained. Carothers considered himself unfit to be a clerk or inventor, but he dominated Du Pont's patent application process for almost a decade.

In addition to his research, trouble-shooting, and writing, Carothers played host to a growing number of famous European chemists. When an Oxford professor visited, Carothers reported tongue-in-cheek, "My vanity was very pleased to show him things sufficiently impressive to startle even an Englishman." On another red-letter day, he hosted Richard Willstätter, who "in his field corresponds to God in some others." As Carothers' research focus and his workload changed, his mood swings accelerated in both intensity and frequency.

Early in 1932, he vividly described an agitated mood for Frances Gelvin. After she asked twice about his work, he replied almost onomatopoeically, "I manage to balance myself in a swivel chair by clinging desperately to the edge of an oaken table. This lasts for 7¼ hours a day. Physically my activities consist in shouting into a dictaphone, jumping up and down to go for a drink of water or milk, lighting cigarettes, answering the telephone and fitfully rushing into the laboratories. All very thrilling . . . There isn't anything in the way of recent results to report—unless 17 papers written during the last 2 months constitute a result. In the evenings I just sit and brood, or else read *Chemical Abstracts* in a mood of excited absent-mindedness." He signed off, "(Unfortunately) alive."

By May 3, the agitation had faded and he was writing, "Dear Fran, No, I am not dead, but only moribund. Feeling rather feeble, smelly and cockroach-like. . . . I go through at least a dozen violent storms of despair every day. [I feel] agitated in a febrile sort of way. I never seem to know 30 minutes ahead now a days whether I shall be able to sit up or not." Yet he continued functioning, enjoying the "lordly" springtime, dining with friends almost every evening, and looking forward to becoming a university "Prof" again, should a tempting offer appear.

A few weeks later, he was in an elevated mood. When Du Pont's librarian inquired about a missing volume, he replied in happy doggerel:

> "I have not stolen from its place your book
> Nor swiped, nor in any other manner took;
> Nay I never saw the blasted thing,
> Know not its color whether blue or pink.
> In fact, your book I didn't even covet;
> I have a private persnl copy ovet."

In the chaos of his mood swings, music was Carothers' lifeline. He avidly attended concerts at Philadelphia's Academy of Music and amassed a large classical music record collection. After recording studios adopted the use of Bell Telephone Laboratory's new electronic microphones, they could reproduce a louder and more brilliant and resonant sound. One side of a record lasted four minutes, and when the first complete classical compositions were recorded at 78 revolutions per minute, Bach's Mass in B minor occupied 34 records. During the Depression most people listened to free radio music, and only about 500 fans could be counted on to buy an enormous and expensive classical music set. Carothers was among the few. He also acquired a shockingly expensive Gramophone Robot record player, repaired it constantly, and called it "a miracle. It will play two dozen records in the selected order (turning them over as the occasion requires) completely automatically . . . What it brings out is really music and if you want you can have it loud enough to rattle the doorknobs at certain frequencies." He often arranged complete concerts for friends: Sibelius and Bach one Friday and an entire opera or a Gilbert and Sullivan operetta the next, with drinks and cheese for 12 to 15 people until 1 a.m. In addition, his newspaper friend, Bill Mapel, gave parties where Carothers sang duets with a popular local singer. Carothers said that if he could start life over, he would devote it to music.

To help his parents through the Depression, Carothers brought them to Wilmington to share a rented house in Arden, an artists' colony outside town. Carothers described it as "a kind of arty and crafty place . . . now populated by imitation bohemians, Jews of a certain type, etc." The elder Carothers knew no one in Wilmington, and Carothers' crowd of smoking and drinking sophisticates was unlikely to appeal to them. Nor were they likely to approve of Sylvia Moore, who was divorcing her husband. Worst of all, Carothers was trying to care for a family when he could barely care for himself.

Carothers seems to have survived by ignoring his parents much of the time. He said, "I come home, sometimes play a couple of games of deck tennis with a neighbor, then after dinner put 15 or 20 records on the phonograph and drink a few dozen bottles of beer while pretending to work until about 10 o'clock when the well known phenomenon of gassy stupefication accompanying large volumes of beer sets in. Then I go to bed." As his parents ran the errands, his mother fretted about the "hard headed business men" at Du Pont who were worrying her son.

Carothers also escaped the menage by attending chemical meetings. While in Chicago, he visited his favorite sister, Isabel. She was earning a six-figure salary writing and acting in a comic radio show, "Clara, Lu, 'n' Em." The program, aired nationally on NBC, was one of radio's first two soap operas. When her group performed for the chemists, Carothers admitted, "I never realized before that they are actually funny and amusing."

On another occasion, Carothers left his parents in Arden to attend a chemical meeting at Cornell University. Two years before, he had panicked at the Yale meeting, but this time he felt happy and free. "My head was practically on fire with theories," he said. When his parents returned to Des Moines after a year in Wilmington, Carothers celebrated with a little boulder hopping in nearby Brandywine Creek.

While Carothers was eager to identify new scientific problems to tackle, his commercially minded boss Bolton prodded his star scientist to return to the search for synthetic fibers. "Wallace, if you could just get something with better properties, higher melting point, insolubility and tensile strength, you could have a new type of fiber," Bolton insisted. "Look it over and see if you can't find something. After all you are dealing with polyamides, and wool is a polyamide."

One day early in 1934, Carothers entered Bolton's office to say, "I think that I have got some new ideas." Spurred on by Bolton, Carothers, the scientist, became an inventor conducting a deliberate, methodical search for a particular kind of polymer. More than four years after the nylon precursor had been discovered and set on a back burner, Carothers returned to the amides. He thought he needed to make a superpolymer with a molecular weight above 10,000, roughly double the size of the polyesters he had made in 1930 and 1931. He was hunting for a polymer with a melting point high enough to make a fabric that could be washed in hot water, ironed, or dry cleaned. Carothers, the agnostic, joked with friends that he was praying daily for his idea to pan out.

On May 24, 1934, a week after Carothers' parents left town, his idea did indeed pan out. Donald D. Coffman—a chemist and recent Ph.D. who was tall, blond, extremely polite, and exceedingly nervous—dipped a glass-stirring rod into a tiny molten mass of superpolymer. The mass was only as big as a Hershey Kiss, but when Coffman pulled his rod out, a fine filament came with it. The strand seemed fairly tough and not at all brittle. The sample was so tiny that he used a hypodermic needle as a spinneret to extrude more strands. When cold drawn, they formed lustrous filaments that were stronger than silk, and—finally—abrasion-resistant and safe in dry cleaning fluid and hot water. The filament—the first polyamide fiber—was an enormous step forward.

Coffman's synthesis of the first polyamide fiber was so exciting that several days passed before anyone at Du Pont realized that Carothers had disappeared. Far from feeling euphoric about the discovery, Carothers was overwhelmed by "a very large (metaphorical) explosion." Unable to reap satisfaction from his success and unaccountably convinced that he would never have another scientific idea, he climbed into his elderly Oldsmobile convertible and drove 70 miles to Baltimore to consult an eminent psychiatrist, Dr. Leslie B. Hohman.

Carothers liked Hohman and, apparently for the first time, confided openly in a psychiatrist. "My doctor here is Dr. Hohman—a rather young fellow and I never saw any one capable of arousing so much respect and confidence in so short a time," Carothers wrote his thesis adviser, Roger Adams. "He opened a conversation this afternoon with a few very pertinent questions concerning the structure of the benzene ring. That seems fairly good for a psychiatrist—although it is scarcely an adequate indication of his qualities. At any rate, if anyone can do anything for this present nervous collapse he can do it. Already he has restored some of my deflated interest in chemistry."

Hohman and Carothers had much in common. Bachelors of almost the same age, they were former Midwesterners who spoke German and loved classical music. Hohman, who coined the term "depression," believed that many adult problems originated in childhood.

Frantic Du Pont executives ordered Julian Hill to find Carothers and suggested Hohman's clinic as the place to start. When Hill arrived, Carothers was sitting in his dressing gown, looking like death warmed over. Hill was furious when he learned that Hohman had advised Carothers to marry; he thought that Carothers had enough problems already without trying to care for a wife, much less children.

By August 1934, Carothers was well enough to leave Hohman's clinic and stay with Hills' in-laws on Martha's Vineyard. In photographs,

Carothers is smiling, seemingly happy to be playing tennis, swimming, and talking chemistry again. Within a few months, he actually turned down an offer to chair the University of Chicago's chemistry department because his work at Du Pont had reached an "exciting stage."

That fall, Carothers' assistant Edgar W. Spanagel discovered polyethylene terephthalate, *the* polyester that Du Pont later manufactured under license as Dacron fiber and Mylar film. Carothers had made most of the polyesters, but he and others in his group assumed that Spanagel's polyester, like their earlier ones, melted at too low a temperature to be practical. As a result, Carothers did not have this one tested for spinnability. British scientists later used it to make Terylene. When Du Pont executives had to buy a license from the British to make Spanagel's fiber, their faces were bright red with embarrassment.

For the remainder of 1934 and throughout 1935, Carothers' team continued to hunt for fibers. They focused on compounds related to Coffman's exciting polyamide filament. It was stronger than silk but Carothers was looking for filaments that were easier to polymerize and spin. Bolton, on the other hand, urged Carothers to focus on polymers made from cheap and plentiful materials.

On February 28, 1935, Carothers' project succeeded beyond anyone's wildest dreams. The cheerful, lively Frenchman Berchet produced a superpolymer made from chemicals derived from cheap benzene, a by-product of coal; later they would be made from petroleum. A filament teased from Berchet's polymer was, despite its lowly origins, pearly and lustrous. And when it was tested, it proved to be spinnable. Its code name was 6-6 because both its reactants—hexamethylene diamine and adipic acid—had six carbon atoms. Technically, the filament was polyhexamethylene adipamide, a long-chain polymer similar in structure to proteins. It became world-famous as nylon.

Bolton urged Carothers to drop all his other projects to investigate 6-6. It would be difficult to manufacture and spin into fiber, and no one knew how to synthesize its two ingredients in the huge amounts required. These were technical, engineering problems that could be worked out later, Bolton thought. Carothers' scientific insights, together with a shrewd nudge from Bolton, were closing in on the goal. By fall, the first nylon yarn had been prepared, spun, evaluated, improved, and sent to Du Pont's rayon department for further tests.

Remarkably, nylon's properties were even better than those of natural fibers. Compared to silk, nylon was stronger; more elastic; and more resistant to rot, mildew, and moths. Nylon was the first completely synthetic fiber to be marketed; rayon is not synthetic because it is made from wood or cotton cellulose. Moreover, nylon could be extruded as a fiber or molded as a plastic. Although Staudinger and Carothers are the fathers of macromolecular chemistry, the European had only theorized about polymer molecules. Carothers not only theorized about polymer molecules but produced them and launched an industrial revolution.

Over the next two years, as work continued on nylon 6-6, Carothers' health disintegrated. His breakdowns became more frequent and more serious. One evening, he stalked like a madman into the laboratory, shouting, "Damn, it's hot in here!" His assistants looked at each other in surprise. It was the only time they had seen him excited, and it was not particularly hot. The next morning, Carothers was hospitalized again.

During Carothers' years in Wilmington, he was diagnosed with several mental disorders. In 1936, a year before his death, he was almost certainly diagnosed with neurocirculatory asthenia, a term suggesting recurring bouts of the lassitude that is a major symptom of anxiety or depression. Carothers did not use the term "manic depression" in letters to friends, but the condition had been known since ancient times and at least two colleagues, including the future Du Pont president Greenewalt, later recalled Carothers' talking freely about having manic depression, now called bipolar mood disorder. After Carothers' death, the term "manic depression" stuck. The psychosis is characterized by alternating moods of depression and mania, the latter including excessive excitement, elevated moods, or overactivity. Whether Carothers was actually diagnosed as a manic depressive and informed of it is not known. In fact, given his complicated medical history, it cannot even be said with certainty that he had the disorder. What is clear is that, as he reached the pinnacle of success, his health rapidly deteriorated.

With nylon evolving from a scientific to an engineering problem, Carothers' basic research department became a division devoted to developing nylon. Since few engineers knew anything about polymers, several of Carothers' assistants moved into engineering and development. Only a skeleton crew, including Flory, Coffman, and Berchet, remained to work for Carothers on theoretical or exploratory problems.

While nylon was transforming his laboratory, Carothers left the United States for a month in Europe. The Faraday Society had organized the second international meeting of polymer scientists, to be held at the University of Cambridge in September 1935. Carothers' presence was the high point of the conference, although his speech about high-molecular weight polymers gave no clue that he had already discovered a marketable synthetic fiber. Meeting privately with leading polymer scientists, including Staudinger, he thoroughly enjoyed the intellectual stimulation of "a real chemical argument . . . [with] chemical fanatics," something he missed in Wilmington. Later, Carothers traveled alone to Paris and the Black Forest, growing increasingly depressed as he went. Walking for days through the woods, he contemplated suicide.

He was obsessed with the idea that he would never have another original idea. Yet at the same time, he considered several prescient research subjects, including Midgley's polyfluorinated compounds and silicon chemistry. Most of all, he thought about biochemistry and how proteins are synthesized. He already realized that shape and fit determine a protein's structure, and he understood that a geometric scaffolding was involved. He also pinpointed the most useful laboratory tool for studying protein structure. "One of the things I'm intrigued with is tobacco mosaic virus," he told a friend. During the 1950s, the virus would be used to establish basic scientific principles about structural molecular biology. Thus, Carothers was one of a small number of scientists who were thinking about protein structure 15 years before Linus Pauling determined the helical structure of proteins and Rosalind Franklin, Francis Crick, and James Watson worked on the double helix of DNA. Had Carothers shifted to biological chemistry, he might have worked with one or more of them.

In February 1936, Du Pont assigned Carothers what was to be his last job for the company, a history of his contributions. Sylvia Moore had ended their relationship, and two days after Carothers completed the history, he surprised friends by marrying a pretty young woman from Du Pont's patent office. Helen Everett Sweetman was not a socialite, like the wives of some of Carothers' friends. Her father was a Du Pont administrator, neither a scientist nor a top executive. But Helen had graduated from the University of Delaware with a degree in chemistry, she played a good game of tennis, and she adored Carothers.

Newspaperman Bill Mapel loved Carothers like a brother, and he organized the wedding in his sister-in-law's New York apartment on February 21, 1936. After the wedding, the guests took the bride and groom to a posh nightclub for dinner and a floor show. After a week in New York, the newlyweds returned to Wilmington. "No doubt this [marriage] properly calls for condolences to the lady," Carothers wrote a friend.

That spring, Carothers was elected to the National Academy of Sciences, along with Orville Wright and Leo Baekeland, the inventor of Bakelite plastic. Carothers and Baekeland were the first industrial organic chemists given the nation's highest scientific award.

Within four months of his marriage and two months of his admission into the National Academy, Carothers collapsed. Instead of returning to Dr. Hohman in Baltimore, Carothers checked into what he called "an especially elegant, large, and elaborate semi-bug house." The Institute of the Pennsylvania Hospital in Philadelphia had hotellike rooms, tennis courts, bowling, badminton, occupational therapy, roof gardens, and a pool for water therapy.

Carothers did not return to Du Pont for three months. In Philadelphia, he was treated by an eminent psychiatrist, Dr. Kenneth Ellmaker Appel, who believed in the effect of childhood and family life on mental health. Carothers was unimpressed. "Treatment consists in conversation, rambling, inconsequential, pointless, and sometimes so repetitive and puerile as to be the source of laughter, amazement, or anger," he wrote. The circumstances under which Carothers was hospitalized are unclear but he told a friend that "this is an involuntary business so far as I am concerned. It was sprung on me suddenly about 5 weeks ago . . . At the moment this assignment seems permanent unless I simply walk out. They can't very well prohibit that."

Du Pont gave Carothers a leave of absence, but Carothers misinterpreted their motives. "They practically packed him in cotton," Julian Hill said later. "He thought they were trying to ease him out. Of all things. This was about at the all time high in misinterpretation, I would think. When they gave him the health leave, he thought this was just the first step."

Carothers was permitted to leave the institute whenever he wished. That summer, Carothers, his wife Helen, and a nurse attended a colleague's party. Several times that afternoon, Carothers called Helen "Sylvia." In July, he decided in an excited rush to board a ship a few days later and join Roger Adams for a hiking trip in Austria. "I am not very optimistic concerning the sudden healing qualities of Bavarian air, but Bavarian beer will undoubtedly provide at least a temporary solace."

When Carothers arrived in Munich on July 31, Adams thought, "He looked rather dejected—had been drinking heavily." After two weeks hiking in the Alps, Carothers was "a changed man—quite normal & enjoying it." But when Adams left, Carothers hiked on alone and became despondent again. Du Pont executives frantically wired Adams, trying to locate Carothers.

Returning to the United States after almost a month on his own, Carothers alternated between the Philadelphia institute, the Baltimore clinic, his laboratory, a room in Whiskey Acres, and home with Helen. In January 1937, his favorite sister Isabel, the radio star, was hospitalized with a streptococcal infection. When she died suddenly at the age of 36, Carothers was devastated. Research later conducted on bipolar mood disorders suggests that depression can be triggered by stressful events, including the death of a loved one, a job loss, or a move from one therapeutic program to another. Within a short time, Carothers had experienced all three: a new psychiatrist, the disbandment of his research staff, and the death of his dear sister.

An almost inexorable series of events followed. An observer today might recognize the signs, but even now, with new pharmaceutical treatments, one in five people with bipolar mood disorder commits suicide. In 1937, few laypeople knew about depression. Carothers resigned his editorship of the *Journal of the American Chemical Society*. Later that month, he wrote his mother, telling her, "I just wanted to give you my love. Also to dad and [aunt] Helen." It was the "the longest and dearest letter I ever had from him," his mother said later. "We never dreamed that he was desperately ill— we know now how he suffered."

On April 15, 1937, a disturbing incident occurred at work. Carothers called his assistant, Joe Labovsky, in at night to run an experiment and witness laboratory reports. Instead of the usual literary or musical chat, there was complete silence. When Labovsky finally spoke, Carothers spun around in his chair and shouted, "Damn it, read it, *read it*," and stalked out. Labovsky was stunned. Carothers had always been so polite and formal.

Within a short time he evidently felt better, for he wrote Jack Johnson planning four days together at the seashore. But in a few days, late in the evening of April 28, 1937, he admitted himself to the psychiatric institute in Philadelphia, only to leave early the next morning to check into a nearby hotel. Twelve hours later, after carrying the cyanide capsule in his pocket for more than 15 years, he mixed its contents with the juice of a squeezed lemon and drank it. Hotel guests who heard his dying groans called the hotel manager. It was two days after Carothers' forty-first birthday.

Carothers' ashes were buried in Glendale Cemetery, Des Moines. Seven months later, his daughter Jane was born. When Carothers died, his estate was worth less than $45,000, but Du Pont paid Mrs. Carothers his bonuses, worth more than one-third of a million dollars. At the request of Wallace's father Ira, the company also paid Wallace's parents a small yearly stipend.

Du Pont introduced nylon commercially five years after Carothers invented it and three years after his death. Du Pont marketed nylon as cleverly as it had Neoprene. The first bits and pieces appeared in Dr. West toothbrushes to replace Chinese pig bristles, which became unobtainable after the 1937 Japanese invasion of Manchuria. The key to selling nylon in large quantities, however, was women's stockings. Women were a captive market because few of them wore pants. Well-to-do women averaged eight pairs of opaque but fragile silk stockings yearly, while less wealthy women wore baggy rayon hose in winter and painted their legs and drew lines up the backs of their calves to simulate seams in summer. A nylon stocking required only a few grams of the precious fiber but commanded a high price. As Hitler invaded the Low Countries in 1940, five million pairs of nylons went on sale in the United States; they cost as much as silk hose but sold out in a day. Nylons were so sheer that American women began shaving their legs. Because most of the Japanese silk used in the United States was knitted into hosiery, women's nylon stockings had as revolutionary an effect on world trade as the artificial dyes that ruined India's indigo planters and as the Haber-Bosch process that ended Chile's near monopoly on nitrates.

During World War II, nylon became an Allied weapon, along with Carothers' Neoprene, Midgley's tetraethyl lead and Freon, and DDT (Chapter 8). The military diverted all available nylon for use in parachutes, airplane tire cords, glider towropes, tents, and the like. Nylon tires enabled bombers and carrier planes fueled with tetraethyl lead to withstand overloading.

Today nylon is used for clothing, tire cords, rug and upholstery material, injection-molding, sails and rigging, fishing lines, racket strings, rope, surgical sutures, machinery parts, and an amazing variety of other articles—enough for approximately 1.5 pounds annually for every person on Earth. Nylon doubled the size of the world's largest chemical company, making polymers Du Pont's core technology. At the end of the twentieth century, nylon still accounted for 40 percent of company sales. Half of all professional chemists and chemical engineers in the United States now work with polymers.

After the war, Carothers' work spread to American universities and became the prototype for science-based industrial research. Polymer scientists, including Flory and Staudinger, won four Nobel Prizes. The prize is not awarded posthumously but, had Carothers lived, he might well have shared one of their prizes.

With peace and prosperity, American scientists began questioning the effects of their products on the public welfare. Nylon's manufacture produced less pollution than rayon but, during the 1960s, Carothers' two closest associates at Du Pont, Flory and Hill, protested publicly about the production of disposable plastic items. At the time, there were no systems for collecting or recycling them. Flory said, "The development of an abundance of cheap, low-grade polymeric materials for everything under the sun has spawned a throw-away economy that is wasteful to a degree that we cannot long tolerate."

Much later—more than half a century after Carothers invented nylon—scientists at the University of California at San Diego discovered that the production of nylon seemed to contribute a small but significant amount of nitrous oxide to the atmosphere. By that time, it was well known that nitrous oxide, N_2O, is a potent greenhouse gas and ozone destroyer. Within a month of the discovery's publication in 1991, Du Pont and several other nylon producers announced plans to phase out nitrous oxide emissions within five years.

As nylon and the plastics revolution became a part of modern life, the figure of Carothers receded tragically into the shadows. The horror of his death, the social stigma attached to mental illness and suicide, and prevailing social codes that discouraged the discussion of personal tragedies contributed to an atmosphere of secrecy that surrounded his life. As late as 1979, the *Encyclopaedia Britannica* credited Father Nieuwland with the discovery of Neoprene.

Two Delaware women preserved the details of his career until the 1980s when historians David A. Hounshell and John Kenly Smith, Jr., began a thorough study of Du Pont research. Motivated by a fear of antitrust lawsuits in the 1960s, Du Pont destroyed decades of company records. Managers were allowed to save historical documents, but few did so. Fortunately, Margaret B. Thome, who was nearing retirement, understood the significance of Carothers' work at the Experimental Station. Thanks to her, Carothers' story survives in several filing cabinets of departmental annual reports and in correspondence related to his hiring and work.

Also during the 1960s, a Wilmington resident interested in history interviewed many of Wallace Carothers' personal friends and colleagues. Until then, Adeline C. Strange had known only that Wallace Carothers had invented nylon and committed suicide.

"So one summer, I took off in my car with a tape recorder to pursue them all. It was sort of an impulse, encouraged by Julian Hill," Strange said. "I didn't want Wallace Carothers to just die. I wanted him to have a life."

8

DDT and Paul Hermann Müller

January 12, 1899–October 13, 1965

When DDT's Swiss inventor, Paul Hermann Müller, won a Nobel Prize for medicine shortly after World War II, the insecticide seemed as miraculous as penicillin. Without DDT, millions of civilians and soldiers would have died of insect-borne typhus and malaria during the hostilities and their aftermath. The Nobel Foundation itself called Müller's pesticide a God-given substance.

Müller's invention launched both the synthetic pesticide industry that exploited his discovery and the environmental movement that opposed its use. Yet Paul Müller, a shy and determined nature lover, shared many of the same reservations about using DDT in the environment that Rachel Carson popularized in her best seller, *Silent Spring*, 14 years later. In the 1990s, three decades after DDT was banned in most of the industrialized world, international health workers revived the debate over its use. DDT is a cheap and effective insecticide against malaria, which kills nearly three million people annually, most of them young children and pregnant women in sub-Saharan Africa.

Paul Müller was born on January 12, 1899, outside Basel, a wealthy railroad and chemical center on the Rhine River where Germany, France, and Switzerland meet. His father, Gottlieb, the son of an inn and tavern owner, worked for the Swiss Federal Railways. His mother, Fanny Müller-Leypoldt, was the family disciplinarian and had belonged to a Lutheran order of deaconesses in her native Germany.

Until he discovered the joys of scientific experimentation in high school chemistry and physics classes, Paul was only an average student. Afterward, his grades fell even lower because he spent all his free time in his little home laboratory. Paul's mother and school principal lectured him sternly to raise his grades, but to no avail. As an adult, Müller was known as a loner who went his own way; to use a homely German expression, Müller was an *Eigenbrötler*, someone who "makes his own bread." So, fed up with school at the age of 17, Müller dropped out. For two years during World War I, he worked for chemical companies in Basel, gaining a wealth of practical knowledge that would help him later as an industrial chemist. The experience matured him too, and with a sense of purpose he resumed high school in 1918 and graduated the following year.

Müller's formative student years coincided with two dangerous crises caused by a lack of effective insecticides. During World War I, when Müller was in high school, neutral Switzerland suffered from serious food shortages. The country is largely mountainous, and most of its arable land is pasturage. Able to raise only half the grain it needed, Switzerland needed to protect every possible kernel from insects but could not.

An insect-borne catastrophe, the greatest typhus epidemic in history, erupted while Müller was a student at the University of Basel. Shortly after World War I and the ensuing Bolshevik Revolution, an estimated 25 to 30 million Russians contracted the deadly lice-borne disease and almost three million died. Hundreds of thousands more perished in Eastern Europe. During the epidemic, large numbers of people were sprayed with insecticides against typhus, a practice that would encourage the development of more toxic gases during the 1930s.

Entering the University of Basel, Müller was so thin that friends called him "The Ghost." A chemistry professor, F. Fichter, recognized the young man's abilities, however, and befriended him. In Müller's Nobel Prize lecture, he credited his perseverance to Fichter's strict training. Müller concentrated on chemistry with minors in physics and botany, and Fichter assigned him a Ph.D. thesis topic on a compound used to manufacture dyes, the main business of Basel's chemical companies. When Müller received his degree in 1925, he started work at the J. R. Geigy Corporation, which through a series of mergers with other Basel chemical companies became Ciba-Geigy, which in turn merged with Sandoz to become Novartis.

Geigy specialized in dyestuffs for woolens, the mainstay for winter clothing, bedding, and carpeting before Wallace H. Carothers invented nylon and polyester (Chapter 7). At first, Müller worked in Geigy's dye department but its fumes gave him asthma, so he transferred to research. As in many other Continental chemical companies, research was an integral part of Geigy's culture. The company had been making synthetic magenta dye since the 1860s, and dye companies survived by inventing new colors.

It was a good move for Müller. As a scientist, he was doggedly determined and methodical, his perception was acute, and his outward reserve covered a passionate devotion to science. He often became so absorbed in chemistry that he seemed to be wearing blinders that blocked everything else from view.

Müller found that he had a good deal of free time in Geigy's research laboratory, so, on his own, he invented a synthetic tanning material that turned preserved and disinfected animal hides pure white. When light discolored them, he persevered until he produced a light-resistant tanning material. Thus, even at the beginning of his career, Müller enjoyed working alone on the stability of compounds and on biological problems.

He also developed a seed disinfectant that was free of poisonous mercury, then widely used in agriculture. The disinfectant helped control *Tilletia*, a smut fungus that causes diseases in cereal crops. The product was introduced to Swiss agriculture in 1942, when grain supplies were extremely precarious.

In the meantime, Geigy had moved into a new field of research: insecticides. After six years of work, company chemists discovered a compound that permanently protected woolens from clothes moths and their rapacious larvae. The mothproofing compound would play a key role in the development of DDT, and the two men who developed the mothproofing agent—Geigy's ambitious research director Paul Läuger and its chief pharmaceutical chemist Henri Martin—would become involved in heated power struggles involving Müller and his Nobel Prize.

Geigy's mothproofing agent was a stomach poison for moths and other keratin-eating insects. It had a strong affinity for woolens, was harmless to warm-blooded animals and people, and had no offensive odor. As a chlorinated hydrocarbon, it was extremely persistent despite exposure to light and moisture.

After mothproofing wool, the next logical step for Geigy was to invent an insecticide that killed more kinds of pests. Imported natural insecticides made from plants, including pyrethrum from tropical chrysanthemums, rotenone from a tropical vine, and nicotine from tobacco, could be quite expensive; they were also not persistent and were easily destroyed by light and heat. American and European attempts to synthesize their active ingredients had failed. Arsenic compounds remained the only cheap and effective insecticides.

By this time, Müller had a wife and children. His wife, Friedel Rüegsegger, took charge of the household and raised their two sons and daughter so that Paul could concentrate on chemistry. Together, Paul and Friedel enjoyed playing flute and piano duets from, for example, Gluck's *Orfeo and Eurydice*. The Müllers lived in suburban Basel but bought a weekend cottage in the nearby Jura Mountains where Paul resumed his longtime interest in botany. He relaxed while gardening, photographing mountain wildflowers, and taking the children on early morning nature walks.

Reading on the weekends in the mountains, Müller immersed himself in the science of plant protection and pest control. The most popular insecticide in Europe and the United States was lead arsenate, a combination of two dangerous poisons. The United States used more than ten million pounds of lead arsenate yearly, and residues on West Coast apples had poisoned customers as far away as Great Britain. Medical doctors realized that ingesting small amounts of lead arsenate could make people chronically sick or even kill them, but entomologists assumed the contrary: that low doses were harmless. Most organic chemists looked down on pesticide research, and it is not certain whether Müller decided on his own initiative to work on pesticides or whether his boss, Läuger, told him to. In any case, in 1935, Müller began work on insecticides.

German scientists, who were beginning to mobilize for World War II, had a big head start. They had been trying to develop synthetic pesticides for years. The German chemist, Fritz Haber (Chapter 5), had organized the gassing of large German flour mills during World War I, using highly toxic cyanide compounds to kill flour meal moths. The German Army helped fund Haber's institute during the 1920s to develop insecticides for gassing, not just insect pests but also, apparently, human beings. In addition, the chemical giant I. G. Farben discovered and patented a new family of chemicals that includes organophosphate insecticides and nerve gas, chemical warfare agents.

To Müller, just starting out on his search for an effective insecticide, the situation looked desperate indeed. A flood of patents had already been issued, and he realized that "the chances were worse than poor; only a particularly cheap or remarkably effective insecticide had any prospects of being used in agriculture." Yet there was hope. After experimenting with products described in the patent literature, he realized that practically none of the new compounds was being sold; the existing arsenates, pyrethrum, and rotenone insecticides were more effective. Reassured about the competition, Müller had the courage to press on.

As he recalled later, "I relied upon my determination and powers of observation. I considered what my ideal insecticide should look like, and the properties it should possess." Geigy's research director, Läuger, was interested in gastric poisons that insects or their larvae had to swallow along with their food. Müller, however, realized that not all insects eat in the same way. Many serious diseases are spread by insects that suck human blood for food; only a contact poison would affect them. So Müller, the man who made his own bread, apparently made the key decision to search for a contact insecticide.

Making a list, Müller outlined the desirable characteristics of an ideal insecticide. It should be toxic to insects but harmless to mammals, fish, and plants; act rapidly; have no irritating odor; and be inexpensive. To his list, Müller added two more properties. The ideal insecticide should affect as many kinds of insects as possible, and it should be chemically stable for a long time. Finally, Müller decided to use as a starting point Geigy's moth-proofing compound, the chlorinated hydrocarbon that was extremely stable on woolens. Thus, from the beginning, Müller's search contained the seeds of its own disaster. In the future, it would kill beneficial as well as harmful insects, and it would persist for decades in the environment.

For four years, Müller synthesized his own compounds and almost single-handedly screened them for their effect on houseflies. They were known to be transmitters of intestinal diseases like dysentery, and it was speculated at the time that they might spread polio. Müller built a cubic-meter glass chamber for insects and sprayed compound after compound at them. As soon as one compound seemed promising, he searched more carefully among its close rel-atives, using the natural insecticides, rotenone and pyrethrum, as controls.

By choice, he worked alone in two highly specialized fields—chemistry and biology. He found biology stimulating but thought, perhaps somewhat condescendingly, that biologists would find his chemical formulas boring and incomprehensible. He, on the other hand, tested his compounds with "keenness and understanding."

As his search lengthened, Müller was increasingly ridiculed as an "odd person," "a lone wolf," and, of course, as a man who made his own bread. With dogged determination, Müller realized that "new substances do not always fulfil expectations; on the contrary they are often bad and only sel-dom better." Recalling his strict university training under Professor Fichter, Müller told himself, "In the field of natural science only persistence and sus-tained hard work will produce results . . . Now, more than ever, must I con-tinue with the search."

Müller had several clues to guide his search. First, he knew from Henri Martin's mothproofing work that a chlorinated hydrocarbon worked as a gastric moth poison. Second, his early experiments showed him that com-pounds with the group CH_2Cl had some insecticidal effect. Third, a 1934 article in the *Journal of the Chemical Society* of London described the prepa-ration of diphenyltrichloroethane, which Müller found to be somewhat poisonous to the flies in his glass box. Taken together, these hints convinced him that a compound containing chlorine should make a good insecticide. Müller's boss Läuger may have also played an important role. Earlier, Läuger had criticized Müller's theoretical understanding of the scientific issues involved, and he may have supplied Müller with a key chemical compound to screen.

By the autumn of 1939, Müller had tested 349 compounds. For his 350th compound, Müller combined the soporific chloral—the active ingredient in Mickey Finn knockout drops—with chlorobenzene and a catalyst, sulfuric acid. His product was dichlorodiphenyltrichloroethane, later known worldwide as DDT:

$$Cl-\hexagon-CH-\hexagon-Cl$$
$$| $$
$$CCl_3$$

Spraying DDT on the flies in his glass cage, Müller was amazed to see them fall helplessly onto their backs in ten minutes. In every test he tried, the insects died, although it sometimes took them several hours or days. He was even more astounded when his cage remained poisonous for weeks and killed any fly that touched its walls. Only after the cage was dismantled, thoroughly scrubbed to high Swiss standards, and aired outside for weeks could he continue his experiments. He tested his compound on mosquitoes and aphids too, not only in the laboratory but also in his office and at home. In September 1939, as Germany invaded Poland and World War II began, Müller carefully wrote in his calendar the chemical formula for DDT and its lethal effect on houseflies.

At first, Geigy's biologists were puzzled because the insects sprayed with DDT did not die immediately. Accustomed to the quick action of pyrethrum and rotenone, they dismissed Müller's discovery as unimportant. They did not realize that DDT's long period of activity could be far more important than sheer speed. In the parlance of insecticides, DDT had "slow knockdown" but "sure kill." Surfaces sprayed with DDT in 1941 and stored under dust-free laboratory conditions were still toxic to insects seven years later.

Ignoring Geigy's biologists, Müller continued testing. He tried DDT on root-eating May bugs, winter moths, and Colorado potato beetles, the scourge of Swiss potato fields. In a key trial, Müller went outside and sprinkled DDT dust on potato plants infested with Colorado beetles. Almost at once, beetle larvae dropped to the ground. Carefully, Müller dug a spadeful of soil and carried it into the laboratory. Studying it the next morning, he saw that all the larvae were dead. Yet he knew they had dropped off the plants so quickly that none had had time to eat the DDT. Surely, this was the contact poison he had been searching for.

DDT met all but one of Müller's ideal characteristics for an insecticide. It was a cheap, contact poison without objectionable odors. It was stable in air and light. Because it was so powerful, extremely small doses could be used. And finally, it dissolved so poorly in water that warm-blooded organisms absorbed only traces of it. The fact that DDT dissolves well in oils did not seem dangerous; only later did scientists realize that, because DDT accumulates in animal fat and mammals' milk, it becomes increasingly more concentrated in predator species as it moves up the food chain. DDT's only failing, as far as Müller's original conception was concerned, was that it did not kill immediately.

DDT enters an insect by dissolving the thin layer of fatty substances that repel water from the creature's waxy outer skin. Penetrating the layer, DDT reaches the insect's nerve endings and gradually paralyzes vital nerve centers. After a short period of extraordinary excitement, insects sprayed with DDT become progressively paralyzed, fall on their backs, and die. Later, it was learned that DDT allows sodium ions to enter insect tissue through voltage-sensitive channels and make the nerves fire uncontrollably. Because animals and people absorb much less sodium in their tissues, DDT is selectively toxic to insects.

Müller must have been disappointed to learn that he was not the discoverer of DDT. Sixty-five years earlier and seventy miles down the Rhine River, an Austrian graduate student at the University of Strasbourg had synthesized the compound as part of his chemistry doctoral thesis. Although Othmar Zeidler described many of DDT's properties and developed the method used to make it commercially, he overlooked the compound's insecticidal powers. And because DDT was not used to make dyestuffs, it was soon forgotten. Thus, when Geigy took out the basic Swiss patent in March 1940, it was for DDT's use as an insecticide.

Today, marketing a new insecticide can take a decade, but Geigy did it in three years. In 1942, Geigy sold almost a pound per capita of DDT-laced insecticide in Switzerland and saved the country's wartime potato crop from a heavy infestation of Colorado beetles. With the discoveries of organophosphate in Germany and chlorinated hydrocarbons like DDT in Switzerland, the era of synthetic chemical pesticides had begun.

Recalling the three million people who had died of typhus after World War I, Geigy also developed DDT products to kill lice. After studying Müller's compound, a Swiss typhus expert confirmed DDT's usefulness in killing the typhus carriers. Next, DDT was tested on pest-ridden Italian refugees in Swiss internment camps and on soldiers in the Swiss Army.

For centuries, typhus epidemics had been the seemingly inevitable accompaniment of wars, famines, and other disasters. Filth and overcrowding help typhus-carrying lice move from one victim to another, at the same time that people must eat every available fat instead of turning it into cleansing soap. Typhus decimated Napoleon's Grand Army as it retreated from Moscow through Poland and Lithuania, where the disease was endemic. Typhus epidemics flourished during the Thirty Years War, the Irish potato famine, and the Warsaw Ghetto. In prisons, it was known as jail fever.

The louse, *Pediculus humanus*, feeds on blood from human hosts. If a person is infected with the typhus organism, *Rickettsia prowazeki*, the louse ingests it and excretes millions more live and infectious typhus microbes ready to be inhaled, rubbed, or scratched into the skin of other human victims. The typhus organism attacks the endothelial cells that line blood vessels. Within a week or two, a vicious headache and fever begin; nervous disorders can follow. Before antibiotics and vaccines, mortality rates could soar to 70 percent. Because lice like the cozy warmth of 29°C (84.2°F), they seek shelter in winter clothing and bedding. During World War II, the only treatment known was to disinfect a patient's clothes and rooms, shave all the hairy areas of the body, and isolate the patient for 5 to 15 days. Doctors, nurses, and laundresses were particularly at risk.

To sell DDT abroad in wartime, Geigy reported its discovery in September 1941 to the governments of the United States, Britain, and Germany. Switzerland sat uncomfortably between France on the west and the Axis countries—Germany, Austria, and Italy—on the north, east, and south. Switzerland had mobilized an army to defend its borders, but to maintain its neutrality it could not tell one combatant about DDT without alerting the others. While Müller remained in Basel and served in Switzerland's civil defense close to the French and German borders, his family retreated for safety farther inland near Lake Geneva. In letters to his wife, Müller reiterated that the war's outcome was in God's hands.

In August 1942, eight months after the United States joined the war, a neutral Portuguese freighter docked in New York City and unloaded more than 400 pounds of DDT insecticides from Switzerland. Scientific reports about DDT soon followed. Translating them into English, executives at Geigy's New York affiliate found them almost too good to be true. Nevertheless, on October 16, 1942, a Geigy executive took the reports and samples of the company's new insecticide to the U.S. Department of Agriculture in Washington, D.C.

Tests against battle-zone insects revealed DDT's potency. When sprayed on the skin of volunteers, it was lethal to lice for three weeks, whereas pyrethrum's effect lasted only eight days. Sprayed on a pond, DDT killed mosquito larvae in it and a neighboring pond as well; waterfowl had carried traces of the compound from one pond to the other. Today, that sounds alarming; in 1942 it seemed too good to be true. Like computing devices, nuclear energy, penicillin, and aerosols, DDT was developed as rapidly as possible for military use in the war. While Germany used DDT only in Greece and Yugoslavia against mosquito larvae, the Allies prepared to fully exploit Müller's discovery.

At first, the military worried chiefly about DDT's safety on people. But after outside consultants and government agencies conducted tests for a few months, DDT diluted to 5 percent was declared safe for troops. DDT's first big field test occurred after the American Fifth Army captured Naples, Italy, on October 1, 1943. With thousands of refugees entering Naples daily, families crowded three to a room without running water. By one estimate, 90 percent of the population had lice. Naples had been typhus-free for 30 years—largely due to soap, washable clothing, and public baths—so its inhabitants had no immunity. Within a month, a typhus epidemic was underway with a death rate approaching 25 percent.

The military organized emergency delousing stations where more than 1.3 million people—72,000 on a peak day—were hand-sprayed, one at a time, with DDT. An American major drew a widely used diagram for sprayers who pumped manually operated dusters: three squirts in an open waistband fore and aft, three at the neck fore and aft, one up each sleeve, plus hat and head. No one had to undress, and clothing did not need sterilization. The military began its campaign in Naples late in December 1943, and continued until March 1944. A half-ounce of 5 percent DDT powder kept a person louse-free for several weeks with few to no known side effects.

A winter outbreak of typhus had been stopped for the first time in history. DDT also halted a flea-borne plague epidemic in West Africa; a dengue fever epidemic on Saipan in the West Pacific; and a typhus epidemic during the U.S. occupation of Japan in late 1945. When the Allies liberated German concentration and labor camps, their lice-laden inmates were dusted with DDT before they were evacuated. Typhus had been a major cause of death in the camps. The commander of Auschwitz, where three million prisoners died, said that poison gas had killed "only" two million people; the other million died of malnutrition, dysentery, and above all, typhus.

Neapolitans were hand-dusted one by one, but military airplanes sprayed DDT over entire islands in the Pacific to kill malaria-carrying mosquitoes before Allied invasions. Like flying syringes, the females of several mosquito species spread malaria parasites by piercing human skin for blood meals and introducing malarial parasites into the bloodstream. The parasites find shelter in the liver, where they mature and multiply before reentering the bloodstream to destroy blood cells. Malaria parasites can suck a quarter of a pound of hemoglobin from a person's red blood cells. The disease can damage vital organs and cause heart failure, respiratory problems, kidney failure, extremely debilitating anemia, and other systemic breakdowns.

With good reason, Allied military leaders regarded malaria as a dangerous enemy. Quinine was unavailable because the Japanese controlled production areas, and other antimalaria drugs had to be developed. The disease was still endemic to parts of the United States, northern and southern Europe, the Mediterranean, and a broad swath of the Earth from Africa through the Pacific islands. It was—and remains today—the world's most widespread contagious disease.

Malaria cases in Sicily exceeded battle casualties. At some West African airbases, personnel averaged an infection and a relapse yearly. The disease was an important factor in the fall of Bataan in the Philippines and in other early Pacific war disasters. For each battle casualty early in the New Guinea campaign, six to eight malaria patients had to be evacuated. An entire division of U.S. Marines was withdrawn from the front after more than half contracted malaria in the summer of 1942. Unless malaria could be controlled, General Douglas MacArthur said that he would have one division of men hospitalized with malaria and another division recuperating from it for every combat-ready division.

To help soldiers keep their aircraft, barracks, tents, foxholes, and forest areas clear of malarial mosquitoes, the refrigeration industry and the U.S. Department of Agriculture developed an aerosol gun that sprayed a mixture of DDT, pyrethrum, and Thomas Midgley, Jr.'s Freon 12 (Chapter 6). The insect "bomb" became so popular that it launched the postwar aerosol industry.

Along with penicillin and atomic energy, DDT emerged from World War II as one of the wonders of modern science. DDT had been tested on millions of men and women and, as far as anyone could see, no one had been harmed. Winston Churchill praised the compound in a radio broadcast in September of 1944. Even before the war ended in 1945, the American

Association of Economic Entomologists announced that "never in the history of entomology has a chemical been discovered that offers such promise to mankind for relief. . . . [in] public health, household comfort, and agriculture." With DDT, entomologists could see for the first time what potato plants looked like without insect damage. As a result of such lavish publicity, there was enormous pressure on the government to make DDT available for civilian use. At least one bootlegger was already supplying eager customers with small quantities.

Wartime use of DDT had raised red flags, however. Spraying the flies on a government base on a New Jersey island in 1944 killed large numbers of fish. On a Pacific island, the mosquito population exploded after the military stopped spraying with DDT because it had wiped out the insects' predators. Italian flies and mosquitoes were growing resistant to DDT. And early experiments showed that DDT could accumulate in the bodies of mammals and enter their milk. As early as 1944 many government officials were asking privately for more data about the cumulative effects of low doses of DDT.

Before releasing the insecticide for civilian use, several government agencies—including the military, the War Production Board, and entomologists in the Department of Agriculture—wanted to wait for test results. Research on DDT's toxicity was being conducted by the U.S. Public Health Service, the Food and Drug Administration, and the Kettering Laboratory of the University of Dayton, the latter project financed by Geigy. The Kettering Laboratory was a major supporter of the tetraethyl lead industry (Chapters 6 and 9). After studying DDT, a committee of the American Medical Association warned about an "appalling lack of factual data concerning the effect of these substances [pesticides] when ingested with food. The chronic toxicity to man of most of the newer insecticides is entirely unexplored."

Even Geigy's New York representative, Victor Froehlicher, urged caution until tests feeding DDT to animals were completed. "Attempts have been made to determine the fate of DDT after absorption by the animal body but no positive results have been obtained as yet. . . . A word of caution might well be in order. This is a new product and as such would require years of research under normal conditions."

The government had no authority to limit DDT's peacetime development, though, and the pressure to commercialize the chemical proved irresistible. In August 1945, the War Production Board lifted its restrictions and DDT was rushed to market.

That summer, the U.S. Army invited Müller, Paul Läuger, and two other Geigy executives to visit the United States for a month to discuss DDT's role in pest control. Civilian airlines had not resumed operations yet, so the men traveled on a military propeller plane that stopped frequently to refuel on its way to the United States.

The trip was an eye opener for Müller. Coming from a country half the size of Maine, the Swiss chemist had never seen such large-scale agriculture. He was given a flight on a small, crop-dusting plane and was impressed with its technique, but he was appalled by the extent of aerial spraying. He knew that devoting vast areas to a single crop required the massive use of pesticides, but he thought that American farmers used far too much DDT. Clear directions about concentrations and spraying schedules were printed on each package but widely ignored. Pilots sprayed farm workers in the fields along with the crops. Yet when Müller returned home, Swiss authorities at the border sprayed him with DDT too.

DDT was wildly popular with the buying public. Norwegian dairy farmers sprayed it on stable walls and, for the first time, had fly-free milk. Housewives used it on fabrics, furs, and babies' rooms—with toddlers present—to kill lice, fleas, bedbugs, cockroaches, crickets, silverfish, and houseflies. Farmers sprayed everything from farm animals, pets, and stables to orchards, fields, and timberlands. In the United States, Western apple growers switched from poisonous lead arsenate to more benign DDT, and Kansas cattle herds gained 2000 pounds for every pound of the fly-killing compound used. Instead of being targeted only for deadly epidemics or malarial regions, DDT was used for approximately 25 years on almost anything that crawled, jumped, or flew. As a Swiss children's book versified patriotically, "Yes, DDT kills lice, bedbugs, and fleas, And in every foreign country, people thank a Swiss company." For the first time, the permanent eradication of insect pests seemed like a reasonable goal.

DDT helped build a powerful industry. Between 1944 and 1951, U.S. production of DDT increased tenfold, from 10 million to more than 100 million pounds, peaking in 1962 to 1963 at 188 million pounds. Pesticide sales soared from $40 million in 1939 to $260 million in 1954. Although fewer than ten large companies dominated the market, the number of insecticide and fungicide companies jumped from 83 in 1939 to 275 in 1954.

As Müller had prophesied and indeed hoped, DDT stimulated the discovery of more synthetic insecticides. DDT relatives included chlordane, toxaphene, aldrin, dieldrin, endrin, and heptachlor. Popular substitutes for DDT's family included organophosphates such as parathion, which is a powerful neurotoxin, and carbamates, which are also highly toxic to people. Unlike DDT, parathion and aldicarb have killed and injured many farm workers. Malathion was later developed to be several hundred times less toxic than parathion.

In the flush of excitement over DDT's effectiveness against disease during the 1940s, the insecticide's inventor was nominated for a Nobel Prize.
The problem was that no one seemed to know precisely who had invented
the miraculous new substance. Despite the worldwide popularity of DDT,
Müller was scarcely known outside of scientific circles, even in Basel. Most
of Geigy's patent applications credited him with DDT's discovery, and he
was listed as an author of the main scientific report published about DDT
in the Swiss journal, *Helvetica Chimica Acta*. The 1944 article listed three
authors, however, and their order proved to be confusing. Läuger appeared
first; Henri Martin, the pharmaceutical chemist, was second; and Müller
was third. Theoretically, the order could have been alphabetical, it could
have reflected corporate hierarchy, or—despite Müller's name on Geigy's
patent applications—it could have indicated Läuger's preeminent role in
the discovery. Certainly Läuger's position was reinforced when the medical
faculty of Basel's university awarded him an honorary doctorate in 1944.
Whatever their priority was, the three men became embroiled in corporate
squabbles.

One evening, Müller's daughter heard the telephone ring and her father
answer the call. It was Läuger, who said in the course of the conversation
that he was responsible for discovering DDT's insecticidal properties.
Müller protested that he had made the discovery himself. Läuger contended
that, as director of Geigy's research department, he had supervised the discovery, established the broad outlines of Geigy's insecticide research program, and contributed numerous ideas to it by writing notes on little slips of
paper each evening and placing them on his employees' desks for study the
next morning. Significantly, Läuger did not deny that the insecticidal effects
of DDT had been discovered in Müller's laboratory.

As the frontrunner in the contest, Läuger was nominated for several
Nobel Prizes. At the peak of DDT's prestige in 1945, a Swiss pharmacolo-
gist nominated both Läuger and Müller for a Nobel Prize in Physiology or
Medicine. Läuger was nominated as the "father of the idea" and Müller as
DDT's actual discoverer. Although the nomination arrived in Stockholm
too late for consideration that year, it set off a storm at Geigy. Martin and
Müller led an internal fight against Läuger all the way to the ruling board of
trustees, and in 1946 Läuger was dismissed from the company.

The year after the first Nobel nomination, a chemistry professor from
Lahore, India, nominated Läuger and the Geigy Corporation for the chemistry prize, and a Basel physiologist nominated Läuger alone for the medicine prize. Then two members of the Nobel Prize committee studied the
nominations and reported secretly to the committee that Müller alone was

worthy of the medicine prize. The identity of the real discoverer "shines through" the mass of data, the Nobel report declared. It was Müller whose well-delineated research project had produced such unexpected results.

Unfortunately, Müller had not been nominated for the prize that year, so he could not receive one. Only Läuger had been nominated. The prize committee must have sat back and waited for Müller to be nominated the following year, but in 1947, no one at all—especially no one from Basel's divided scientific community—nominated him. Finally, in 1948, Müller's supporters reached farther afield to find a nominator. In the end, five medical school professors from Istanbul, Turkey, nominated Müller for the prize in medicine or physiology. None of these behind-the-scenes machinations was publicly known, of course. Records of the Nobel Prize deliberations were sealed until the late 1990s.

That October, rumors about the Nobel Prize filled the air. On the day of the announcements, Frau Müller became extremely nervous and took to ironing frantically. About 10 p.m. that evening, a telephone call came from Stockholm. Müller had finally won the Nobel Prize.

The Müller family traveled to Sweden in 1948 on a train guarded by soldiers as it chugged slowly through bombed-out Germany. Significantly, Müller did not talk about the glories of DDT in his Nobel acceptance speech. Instead, he voiced his concerns about using DDT in complex biological ecosystems. Plunging into his talk with barely a nod to his audience, Müller emphasized that it had taken scientists 90 years of untiring research before they could explain how William Perkin's synthetic dyestuffs worked. Yet, Müller continued, synthetic pharmaceuticals and pesticides—especially synthetic ones like DDT—are far more difficult to understand. Living organisms cannot be tested with any certainty, and complicated biological systems with many variables require multiple controls. Müller argued presciently, "We are moving into unknown territory where there are no points of reference to begin with . . . We can proceed only by feeling our way." Müller concluded that his invention represented only a beginning. "Gradually, insecticides and other pest-control agents will be available providing a whole range of specific properties. . . . I am grateful and glad that I have been permitted to lay a first foundation stone in this puzzling and apparently endless domain."

In addition to the Nobel Prize, Müller received an honorary doctorate from the University at Thessalonica in Greece, where DDT helped eliminate malaria, and honorary memberships in the Swiss Nature Research Society and the Paris Society of Industrial Chemistry. The list of awards is surprisingly short for someone whose discovery saved millions of lives. Its paucity is testament to the multitude of problems that were rapidly accumulating around Müller and the insecticide he had invented.

Shortly afterward, a scandal erupted in Basel's small chemistry community when Switzerland's Nobel laureate complained publicly that the Geigy Corporation had not paid him the proper royalties on his patented inventions. When Müller hired a politically active lawyer to represent him, the story hit the Swiss newspapers. In the end, Müller became a vice director of Geigy and received a share in the profits.

By that time, DDT was reaching the summit of its reputation. It was credited with saving more than five million lives from malaria alone during the 1940s. As the foundation of the World Health Organization's antimalarial campaign during the 1950s, DDT was sprayed over a larger area of the Earth than ever before. It helped eliminate malaria from the Netherlands, Greece, and parts of Italy—relatively contained areas where malaria had been marginally endemic. In Sri Lanka, the number of malaria cases plummeted from 2.8 million in 1948 to 17 in 1963. In India, where an estimated one million people had died annually of malaria, the numbers dropped to 41,000. Yet after four years of saturation spraying, Sardinia's mosquitoes remained.

DDT was fast becoming a Dr. Jekyll and Mr. Hyde compound, however. At the same time that the Dr. Jekyll side of its personality was saving human lives from malaria, its Mr. Hyde characteristics were causing increasing havoc among wildlife. Even though DDT had been on the open market only a few years, houseflies in Sweden, where DDT was used lavishly, were becoming resistant to the chemical. After each spraying, a few survived to reproduce and form DDT-resistant offspring. In 1948, the year he won the Nobel Prize, Müller himself emphasized in another speech that DDT was not omnipotent. Some insects—including bees, cotton parasites, and grasshoppers—had become resistant to it.

In a puzzling phenomenon, the insecticide did not stay where it was sprayed. In the five years between DDT's release for civilian use in 1945 and 1950, DDT used against flies in cow barns reappeared in cows' milk. DDT was linked to fish-eating birds of prey that produced fewer or no young. Princeton, New Jersey, used 4.5 pounds of DDT per Dutch elm tree per year, and scientists found DDT in the tissue of dead birds and a nestling survival rate of only 44 percent.

Some of DDT's effects seemed counterproductive, too. It actually encouraged some citrus-fruit pests by destroying their predators. It killed all the insects in an area, even beneficial ones, so birds and other small creatures that depended on insects for food also died.

During the 1950s, millions of acres in the United States and Canada were sprayed for mosquitoes, gnats, flies, Dutch elm bark beetles, spruce budworms, gypsy moths, and fire ants. Biologists advised using small amounts of DDT over small areas of land—never near water—and to leave unsprayed strips as wildlife refuges. If DDT had been used that way, insects would not have become resistant as quickly. Entomologists, however, ridiculed colleagues who wanted to combine chemicals with biological controls such as crop rotation. In stores, the popularity of the new cosmetically perfect fruits and vegetables encouraged the use of even more pesticides.

In the public's eye, Rachel Carson's 1962 book, *Silent Spring*, sounded the first alarm against DDT in the environment, but complaints actually surfaced as early as 1945. That year, the same year that DDT went on the open market, the *New Republic* magazine published a prophetic article by J. K. Terres describing a silent spring like Rachel Carson's 17 years later: "The sun arose on a forest of great silence—the silence of total death. Not a bird call broke the ominous quiet." Because DDT accumulates in animal fatty tissues, the U.S. Food and Drug Administration announced that it was "extremely likely that the potential hazard of DDT has been underestimated." *The New York Times* published frequent warnings from scientists in the U.S. Department of Agriculture and State Agricultural Experiment Stations. The Beech-Nut Packing Company complained that it had trouble finding residue-free vegetables for its baby food.

The public was still largely unaware of the controversy, but scientists began gathering data about DDT and other pesticides almost immediately. It took them more than a decade to prove DDT's harmful effects on wildlife. Why did it take so long? First, scientists were accustomed to dealing with lead arsenic pesticides so they looked for cases of acute, central nervous system poisoning among people, not low-level hormonal imbalances among wildlife. If tests had been done on animals, DDT's dangers might have been discovered sooner, but scientists relied on studies of factory workers and convicts, so-called volunteers who were fed high daily doses of DDT for up to a year. All had elevated levels of DDT in their fat stores, but no symptoms of poisoning or illness. Furthermore, until vapor-phase chromatography became available in 1960, scientists could not trace tiny pesticide residues through complicated ecosystems. In addition, chemical companies lacked financial incentives to identify pesticide problems, and government agencies had no authority, funding, or public backing to regulate the chemicals. In fact, government officials and chemical companies often forged close working relationships that precluded tough regulation.

Finally, the scientific community itself was divided over DDT's role. Many in the U.S. Public Health Service and Department of Agriculture thought that DDT was safe if used properly. Pharmacologists and physicians in the Food and Drug Administration, the American Cancer Society, and consumer groups were more skeptical. Although much of the research on DDT's effect on wild birds and fish was done before 1960, there were still not enough data to convince the scientific community at large. Then the disaster at Clear Lake occurred.

At Clear Lake, California, about 100 miles north of San Francisco, a tiny amount of DDD, a close chemical relative of DDT, wiped out a breeding colony of 1000 pairs of western grebes in 1960. The insecticide, applied to kill gnat larvae, became increasingly concentrated as it moved up the food chain through plankton to herbivorous fish to predacious fish and birds, including the fish-eating grebes. After Clear Lake, biologists realized that DDT was extremely persistent in the environment: it did not quickly degrade or disappear.

Silent Spring, serialized in *The New Yorker* magazine in 1961 and published as a book one year later, became one of the twentieth century's most influential journalistic exposés. Rachel Carson, a former writer for the Fish and Wildlife Service of the U.S. Department of the Interior, based her book on the wealth of scientific data gathered by government and university researchers. She herself did no original research, but her electrifying popularization of the issue indicted a technology that had seemed harmless. "It is not my contention that chemical insecticides must never be used," she wrote. "I do contend that we have put poisonous and biologically potent chemicals indiscriminately into the hands of persons largely or wholly ignorant of their potential for harm." Her primary goal, she wrote, was to convince the public that DDT and other organochlorine and organophosphate insecticides threatened human health.

Carson turned a scientific discussion into an impassioned public debate. For the first time, agricultural chemicals, ecological food chains, and birds and fish became objects of popular concern. Membership in environmental organizations doubled and tripled as millions debated complex, hard-to-detect ecological effects. Representatives of agriculture and the chemical industry argued in vain that no one had been killed in 25 years of using DDT and that, when properly applied, it did not harm wildlife populations. In the midst of the outcry, the peregrine falcon population crashed.

Peregrine falcons, crow-sized birds that reach speeds of 200 miles per hour as they dive for prey, nested in eyries that had been used continuously for centuries in Europe and since, at least, 1860 in the United States. When two naturalists checked 133 known peregrine nests between the state of Georgia and Nova Scotia in the spring of 1964, they found not one viable nestling. Similar devastation was reported in Britain.

The peregrine falcon crisis forced scientific specialists to coordinate an interdisciplinary research campaign to learn about the bird. Many scientists suspected DDT was the culprit, but they had no proof. Between 1965 and 1968, ornithologists, chemists, physiologists, and scientists in many other fields led field studies; determined how pesticides were distributed in food chains; analyzed the physiology of pesticides in mammals and birds; and conducted laboratory studies. Amateur birdwatchers alerted scientists to similar problems with fish-eating bald eagles in Florida, and a campaign of coordinated, interdisciplinary studies of their populations was also organized.

A study of eggshells from British museums revealed that they had thinned significantly, beginning around 1947 when DDT spraying started. Studies of bald eagles, ospreys, and Lake Michigan gulls confirmed that DDT interfered with eggshell formation. Metabolic research in laboratory animals showed that DDT, chlordane, and several other insecticides speed the liver metabolism of the sex steroids in female birds that control calcium formation in eggshells. Fed small amounts of DDT and its close chemical relative dieldrin, American sparrow hawks also produced thin eggshells. By 1968, the case against the chlorinated hydrocarbon insecticides was essentially complete. The Environmental Defense Fund was formed to use the scientific evidence in court suits filed against the use of DDT. When the public realized that the national symbol, the bald eagle, faced extinction, public opinion turned against DDT.

Müller had retired at the age of 62, the year that *Silent Spring* was published. After purchasing a small house and remodeling it into a private laboratory, he experimented with insecticides that did not have to be sprayed but instead could be absorbed through plant roots. After a stroke, Müller died on October 13, 1965. As the backlash against his invention grew increasingly bitter, his grief-stricken family took comfort in knowing that he was spared many of the attacks on his discovery.

The world had changed radically in the quarter century since Müller had begun his search for an effective synthetic insecticide. DDT and its chemical derivatives had been the most widely used insecticides for more than 20 years. Because insect resistance was weakening DDT's effectiveness, its use was beginning to decline. Since DDT-associated molecules have a half-life as long as 50 years, however, almost one billion pounds of DDT remained in the environment.

At the same time, the public's faith in science and technology was erod-ing. Radioactive fallout from atomic bomb tests was poisoning cows' milk, and the thalidomide antinausea medicine prescribed to pregnant women in Europe had caused severe birth defects in 8000 children. Above all, the enormous growth of the chemical industry and pollution after World War II put public pressure on Congress to clean up the nation's air and water.

Reflecting the enormous change in environmental attitudes, 20 million people attended Earth Day activities around the country on April 22, 1970, and Congress established the Environmental Protection Agency (EPA) in 1971 to protect air, water, soil, plants, and animals endangered by manufac-tured chemicals. Within a year of EPA's founding, it banned the use of DDT in the United States, prematurely some later argued. Other countries also phased out DDT.

In the aftermath of the DDT bans, many bird populations recovered. Robins, bald eagles, ospreys, and peregrine falcons returned to old nesting grounds. The use of other pesticides continued unabated, however. By 1999, American farmers were using one billion pounds of pesticides and herbi-cides yearly; every dollar spent on pesticides seemed to save $4 in crops.

The ban on DDT had some unexpected results. For example, when Sri Lanka responded to *Silent Spring* by halting DDT spraying in 1963, the inci-dence of malaria exploded in five years to 2.5 million cases. During the 1970s, Sri Lanka switched to parathion, which killed many members of its spraying crews; none had died using DDT. Most public health authorities today believe that a person's risk of being poisoned by the normal use of DDT is low compared to that of other pesticides, and DDT is not widely regarded as a human carcinogen. Malaria remains a problem in Sri Lanka and in India, where it also recurred in epidemic proportions after DDT spraying stopped.

The resurgence of malaria since the 1970s pitted environmentalists against international health officials over the continued use of DDT in poor countries. Each year, malaria infects and enervates half a billion people, roughly 10 percent of Earth's population. It kills up to 2.7 million people annually, mostly small African children and pregnant women. DDT is still used for spraying inside houses in more than two dozen poor countries, including China, India, and Mexico, where approximately 40 percent of the world's population lives.

When the United Nations tried to negotiate a treaty banning hazardous substances in 1999, medical authorities argued passionately for continuing the use of DDT, despite its harm to wildlife. They argued that only small amounts of DDT are used today; the entire nation of Guyana, for example, uses less in one year than a U.S. farmer used to apply to a single, 1000-acre cotton field. In addition, since only the interior walls of homes are sprayed, danger to wildlife is minimized. Most important, the purpose of spraying today is to prevent serious damage to people's health, not to entirely eradicate insects.

As the twenty-first century began, coordinated efforts to combat malaria globally were launched by groups including the World Health Organization, the World Bank, the National Institute of Allergy and Infectious Disease (NIADD) in the United States, the Rockefeller Foundation, and the Bill and Melinda Gates Foundation. A consortium of organizations and several pharmaceutical giants, including Glaxo, SmithKline, Hoffmann-LaRoche of Switzerland, and the International Federation of Pharmaceutical Manufacturers Association, hopes to develop and register a new antimalarial drug every five years. Their goal is to halve the incidence of malaria worldwide by 2010, when its first drugs are scheduled to become available. Perhaps then, Paul Müller's Dr. Jekyll and Mr. Hyde insecticide can be retired for good.

9

Lead-Free Gasoline and Clair C. Patterson

June 2, 1922–December 5, 1995

Best scientists lack the comfort of peers
Their science is always at first incredible,
Even though later it teaches more. . . .
Why do they struggle so?

Because in each discovery of new knowledge
Lies an awareness of the beauty and worth of human life,
Which enslaves them as guardians of human destiny.

—Clair C. Patterson
August 23, 1981

During the 1960s, Americans lived in a lead-drenched society. They fueled their cars with leaded, antiknock gasoline. They ate food and their babies drank milk from lead-soldered cans. They stored drinking water in lead-lined tanks and transported it through lead or lead-soldered pipes. They squeezed toothpaste from lead-lined tubes and poured wine from bottles sealed with lead-covered corks. They picked fruit sprayed with lead arsenate pesticide and served it on lead-glazed dishes in houses painted and puttied with lead-based compounds.

In all, Americans ingested approximately 20 tons of lead each year. Of that, they retained between a tenth and a third in their bodies, depending on the chemical and physical state of the lead. Lead is a neurotoxin, and in massive doses it damages the central and peripheral nervous systems, the blood-forming organs, and the gastrointestinal tract and can result in death. In small doses, it was generally and erroneously believed that no harm was caused. There had been no large-scale studies of the effects of low-level lead contamination on the public health for several decades.

Clair C. Patterson, the geochemist who used lead to determine the age of the Earth and the solar system, fought giant industries, governmental agencies, and even other scientists until lead was eliminated from gasoline and food containers. Patterson discovered global pollution and taught chemists how to analyze environmental contaminants. He made environmental studies an exact and quantitative science by developing microchemical analysis into a powerful tool for Earth scientists and oceanographers and by pioneering superclean collection techniques. Stimulating medical research on lead and learning ability, he helped convince public health and government officials that even low-level, ambient lead pollution poisons people. Above all, he spearheaded the ban on tetraethyl lead in gasoline, one of the few industrial pollutants to be eliminated from the United States. With the removal of lead from gasoline, the amount of lead in the blood of American children and adults declined by 80 percent.

Patterson traced what he called his "renegade" instincts to the small Iowa town where he was born in 1922. Mitchellville, he said, was a community where "creativity is not to be trampled on just because it's divergent from ordinary views." He attended nearby Grinnell College, where social activism flourished as an outgrowth of its abolitionist and Congregational Church background. In college, Patterson was six feet four inches tall, gaunt and intense, with long, waving arms and a goofy sense of humor. He was transparently, exasperatingly, lovably honest. His classmate Lorna "Laurie" McCleary, who married Patterson in 1944, said, "You always knew exactly what he thought." After "Pat" earned a master's degree at the University of Iowa, he and Laurie worked on the Manhattan Project at the University of Chicago and in Oak Ridge, Tennessee, helping develop the atomic bomb.

Oak Ridge introduced Patterson to the technique that built his career. To fuel the bomb, its laboratories were using mass spectroscopy to separate uranium-235 isotopes from uranium-238. Isotopes are atoms of the same element with different numbers of neutrons and hence different weights. As Patterson explained, "You accelerate that sample through an electric field and get it moving and then you put it through a magnetic field, and the magnetic field will bend the lighter isotope more than it will bend the heavier one. So it separates the two isotopes."

Like many others at Oak Ridge, the Pattersons petitioned the Manhattan Project to explode a trial bomb on Japan's countryside before targeting a city. After the bomb developed at Oak Ridge was dropped on Hiroshima, Patterson came to regard the Manhattan Project as "the greatest crime that science has committed yet . . . We burned 100,000 Japanese alive . . . [I] helped burn them alive." His later lead pollution studies and his collaborations with Japanese scientists were penance for Oak Ridge.

After the peace, Patterson entered the University of Chicago as a chemistry graduate student. American universities, especially their science departments, were expanding rapidly and applying wartime techniques and data to new problems. Chicago's interdisciplinary approach to science attracted a host of stars, including Nobel Prize winners, physicist Enrico Fermi and chemists Harold Urey and Willard Libby. Earth science and isotopes attracted particular attention. Meteorology and oceanography had been lavishly funded during the war, and Patterson thought that the chemists and physicists who were tackling geological problems were revealing "magnificent new and rewarding visions." Vast amounts of information had accumulated about isotopes. Libby won a Nobel Prize for a dating system based on the decay rate of radioactive isotope carbon-14. Harrison Brown, an assistant professor at Chicago, hoped to use isotopes of lead—dull, cheap, ordinary lead—to date the age of the Earth.

Many scientists thought that Earth must have formed as long as 3.3 billion years ago, but their evidence was confusing and inconsistent. They knew that some of the lead on Earth was primordial, i.e., it dated from the time the planet formed. But they also understood that some lead had formed later from the radioactive decay of uranium and thorium. Different isotopes of uranium decay at different rates into two distinctive forms or isotopes of lead: lead-206 and lead-207. In addition, radioactive thorium decays into lead-208. Thus, far from being static, the isotopic composition of lead on Earth was dynamic and constantly changing, and the various proportions of lead isotopes over hundreds of millions of years in different regions of the planet were keys to dating Earth's past. A comparison of the ratio of various lead isotopes in Earth's crust today with the ratio of lead isotopes in meteorites formed at the same time as the solar system would establish Earth's age. Early twentieth century physicists had worked out the equation for the planet's age, but they could not solve it because they did not know the isotopic composition of Earth's primordial lead. Once that number was measured, it could be inserted into the equation and "blip," as Patterson put it, "out would come the age of the Earth."

Harrison Brown understood enough about the geochemistry of uranium and meteorites to realize that the lead in iron meteorites should be primordial, unchanged since the solar system formed. So he went looking for a student familiar enough with mass spectroscopy to analyze the isotopes in the lead in ancient iron meteorites and in modern rocks. He found Patterson.

As the first step toward determining the age of the Earth, Patterson measured the lead in zircon, a common mineral that is found in Earth's igneous rocks and often used for jewelry. Patterson was a chemist and knew nothing about geology or mineral separations, but when ordinary igneous rocks crystallize and form from magma, they contain minute traces of zircon crystals. At first, the zircon contains uranium with only negligible amounts of lead. But as the zircon ages, its uranium decays to lead. To establish the ratio of lead isotopes in modern rocks, Brown told Patterson to measure the abundance of the various lead isotopes in zircon. Only a handful of common rocks anywhere on Earth had been dated by radioactivity, and those had been gram-sized specimens of minerals from rare uranium ore deposits. Each zircon crystal was the size of a pinhead; each pinhead contained only a few parts per million of uranium, and the uranium decayed to even smaller amounts of lead. Patterson had to develop techniques to analyze lead samples a thousand times smaller than any observed before.

"Pat," Brown said, "after you figure out how to do the isotopic composition of these zircons, you will then know how to get the lead . . . (in an iron meteorite). You'll be famous, because you will have measured the age of the Earth."

"Good, I will do that," Patterson replied.

"It'll be duck soup," Brown replied.

His recipe for duck soup took seven years.

"Brown thought it was merely a matter of reducing the sample size . . . I reduced the amount. But that wasn't the problem. I could reduce it by a factor of a thousand; that only took me a year or so," Patterson recalled. The real difficulty was his laboratory. Patterson was working in one of the university's oldest and dirtiest buildings, and the lead around him was overwhelming the tiny lead samples he wanted to analyze. He had none of the equipment routinely associated with clean laboratories today, e.g., lead-free Teflon containers; filtered air that enters at positive pressure and excludes dirty, outside air at low pressures; laminar-flow workstations bathed in additionally filtered air; or the subboiling distillation of liquid reagents that evaporate without spattering droplets of chemicals before they have been purified. Nevertheless, Patterson was able to improve his handling and collecting techniques and to identify, quantify, and remove most of the lead from his laboratory's pipes, reagents, electrical connections, metallic instruments, glassware, water, and air. "Getting the lead out" took years longer than analyzing zircon. But in the process, Patterson learned that most of the tens of thousands of statistics published about the lead content of common objects were wrong: everyday life was far more contaminated than anyone knew.

Patterson had identified lead as a source of pervasive, ambient pollution long before anyone else was even aware of its existence. By the time he earned his Ph.D. in 1951, the control blanks he processed in his laboratory contained only 0.1 millionth of a gram of lead, an impressive feat at the time. Today most clean laboratories can produce blanks with only a few trillionths of a gram.

Patterson's Ph.D. thesis, which focused on the lead isotopes in billion-year-old Precambrian rock, has been called one of the most remarkable achievements in geochemistry. An article he wrote with geochemist George R. Tilton and physicist Mark G. Inghram opened new areas of lead isotope geochemistry for terrestrial and planetary studies. For the first time, geologists could measure lead isotopes in ordinary igneous rocks and sediments. Knowing the amount of lead in zircon, they could date granites around the world. Even more important, Patterson's thesis illustrated the power of microchemical analysis to solve geological problems. Over the next several decades, Patterson and other Earth scientists would develop many of chemistry's techniques for determining the composition of incredibly small amounts of material. Most chemists have the luxury of working with relatively large samples, but geologists must often identify the chemical and isotopic composition of small, single grains of matter. Patterson's unyielding perseverance and meticulous drive became the signatures of his research. He argued that scientists should spare no effort to get really good data; their obligation in life was to take every possible precaution.

Despite his accomplishments, Patterson still had not finished his duck soup. He had not yet determined the age of the Earth. He continued to work on the problem for two more years as a postdoctoral fellow at the University of Chicago and, beginning in 1952, at the California Institute of Technology in Pasadena, California.

As a chemist working in a geology building, Patterson needed to build a chemistry laboratory. He promptly asked the Atomic Energy Commission (AEC) for a grant to install a clean laboratory at Caltech to determine the age of the Earth. The AEC was not interested in such an esoteric subject, though, so Brown, a master fund-raiser, dressed up Patterson's grant application. Brown, who had also moved to Caltech, told the AEC that Patterson studied the uranium in granite and that the uranium in a ton of pulverized granite produces as much nuclear energy as ten tons of coal. With the grant swiftly approved, Patterson built the first clean laboratory in lead isotope chemistry. Ironically, he did so in some of the world's most polluted air. Backed up against a mountain range, Pasadena trapped the smog from the entire Los Angeles basin.

By 1953, Patterson finally had enough superclean samples of primordial lead to calculate Earth's age. He took his precious samples to the mass spectrograph at Argonne National Laboratory, located in the midst of cornfields outside Chicago. As he worked late into the night, the laboratory emptied and fell silent. When he finished his experiment and went outside under Illinois' star-filled sky, he knew—after seven years—that meteorites, the Earth, and our solar system are 4.5 billion years old. In one of geochemistry's classic experiments, he had established the first definite boundary for the age of the solar system. As Patterson drove to Iowa the next day to visit his parents, he was so elated that he thought he was having a heart attack. When he arrived, he asked his mother to take him to a hospital.

Years later, he described the moment: "True scientific discovery renders the brain incapable, at such moments, of shouting victoriously to the world, 'Look at what *I* have done!' " Instead, in the "sacred but lonely chapel of scientific thought," he instinctively thundered, "*We* did it." Electrified by the thought that humans can penetrate Earth's secrets, he felt an enormous sense of obligation to the generations of scientists who had gone before him. "A glorious emotion," it instilled in Patterson a lasting passion to protect and nurture the human mind. That night at Argonne, Patterson felt that he had finally become a scientist.

Patterson announced his findings at a scientific meeting in September 1953. Three years later, he refined Earth's age to 4.55 billion years, a figure that stands unchanged 50 years later. As he declared, "The age of the Earth is known as accurately and with about as much confidence as the concentration of aluminum is known in the Westerly Rhode Island granite."

Patterson was disappointed that he did not win a Nobel Prize for the discovery. At the time, the Nobel chemistry and physics prizes did not honor geology, and interdisciplinary science was often ignored. Furthermore, few scientists outside the small, new field of nuclear geochemistry understood how he had calculated Earth's age. Most geology was still descriptive, not yet grounded in mathematics, physics, or chemistry. "It was a dozen years literally before this number got into the geology textbooks," Patterson said later. Even then, virtually none mentioned Patterson's name. A recent survey of more than 50 geology textbooks published in the past three decades found only four that credited Patterson with determining the age of the Earth. Ironically, one of the few who immediately recognized Patterson's achievement was a powerful Pasadena creationist. The radio and television evangelist came to Caltech to inform Patterson that he would burn in hell.

As other scientists rushed to confirm or overturn Patterson's value for the age of the Earth, he decided, "I don't want to work on that stuff anymore." After World War II, many physical scientists were collecting piece-meal statistics such as rainfall, river flow, temperature, carbon dioxide concentrations in the atmosphere, and sediments in oceans and large lakes. Information collected on the global distribution of the elements in rain would prove important for acid rain studies during the 1980s.

As a guide to the evolutionary history of the continents, Patterson decided to measure the lead isotope ratios of Earth's crust as a whole. As rocks erode, their minerals are collected and mixed in the oceans, where they eventually settle in layers of sediment. Patterson organized a formidable series of experiments to measure the lead isotopes on land, in various layers of ocean water, and in sediments on the sea floor.

To get a composite of all the beach sand in the United States, Patterson wrote post offices every 30 miles along the East and Southern coasts. Enclosing bags and directions, he asked them to collect one and one-half pounds of sand and send it to Cal Tech. He and Laurie, together with their children, piled into a car and one summer drove from Baja to Vancouver Island collecting sand from the West Coast.

To fund Patterson's project, Harrison Brown convinced the American Petroleum Institute that information about ocean sediments would help locate oil. "Harrison got money from them every year, huge amounts, to fund the operation of my laboratory, which had nothing whatsoever to do with oil in any way, shape, or form," Patterson recalled. "To me it was just a falsehood . . . a fib." But Brown continued to get Patterson the money he needed for several years.

Quite by accident, Patterson and his postdoctoral fellow, Tsaihwa J. Chow, discovered an enormous modern surge in the amount of lead flowing from rivers into oceans and their sediments. In estimating how much lead the ocean sediments should contain, Patterson had analyzed another element, barium, which behaves much like lead but is not heavily used by industry. The amount of barium in terrestrial rocks and ocean sediments became Patterson's guide to the flows, pathways, and abundances of lead one would expect in an uncontaminated world. But while barium was more concentrated in the lower ocean waters, the concentration of lead was much higher in surface waters. Patterson and Chow were surprised to find that the surface layers of the Pacific Ocean off Southern California contained roughly 80 times more lead than the natural erosion of ordinary, igneous rocks on land could have produced. "Why should the lead be (up) so high?" Patterson wondered. "Now, the waters don't mix that rapidly. And the waters up here are much younger than the waters down there. It takes a long, long time for them to mix."

Patterson thought he could identify the culprit: "If the high concentrations of lead observed in a few surface waters of the Pacific were representative of the sea surface of the entire northern hemisphere, the bulk of this lead could be readily be accounted for as originating from leaded gasolines." The hypothesis was unproven, but Patterson immediately understood its social implications. Automobile exhaust emitted lead as soluble lead-halide particles, which humans and other mammals easily absorb. When Patterson reported his ocean sediment research in an encyclopedic, 45-page article in 1962, he handed a copy to a colleague saying, "Read it. It's important."

To determine whether his Pacific samples were in fact representative of other oceans, Patterson and a Japanese colleague, Mitsunobu Tatsumoto, began developing profiles of the lead in ocean layers in Atlantic and Mediterranean waters. Patterson hated ocean-going field trips; he often became violently seasick, once so seriously that he had to be given oxygen. Because the ships were coated with leaded paints and compounds, sampling was tricky, too. Despite the problems, Patterson could see that, as in the Pacific, lead was concentrated in the upper portions of the Atlantic and Mediterranean.

Since snow and rain feed the ocean's surface waters, Patterson needed to know whether precipitation contained normal amounts of lead from airborne dust or abnormally high amounts of lead from tetraethyl lead. Clean air naturally contains tiny amounts of lead from volcanoes, soil dust, forest fires, sea spray, and the like. To find the answer, Patterson hiked into a pristine alpine meadow inside Lassen Volcanic National Park, 500 miles north of Los Angeles' smog. Again he was pioneering, adapting the clean-laboratory techniques he had developed for his age-of-the-Earth studies to field conditions in remote areas. To escape the effects of leaded gasoline, he collected clean snow samples from a branch road that had been closed to cars since the year's first snowfall. Yet even in this protected valley, he discovered 10,000 times more lead than could be expected from natural airborne dust alone. In fact, the concentration of lead in the snow was 10 to 100 times larger than that in seawater. A relatively few years worth of snow could account for all the lead in the oceans' surface layers, without even considering lead from natural airborne sources. The evidence against leaded gasoline exhaust was building rapidly.

In a climax to his sediment studies, Patterson reported tersely that "we have found the composition of lead in snow to be very different from the composition of lead which has been deposited on the ocean floors during the past 100,000 years." The lead in Lassen Volcanic National Park had a signature mix of lead isotopes, a characteristic fingerprint identifying it as a "man-made mixture from a few lead mines instead of a natural mixture from large continental surface areas."

Nature published Patterson's paper describing industrial lead in snow and seawater in 1963. A footnote to the article cited the American Petroleum Institute as his funding source. With oil companies financing his work, even an idealist like Patterson realized, "We're in serious trouble." As he summarized the experience, "I wrote a big paper, and I said, 'This lead is coming from leaded gasoline.' Wham!" The lead industry took notice.

Leaded gasoline was one of the country's top ten industrial chemicals during the 1960s; it accounted for 90 percent of all automobile fuel sold in the United States. As Esso ads proclaimed, there was "a tiger in the tank" of almost every American car. Between 1926 and 1985, more than seven million tons of lead were burned as fuel additives. In terms of sheer volume, leaded gasoline was one of the most important organic chemicals that modern society has produced.

For two decades, the Ethyl Corporation had controlled the worldwide market for the tetraethyl lead additive discovered by Thomas Midgley, Jr. (Chapter 6). Ethyl's $2 million annual advertising budget identified tetraethyl lead with baseball, football, and "the American Way of Life." The company funded almost all the research about tetraethyl lead's effect on human health. As a result, research on tetraethyl lead had focused on safety in the factory workplace rather than on the health of the general population.

Three days after *Nature* published Patterson's article describing industrial lead in snow and seawater, he arrived at work early in the morning as usual. Four men from the lead industry were already waiting for him in his office. Patterson wrote years later that the delegation came from the Ethyl Corporation, but Laurie Patterson remembers that the group also included representatives of the petroleum and chemical industries. In any event, Patterson regarded all four as "white shirts and ties," his scornful term for corporate types.

Looking up as Patterson entered his office, the executives would have seen a gangly guy with an intense voice, a man without vanity, dressed as always in khakis, desert boots, and a short-sleeved white shirt. Patterson had quit smoking and become a physical fitness addict, lifting weights in his backyard, jogging five miles three times weekly, and competing against high school runners. The businessmen would not have known that Patterson generally jogged around a track *against* the flow of other runners—"to strengthen his weaker side." Had they known how rarely Patterson trod the beaten track, they might not have bothered to visit him.

"He assumed they were interested in his paper," Laurie Patterson recalled. "He assumed they'd change their ways if they understood the dangers. So he told them."

As Patterson described the meeting: "They presented a brief resume of their operations with the apparent aim of working out with me some way to buy me out through research support that would yield results favorable to their cause. I sat them down before a lectern and explained in principle how some future scientists would obtain explicit data showing how their operations were poisoning the environment and people with lead. I explained how this information would be used in the future to shut down their operations. They thanked me and left. Soon thereafter, the following things happened:

"1) The U.S. Public Health Service (superseded by EPA) refused to renew my research contract with them.

"2) The American Petroleum Institute refused to continue a substantial contract that had supported my research for years."

"They. . . . not only stopped funding me, they tried to get the Atomic Energy Commission to stop giving me anything—they were still giving me some money. They went around and tried to block all my funding. But I'm so stupid that I didn't even know."

Patterson's passion was scientific research and, by canceling his grants, industry was striking where he was most sensitive. He would have trouble funding research projects for the rest of his career.

Patterson was vulnerable on another score, too. Patterson realized that he was a poor lecturer, and he wanted to do research full-time, so he had refused to become a tenured faculty member at Caltech. He sometimes complained about not being a professor and once demanded—without success—a more elegant title, like "Geochemist." "Lawyers for the Ethyl Corp. testified at Legislative hearings that I was a mere technician at Caltech, without academic stature and credibility in the scientific arena (no tenure), who was held in low esteem by the medical world."

Even more important, his decision to remain an untenured senior research fellow meant that he could be fired at any time. After the Ethyl Corporation's representatives visited Patterson's office, the petroleum industry upped the pressure a notch. A member of Caltech's board of trustees was a vice president of a petroleum company that used tetraethyl lead in its gasoline. The trustee telephoned Caltech's president, Lee DuBridge, about Patterson. DuBridge in turn phoned Patterson's boss Robert P. Sharp, chair of Caltech's geological and planetary sciences division.

"I won't say the trustee urged Lee to fire Patterson, but he wanted Patterson curbed, so to speak, and Lee called me," Bob Sharp said. "It was this very mild telephone call from Lee DuBridge reflecting the concern of a trustee. I said, 'Oh, Lee, you know better than that. This guy is doing tremendous research and to fence him in any way is a mistake. You can't do that.' So Lee told the trustee, 'Too bad, we're going to let him run free.' So we did. I'd have gone to the mat for Pat, but I didn't have to."

Sharp added, "Of all the people in our division, Pat was the most original thinker, the guy who did the most significant research, and what else could you ask? He thought deeply on a lot of things. . . . I loved the guy." Patterson believed the oil industry was trying to get him fired and thanked Sharp for protecting him. Sharp knew the oil executive personally and thought that "he knew better, but was under strong pressures from executives higher up in his company to do something about 'that nut at Caltech.' "

"That nut" had to choose. If he gave in to the oil industry, he could return to purely academic research on Earth's evolution. Chemistry's reforming zeal had declined over the first half of the twentieth century as American university chemists focused on building, almost from scratch, a world-class scientific community. During two world wars and the Depression, training students and faculty, writing textbooks, organizing research laboratories, starting journals, and conducting military research had left chemists little time for attacking social problems. Thus, Patterson would not be alone if he chose to focus only on basic research.

On the other hand, Patterson could decide to face down the lead, petroleum, and chemical industries by continuing his environmental studies. If so, he would not be alone either. During the 1950s and 1960s, growing numbers of scientists were gearing up to attack public health and environmental problems, particularly those caused by the radioactive fallout from American and Soviet nuclear bomb tests, the rampant use of insecticides like DDT, the damage to waterways caused by phosphorous and surface reactive agents in detergents, and the air pollution caused by automobiles.

A broadly based environmental movement was also forming in Western Europe and the United States. Rachel Carson's *Silent Spring* dramatized in 1962 the danger of releasing pesticides promiscuously into ecosystems. When a power breakdown left 80,000 square miles of the Northeast without power in 1965, biologist Barry Commoner could write, "The age of innocent faith in science and technology may be over. . . . Science has unleashed vast forces without knowledge of what the long-range effects on the environment will be." Once assumed to be beneficial, science was coming under attack as a branch of the military-industrial complex. Environmentalism joined civil rights, peace, and participatory government as foci for antiestablishment protests.

The environmental movement culminated in 1970 with the first Earth Day, when university campuses nationwide protested Dow Chemical's manufacture of napalm for Vietnam and targeted the chemical industry as Earth's despoiler. A year later, Congress established the Environmental Protection Agency (EPA). The number of ecologists tripled between 1945 and 1960 and doubled again during the 1970s. The American Chemical Society broadened its approach by changing its Division of Water, Sewage, and Sanitation Chemistry gradually over 15 years into a Division of Environmental Chemistry.

If Patterson had any remaining doubts about pursuing lead pollution instead of conducting purely academic geochemistry, they were dispelled during a sabbatical that he spent at the Massachusetts Institute of Technology in 1963. An eminent MIT toxicologist, Harriet Hardy, cornered Patterson one day. Hardy was a protégé of the founder of occupational medicine, Alice Hamilton, and was herself an authority on beryllium poisoning. Buttonholing Patterson, Hardy told him urgently, "A lot of kids are dying of lead poisoning in Boston." Only he knew how to test tiny amounts of lead, she stressed.

Patterson felt he had no choice. He would have to focus on lead in the environment. He would have to demonstrate that the preindustrial world had been virtually free of lead pollution. He would have to challenge the giants of American industry: carmakers, petroleum companies, lead producers, and chemical corporations.

Ultimately, Patterson decided, his refuge lay in facts. "I was driven to . . . prove my theoretical points unequivocally with solid experimental data." Instead of collecting reams of sloppy data, he chose problems where a few bedrock values would illuminate broad scientific vistas. His theories and chemical analyses would have to be painstakingly perfect in every detail because his thesis was premised on his laboratory's being right and almost every other trace metal laboratory's being wrong.

Patterson could be relaxed and garrulous at times, but in his laboratory he was often domineering and impatient. He might grab something out of someone's hands or become angry if anything was moved from the stacks of papers in his office. Laurie Patterson taught physics in a nearby school, and she conducted an experiment in his laboratory to demonstrate that high school joggers absorbed more lead from Pasadena's smog than nonjoggers did. "I felt like a leper. I just couldn't do it right. But I understood. Cleanliness caused most of his explosions. If people did things in the lab that contaminated it, it could upset someone's year of work." Laurie never did an experiment in her husband's laboratory again.

"He was a lonely warrior," Bob Sharp said. "But he'd have taken on the President of the U.S. if it was necessary. He was utterly fearless. . . . He believed almost fanatically in what he believed." He could be prickly and cantankerous, but Patterson's friends agree that he did not enjoy fighting battles. The human propensity to pollute Earth distressed him, and when he was depressed, he often sought out a close friend, Caltech professor Samuel Epstein, or wrote a poem venting his frustration.

Over the next 30 years, Patterson used mass spectroscopy and clean laboratory techniques to demonstrate the pervasiveness of lead pollution. He traced the relationships between America's gas pump and its tuna sandwiches, between Roman slaves and silver dimes, and between Native American Indians and polar snows. He forged as close a connection between science and public policy as any physical scientist outside of medical research. He made the study of global pollution a quantitative science. And marrying his stubborn determination to his passionate conviction that science ought to serve society, Patterson never budged an inch.

His basic concept was simple: to know how polluted the world is today, one must first learn what the world was like before industrialization. To demonstrate that modern levels of contamination were unnatural, he traveled—literally—to the ends of the Earth. He called his first project "A Snow Job."

Patterson's friend Edward D. Goldberg at the Scripps Institution of Oceanography in La Jolla, California, had tipped him off that one of the best records of the world's climate is embedded in thin layers of glacial ice at high altitudes or near the poles. Snow, dust, and fog deposit chemicals from the atmosphere onto the ice, where they remain undisturbed for thousands of years. As Patterson quickly realized, "Only the quiescent ice sheets in the arid, perpetually frozen polar regions of the Earth provide annual layers of precipitation that are undisturbed by percolation and mechanical mixing, that are relatively free of dusts and salts, and also are thin enough to be accessible even when centuries old."

Months of planning preceded two summers spent in Greenland and one winter in Antarctica in the mid-1960s. In his Caltech office, Patterson thought through every motion of his experiments in advance. He would have to analyze traces of lead a thousand times smaller than those in the so-called pure distilled water used in most laboratories. Few scientists could detect trace amounts, so he once again would have to invent new techniques for collecting and analyzing lead samples.

In preparation for one trip, Patterson and his colleagues cleaned 500 plastic containers in vats of nitric acid, rinsed them in pure water, filled them with pure argon to displace lead-contaminated air, and sealed them in plastic bags equipped with breath filters. Even then, the containers contributed about 0.05 millionths of a gram of lead to each sample; as they were trucked from the factory to Caltech, automobile exhaust had sprayed them with thousands of micrograms of lead. For Patterson's next trip, he collected the containers directly from the factory production line and sealed them immediately into plastic bags before their trip to his laboratory.

At the north and south poles, Patterson's biggest problem was collecting superclean samples under arctic conditions. The quantities involved were not negligible; for each analysis, for example, he needed 100 gallons of melted ice, and he did four analyses for each time period. When Patterson arrived in Thule, Greenland, he checked the tunnel where he planned to dig. To his disgust, he discovered that Army engineers in the tunnel smoked profusely and guzzled soda from lead-soldered cans. They ingested 100,000 times more lead than the polar ice contained naturally. Every fiber and particle of their hair, skin, and clothing was contaminated with industrial lead, and they sprayed their lead-contaminated urine, spit, and mucus around the tunnel. To make matters worse, the tunnel had stored lead-rich sewage, tools, electrical wires and connections, fuel, hydraulic fluid, and painted equipment. Vehicles fueled with leaded gasoline had been driven inside the tunnel, and aircraft twice dumped leaded fuel into the air nearby. Encased in plastic suits and gloves over Army-issue down jackets and mukluks, Patterson and his Caltech graduate students laboriously scraped off the polluted layers of ice and chopped free block-sized samples. As sweat collected, it froze at their wrists and their noses dripped from the cold. The ice blocks were sealed in drums and melted electronically; the water was poured into Patterson's superclean plastic containers for shipment to Caltech.

On a trip to Antarctica, Patterson led four graduate students from New Zealand and assorted military personnel on a sled traverse to a virgin area 130 miles upwind from vehicular pollution. Told that visibility was too poor for the trip, Patterson went anyway. He perched on a Sno Cat's front fender and marked the route by poking flagpoles into the snow every few yards. For two weeks, the group tented next to the Sno Cat and its kitchen. Instead of 15 feet of soft snow as expected, the group found ice. A student figured that they hauled out 1000 banana boats worth of polluted ice as they dug a clean "slanting hell-hole" 50 feet deep and 100 feet long.

Morale must have suffered. Patterson could be downright irascible with mere graduate students; in turn, his perfectionism must have overwhelmed some of them. Patterson forbade the team to grow beards or practice for a New Year's Eve ice bowl game; hairs were contaminants, and a broken leg would prevent Patterson from getting his data. The students grew beards anyway. Patterson tried to lift their spirits by drawing a daily comic strip that he titled, "The Pit Diggers."

Analyzing the samples back at Caltech, Patterson, Masayo Murozumi, and Chow demonstrated that polar ice is naturally extremely pure but that snow deposited in modern times on Greenland contained roughly 100 times more lead than did preindustrial snow. Most of the lead deposits dated from the twentieth century. Geochemists later used the unique ratio of lead-206 and lead-207 isotopes in the lead to prove that these deposits originated in the United States.

Patterson's extraordinary polar studies, published with Murozumi and Chow in 1969, provided the first clear evidence that air pollution reaches even the most remote areas of the Earth. As he often did, Patterson listed his colleagues' names before his own on the article's list of authors; in some joint projects, he did not include his name at all. "It will be better for your career," he told one young man. Years later, he listed some of those articles in a geology department brochure describing faculty accomplishments. The flier was an unobtrusive way of stating for the record that those research projects had been his work too.

In his polar studies, Patterson analyzed such small traces of lead that, for 20 years, no other scientist could replicate his data. As the French glaciologist Claude Boutron noted in 1994, "The difficulty of making these measurements was not fully appreciated at the time." With no attempt at diplomacy, Patterson said, "It was beyond their ability by factors of thousands, or tens of thousands." Ten years later, Patterson and a graduate student, Amy Ng, used more sophisticated techniques on lead samples 100 times smaller than those he had analyzed in the 1960s and confirmed his earlier data.

At the same time that Patterson was planning his ice studies, he also investigated the lead pollution created by ancient Greeks and Romans. Lead smelting for silver—a veritable protochemical industry in the ancient world—financed the Golden Age of Greek democracy, Hannibal's march over the Alps, and the glories of Imperial Rome. The ancients' open-pit smelters spewed out dense, white clouds of poisonous fumes that were easily absorbed by plants, animals, and people. Clouds of lead wafted north over Europe, Great Britain, and Scandinavia to the North Atlantic Ocean.

Over the polar regions of the north, snow, fog and dust precipitated out the lead. Unknown to mankind, the lead lay there, encased in Greenland's glacial ice cap, for 2500 years.

During the 800 years of the Greco-Roman era from 500 B.C. to 300 A.D., Athens and Rome discharged enough lead into the planet's atmosphere to equal 15 percent of the lead pollution produced by American leaded gasoline in the twentieth century. Although Patterson suggested the experiment in 1970, it was not carried out until 1994. Then a French team showed that Earth's first example of large-scale, hemispheric pollution occurred 2000 years before the Industrial Revolution.

Patterson tabulated the social costs of ancient lead mining: to refine ten tons of silver, the Romans produced 400 tons of lead and 1500 tons of slag at a cost of approximately 500 to 1000 slave-years, 10,000 tons of trees, 300 tons of olive oil for illumination, and 200 to 900 tons of various compounds used to improve extraction rates. An ancient mine was "a truly formidable thing, a monstrous parasite that gobbled up vast quantities of food, forests, tools, oil, and slaves, that immobilized armies and required the attention of whole populations." Patterson collected 4620 U.S. silver dimes in Los Angeles and calculated their half-life at only 30 years. Historians had not realized that over time silver coins degraded or got lost. Patterson's work explained why, after Rome's silver mines were exhausted in the third century, its silver coinage had to be replaced with debased metals; the resulting inflation and financial chaos contributed to the downfall of the Roman Empire.

Fascinated by the Greeks and Romans, Patterson cooked up a batch of sapa, the grape juice concentrate used by the ancients to control the fermentation of their wine. Roman recipes called for simmering the juice with herbs and spices in a pure lead cauldron for days. The lead pot both sweetened and contaminated the sapa; Patterson discovered that one teaspoonful of sapa a day was enough to cause chronic lead poisoning. One out of every five recipes in a fourth-century cookbook called for sapa, and the average Roman consumed between one and five liters of wine daily. Patterson concluded dryly, "Most modern people, consuming 1 liter of such wine per day for a year would afterward be readily diagnosed as suffering from clinical forms of overt lead poisoning. If they didn't die, they would, among other things, be infertile and recognized as mad by less-poisoned observers."

In the midst of Patterson's ice core and Greco-Roman studies in 1965, Dr. Katharine R. Boucot asked him to submit an article about lead pollution to *Archives of Environmental Health*. Boucot was chief editor of the journal, considered the bible of industrial toxicology.

Patterson was a poor writer. He generally started in the middle of his subject and worked forward and backward simultaneously. Colleagues called him "Page-a-Day Patterson" and helped him rewrite, but afterward, he took his manuscripts to his secretary. Shutting her door and forbidding her to answer the phone, he sat beside her, dictating his own revisions and additions back into the manuscript until every phrase was as precise and accurate as possible. Some colleagues thought that if he had been a more graceful writer, he would have earned more accolades.

In his *Archives* article, Patterson sharpened his attack on the lead establishment. In a relentless volley of charges, he argued that "the average resident of the United States is being subjected to severe chronic lead insult." A mere doubling of the lead burden would give the average American the classic symptoms of acute lead poisoning: anorexia, vomiting, diarrhea, headache, stupor, convulsions, coma, and even death. The atmosphere contained 1000 times more lead than is natural. About nine-tenths of the lead in the upper layers of the oceans in the Northern hemisphere probably came from lead mines. He added presciently that "an additional important contribution to respiratory lead exposure originates from tobacco smoke."

During the 1960s, the lead industry and most occupational and public health workers believed that lead was hazardous only at the high levels of exposure experienced by paint-eating children and some lead workers. Average levels experienced by the general population were considered normal and acceptable. Dr. Robert A. Kehoe, a "founding father" of the Ethyl Corporation and the era's leading authority on the toxicology of lead, believed in a sharp dividing line between well-being and lead poisoning. He placed the line at precisely 75 micrograms (or millionths of a gram) of lead per deciliter of blood. Outside the workplace, he said that responsibility for lead poisoning rested with users of the metal, including "the infant, usually poorly cared for, who habitually, for weeks or months, eats dangerously large quantities of lead-containing paint . . . [or] the art-conscious but technically incompetent potter who puts out a badly glazed brand of tableware with which to beguile aesthetic housewives."

Patterson, however, was already convinced that lead poisoning occurs over a wide range of exposure. In his *Archives* article, he argued: "We cannot assume that there is a sharp dividing line between what is obviously toxic, giving rise to lead colic or other symptoms, and what is completely harmless. In all probability there is a range of lead intake between these two extremes. . . . Pathologic and histologic changes of the brain and spinal cord together with functional shifts in the higher nervous activity are induced by exposures to atmospheric lead concentrations corresponding to those exposures now experienced by dwellers in most large American cities." Patterson went two steps further in the article. He called for a ban on lead's "technological filth" in gasoline, insecticides, food-can solder, water pipes, kitchenware glazes, and paints. And he imperiously ordered public health officials to reassess their responsibilities.

Although few attempts had been made to test the subclinical effects of low-level exposure, evidence was already accumulating that children with low concentrations of lead in their blood could experience blood abnormalities and mental retardation. Within ten years, it would be known that low levels of lead in early life are associated with metabolic disorders, neuropsychological deficits, hearing loss, retarded growth and development, and, in adult males, cardiovascular problems. During the 1960s, the Centers for Disease Control (CDC) considered 60 micrograms of lead per deciliter of blood acceptable. To protect children from brain damage, however, the CDC gradually lowered the acceptable level for children to 40 in 1970; 30 in 1975; 25 in 1985, and 10 in 1991. Today, many scientists believe that mammalian cells can be damaged even below 10 micrograms.

When Patterson's article was published in August 1965, it created a sensation in the lead community. Herbert E. Stockinger, chief of toxicology with the U.S. Public Health Service (USPHS) in Cincinnati, Ohio, was enraged. He had just returned from a World Health Organization conference that concluded that environmental lead levels had not increased in human blood or urine in 20 years. Stockinger complained, "I had hardly returned from Europe when I received calls from industrial hygienists interested in lead problems asking whether I was out of my head to let an article like that be published. Even while in Europe, individuals embarrassed me in discussions of this article. What I can't understand is, how did such an article not come to my attention, since it is directly in my major field of interest. I certainly would never have sanctioned its publication because of all of its conclusions which are rabble rousing. . . . science fiction." Stockinger signed off, "Is Patterson trying to be a second Rachel Carson?"

Within months, *Archives of Environmental Health* was distancing itself from Patterson. The Ethyl Corporation brought the 73-year-old Kehoe out from retirement to answer Patterson's charges. In a four-page statement published in the *Archives*, he attacked Patterson personally. Among other things, Kehoe called Patterson a zealot venturing into the alien area of biology and a disingenuous geologist suffering from naiveté, credulity, and even magic.

Kehoe, who was considered the leading authority on workers' industrial exposure to lead, had been the Ethyl Corporation's medical director for many years. The lead industry had built the Kettering Laboratory for him at the University of Cincinnati and paid his salary. Just two years before, his facility had been expanded with $1.5 million from industrial and U.S. Public Health Service grants. The laboratory employed nearly 150 people and performed research for more than 100 industries and governmental agencies. Kehoe was so powerful that when he ignored the scheduled speakers at a conference and spoke eight hours daily for five consecutive days, no one objected. "All who attended recognized who the ultimate authority was," one of his employees wrote respectfully in the *Archives for Environmental Health*. Kehoe and the occupational health establishment had not investigated the effects of low levels of lead on the public health for more than 30 years. A year after Patterson's attack on the lead industry was published, the *Archives* dedicated an entire issue to a glowing "Tribute to Robert A. Kehoe, M.D." Pointedly, editor Katharine Boucot, who had commissioned Patterson's article, did not participate. In her editorial that month, she blithely discussed the innocent joys of spring flower bulbs without so much as mentioning Kehoe.

As for Patterson, he was relieved to be finished with a "trying situation." Toxicologists, sanitary engineers, and public health officials had subjected him to "derisive and scornful insults," and he had not worked in mainstream, evolutionary geology for a year. Within months, though, he was back in the fray warning California Governor Edmund G. Brown that "one cannot distinguish . . . between the views of the California State Department of Public Health and the Views of the Ethyl Corporation." While European countries established ministries for the environment during the 1960s, the United States still relied on regional approaches, and Southern California's efforts to combat smog were making it a national leader. California's governor ignored Patterson's first letter, however, so Patterson asked a friend in state government to intercede. She wrote Governor Brown's executive secretary, "Patterson is not a nut." In the end, the governor signed a bill directing the State Department of Public Health to establish air quality standards for California. Patterson, who never threw anything away, filed the correspondence in a folder with a happy, handwritten note:

> "Educating the
> Calif. State Dept of Public Health
> Gov. Brown knuckles under."

Despite the attacks on Patterson's *Archives* article, it marked the beginning of a major change in USPHS's attitude toward lead in the environment. In response to the article, the agency sponsored the Symposium on

Environmental Lead Contamination in December of 1965. More than half of its 32 participants represented the lead industry or federal health and research groups from Ohio and Michigan, strongholds of the automobile industry near Kehoe's laboratory. Attendees abandoned any pretense at neutrality and let their emotions and biases bubble over. "Perhaps it's because the trigger, Dr. Patterson's article, is so obviously an emotional article," an observer commented.

Deputy Surgeon General L. H. Gehrig spoke frankly: "Some maintain that a large segment of the population is already perilously close to the threshold of lead toxicity as a result of environmental exposure; others take an almost diametrically opposed position." He also conceded that "across the entire range of environmental health problems, we are making a rather belated start." Until the conference, the USPHS had focused on hydrocarbons and sulfur dioxide and rarely referred to tetraethyl lead as a pollution problem.

After two days of speeches, Dr. Harry Heimann, a physiologist at the Harvard University School of Public Health, stood up in disgust and declared, "The first thing I'd like to point out is that there has been no evidence that has ever come to my attention, including at this meeting, that a little lead is good for you. I say this because I believe there are some persons who imply that this is so." Noting the geographic proximity of many proindustry scientists to Kehoe's laboratory in Cincinnati, he declared, "It is extremely unusual in medical research that there is only one small group and one place in the country in which research in a specific area of knowledge is exclusively done." Urging other scientists to investigate the effects of lead on the public health, Heimann attacked Kehoe's idea of a threshold of safety. "To use a single figure as the safe one beyond which all poisoning will probably occur—and below which poisoning will not occur—is a most unusual kind of a situation in Public Health and in Medicine."

The symposium's only conclusion was to call for more research, and Ethyl officials were pleased that there were "no adverse effects flowing from that particular meeting; the press releases underscored the economic hardships that would be caused by the disappearance of lead anti-knocks."

Although Patterson insisted that he had no political acumen, he continued his campaign to reach the people who could affect public policy. That fall, he wrote to Senator Edmund S. Muskie of Maine, who chaired the Senate Special Subcommittee on Air and Water. Muskie had just spent two years holding public hearings throughout the United States on air quality; he would be the Democratic vice presidential candidate in 1968 and a presidential candidate in 1972. Patterson confided to Muskie that Kehoe was decades out-of-date in believing that the lead in the atmosphere came from meteorites. In reality, meteorites have less lead than virtually any rock on Earth and at most *one-billionth* of the lead in the air of most large American cities.

Muskie's public hearing, held in Washington, D.C., in June 1966, revealed that $480,000 of petroleum industry money was helping to finance a Bureau of Mines study of antiknock compounds. With no funds to conduct its own research, the government agency had agreed to publish the petroleum-funded study only if the American Petroleum Institute approved its contents.

The hearing came at a critical time for the Ethyl Corporation. The company was in serious financial difficulties. When its patents and cartel arrangements ended in 1947, other companies began selling tetraethyl lead. Ethyl could not compete. Its share of the North American market dropped from 100 percent in 1947 to about 55 percent in 1960, with no end in sight. In the largest leveraged buyout that Wall Street had ever seen, General Motors and Standard Oil Company of New Jersey sold Ethyl to a Virginia paper bag company a fifth Ethyl's size in 1962. "Jonah Swallows the Whale," laughed newspaper headlines. The Albemarle Paper Manufacturing Company of Richmond, Virginia, borrowed the entire purchase price of $200 million to turn the Ethyl Corporation into a diversified chemical empire. Stanford University, Yale University, the University of California, the Teachers Insurance and Annuity Association, and the Ford Foundation were among those who helped finance the sale. To pay off its enormous debt, Albemarle desperately needed to continue selling tetraethyl lead for ten more years.

As in 1925, when dozens of workers went insane from tetraethyl lead poisoning, Kehoe was the Ethyl Corporation's "key man" at a hearing. Patterson was a "key" critic, and corporate executives looked to Kehoe to give them the ten years they needed. According to the corporation's own official history, "Kehoe had the fate of the company in his hands. If he wavered, the company would have been faced with disaster."

Kehoe was a smooth and practiced expert witness at government and judicial hearings. He opened his testimony by boasting that he knew more about lead than anyone else in the world. He boasted that he had served as the Ethyl Corporation's medical director because "I was the only person who was familiar with the toxicology of tetraethyl lead and with the occupational hazards associated with its manufacture and distribution. . . . In developing the information on this subject (lead), I have had a greater responsibility than any other person in this country." Kehoe proudly declared that most of the research on lead in the environment was funded by the tetraethyl lead industry and conducted in the Kettering Laboratory.

By the fifth day of the hearing, reporters were bored and restless. Then, suddenly unexpectedly, Patterson appeared, heavily tanned from his Antarctic trip. Muskie's aides had urged him to prepare a written statement, and Patterson must have spent the night agonizing over his speech. He was a poor lecturer; as a friend said, "I don't know if Patterson ever gave an interesting talk." He also hated summarizing his work; invited once to give a 50-minute colloquium at Caltech, he arrived only to announce that he would not even start speaking unless he was asked to return the following week to talk for *another* 50 minutes. Nevertheless, in his hotel room early that morning, Patterson managed to pull together a 15-minute statement.

"It's not in very good shape," Patterson apologized to Muskie's committee. Then, gritting his teeth and inhaling, he began. His first sentence was a mouthful—five lines long—followed by a torrent of densely packed facts, including his news that lead pollution had found its way to the North Pole and was the first known global pollutant. He charged that low levels of lead, far below what a worker might experience on the job, harm the public at large. Based on the behavior of other elements, Patterson calculated that a 165-pound man should naturally have about 2 milligrams of lead in his body, although the typical American in the 1960s had 200 milligrams, 100 times more.

Children are particularly at risk, Patterson complained. The blood-forming mechanisms of children are disrupted when they breathe air containing three-millionths of a gram of lead per cubic meter, the average concentration in the Los Angeles basin during the 1960s. In four years, children living in apartments near freeways could absorb enough of the metal to get the classic symptoms of lead poisoning. The air in American cities had 100 times more lead than 30 years before, nearly all of it from the tetraethyl lead in automotive fuel. Despite these facts, Patterson charged that the USPHS, the California State Department of Public Health, and most professors of occupational medicine and environmental health engineering defended industry's "economically expedient" policies.

When Patterson finished, Muskie quickly summarized Patterson's entire testimony in a sound bite: "In your statement there is a sentence, and I quote: 'It is possible that deleterious effects to the health of large numbers of people are being caused by these high levels of exposure.' That appears to be the question which you raise."

"That is right," Patterson answered.

Skillfully, Muskie summarized other points. Are the differences between the natural and typical levels of lead "recognized distinctions in the scientific world?"

"This is my own terminology devised—this particular matter has never been considered until last year or a year and a half ago when I initiated this study."

"Why not?" Muskie asked. "It seems such a logical approach to a lawyer."

"Not if your purpose is to sell lead," Patterson countered. The two men were developing a rhythm, one questioning, the other answering in a quick staccato.

"An American Medical Association committee concluded that the general public does not now, or in the immediate future, face a health hazard. Do you agree with that?" Muskie persisted.

"No, of course, I don't agree with it." Patterson insisted, "If their income, their economic dependency involve the interests of lead-using industries, then their viewpoints are oriented this way."

Once again, Ethyl Corporation officials were pleased with the hearing, at least in the short term. Kehoe "bought us time. . . . In general, there was no undue emphasis given to the company's product and no adverse publicity with regard to the additive."

But Muskie was pleased too. Patterson had transformed lead into a public enemy. Newspapers reported that all the accepted medical knowledge about the hazards of leaded gasoline was provided by doctors paid by or working for the Ethyl Corporation. The ethics of the 1920s, in which industry controlled the technical information required to make public policy decisions, was giving way to calls for direct government regulation. Muskie's public health hearing ended 40 years of cooperation between the lead industry and university, state, and federal health agencies. Patterson's stubborn refusal to give an inch had stood him in good stead. Over the years, as the government struggled to develop health standards for lead, Muskie and Patterson continued to confer.

Five years after the hearing, Congress passed the Clean Air Act of 1970. It was the first legislative attempt to reduce the lead in gasoline. The law did not ban leaded gasoline outright, a point that disappointed Patterson. Instead, it gave the newly formed Environmental Protection Agency authority to ban any fuel additive that harmed emissions control devices, and tetraethyl lead did just that. An Ethyl executive fumed that the company's image was changing from "the *good* guy that made engines run smoother to the *bad* guy that must be eliminated if the nation wants to clean up its air."

To meet the new federal emissions standards, General Motors Corporation decided in 1970 to equip its cars with catalytic converters, which lead inactivates. Other carmakers followed suit, and leaded gasoline became one of the few "environmentally unsafe" products to be forced out of the market place. "Get the lead out" replaced "put a tiger in your tank" as the slogan of the environmental 1970s. Ethyl Corporation officials felt betrayed: how could General Motors, the father of tetraethyl lead, sell its share of Ethyl for millions of dollars and then arrange for the product's demise?

The use of leaded gasoline dropped precipitously in the United States, from 253,000 metric tons in 1972 to 17,000 in 1988. The effect on the public's health was dramatic. By 1980, the average blood lead level in the United States had declined about 40 percent, to 10-millionths of a gram or about 1 part per million. Since 1991, it has dropped to 3-millionths of a gram. As American lead consumption fell, the amount of lead settling on Greenland's polar ice cap plummeted almost 90 percent and, by 1989, approached preautomobile levels. That same year, the *Washington Post* declared that the single greatest achievement of the Clean Air Act was the elimination of leaded gasoline in the United States.

In other antilead legislation, the United States banned the metal from indoor paint, albeit 44 years after most of Europe. As of 2001, lead chromate is still permitted to color school buses and the yellow stripes on roadways while "red lead" oxide is still used in corrosion-resistant paints for bridges and other metal structures. Other countries also took action against tetraethyl lead in automobile fuel. Brazil and Canada phased out leaded gasoline by 1990. Many other countries, including most European nations and Argentina, Iran, Israel, Mexico, Taiwan, and Thailand significantly reduced the lead concentration in their leaded gasoline. With new cars in Europe and Mexico required to have catalytic converters, their use of lead will decline further. However, as developing countries produce more automobiles, lead levels will rise again, because unleaded gasoline is unavailable in many parts of Africa, Asia, and South America. Most of the lead now settling on Greenland's snow comes from western and eastern Europe and from the former Soviet Union.

The Ethyl Corporation survived. EPA's phase-out and a series of lawsuits gave Ethyl five years before the full impact of tetraethyl lead's demise went into effect, and Ethyl used the time to diversify. During the 1980s, Ethyl ranked among the 200 largest corporations in America. The company no longer makes tetraethyl lead but contended, as late as February 2001, that research has failed to show that leaded gasoline poses a threat to human health or the environment.

Although Patterson's research paved the way for the passage of the Clean Air Act of 1970, he had not yet convinced the scientific community that natural, preindustrial pollution levels must be measured before the amount of global pollution can be determined. To do that, government and university scientists would have to adopt his pioneering superclean laboratory techniques. As Patterson described the situation, "The laboratory at Caltech is a special sanctuary. We exclude lead like we exclude germs." His argument with the scientific community over the need to identify preindustrial pollution levels would last 20 more years. Nevertheless, his clean-laboratory research—and his ability to detect smaller and smaller quantities of trace metals—marked the beginning of the EPA era and the age of highly sophisticated chemical analysis.

Patterson worked throughout the 1970s on establishing the natural lead levels in food chains on land and in the ocean. Using information from atomic bomb tests about the poisonous element barium, he found that the barium-to-calcium ratio in rocks is 100 times greater than in food and 100 times greater in food than in people. Then he used those figures to hypothesize that lead levels should be 100 times lower than they were in the average 1970s person. Eventually, refinements in his measurement techniques showed that typical lead levels were actually 1000 times higher than they were before primitive man invented smelting.

Patterson's assistant, Dorothy Settle, was an important key to Patterson's ability to pursue land and sea studies simultaneously. She had a master's degree in chemistry, she was tough and well organized, and she became a close colleague and friend of Patterson's. "He truly considered me his equal," Settle said. "He was a very gentle, very caring person. Most people saw the rough, gruff façade. But he valued each person, no matter who they were." When a secretary had personal problems, Patterson helped her. When he heard that a hospitalized Caltech custodian had no family, it was Patterson who sat at his bedside evenings. And when Settle's husband became gravely ill, Patterson said, "Dorothy, I've put the phone on my side of the bed. You call me any time day or night if you need me." Settle said, "And I did. Before and after my husband died, he was there for me."

Throughout their friendship, Patterson and Settle fought and argued tooth and nail. But after Dorothy Settle spent two years measuring the lead in tuna muscle, Patterson made her the first author of their 1980 report. To determine the lead levels in the purest animal tissue on Earth, Patterson had chosen tuna because it is at the top of the marine food chain, which is far less polluted than the terrestrial food chain. Settle's work showed that a gram of fresh tuna contains only 0.3 nanogram of lead but that canned tuna contained almost 5000 times more lead because the containers were sealed with lead solder. At the time, government and industrial laboratories considered the amount of lead in canned tuna normal and healthy because their laboratories were so contaminated that they could not differentiate between the two lead levels. Canned food constituted about 20 percent of the American diet during the 1970s, and most cans—including those of evaporated milk used for infant formula— were soldered with lead.

During the media blitz that followed, Patterson urged the public to buy Chicken of the Sea tuna because the Van Camp Sea Food Company's molded steel cans were lead-free. With characteristic bluntness, Patterson lambasted a host of government laboratories from the Environmental Protection Agency and its Bureau of Foods to the National Marine Fisheries Service and the Food and Drug Administration (FDA). Asked if any other laboratories agreed with his findings, Patterson declared loftily that scientific questions are not determined by majority vote.

At a 1981 EPA conference called to discuss the issue, Patterson offered to train government scientists in his clean laboratory techniques. Soon afterward, a parade of key scientists visited Pasadena to study with Settle. Within six months, Patterson announced that the FDA had made "considerable improvement" both in its laboratory and in reducing lead levels in infant formula.

As usual, Patterson was also juggling a spectacular variety of side projects. He analyzed the lead in tree stem wood and made the first accurate measurement for a material that constitutes a major part of Earth's biosphere. When he analyzed the skeletons of Native American Indians who had lived in the Southwest and the Andes thousands of years ago, he showed that before the Americas discovered metal smelting and ceramic glazes, lead levels were only one-thousandth as high as in modern times. When the novelist Saul Bellow visited Caltech for a year, Patterson convinced him to write a novel about lead pollution. In *The Dean's December*, Bellow closely modeled the character of Sam Beech after Patterson, who liked to joke that the name stood for "son-of-a-bitch." He kept track of his various projects by saving everything; his clean laboratory was meticulously organized, but his office was a packrat's clutter of paper. After his death, Caltech archivists threw out lunch receipts, library renewal slips, phone bills, and application blanks dating back decades—and still had 70 cartons of documents worth cataloging.

When Russell Flegal joined Patterson's laboratory as a postdoctoral fellow to measure lead in the oceans, he ran up against Patterson's well-known crotchety style. During his first week at Caltech, Flegal saw Patterson only once for a few minutes. At the end of the week, Flegal told Patterson that he was leaving. "Listen—I came 300 miles to work with you and you're treating me like—!" Patterson immediately apologized and said he was rushed because he had cancer and only six months to live. In fact, he added, he had two kinds of incurable cancer. The next morning, when Flegal asked if he had gotten a second opinion, Patterson said he had never gotten a first opinion. "It was self-diagnosis. . . . It was really important to him to get as much done as possible, so he was always coming up with different self-diagnosed diseases. After a while I stopped paying attention to him. It was the start of a beautiful relationship. . . . He'd do anything for me, and I think he'd do anything for anyone he cared about."

Patterson enjoyed polishing his image as a cantankerous curmudgeon. When a Caltech undergraduate's stereo set blasted rock music across the campus, the faculty stewed in fury, but Patterson took action. He camped under the student's window the better to curse him. Then Patterson had double doors and windows installed to soundproof his office. To remind colleagues that machines are fallible, he glued an artistic arrangement of bird droppings to a mass spectrometer in Caltech's basement. And when two distinguished Japanese scientists came to his house for dinner one evening to urge him not to hire a disrespectful, young postdoctoral student, Patterson made them cool their heels while he did a rambunctious series of calisthenics outside. Then he hired the young man. "I'm not a brilliant person," Patterson contended. "I can see the naked emperor just because I'm a little child-minded person."

Patterson needed every ounce of cantankerousness that he could muster in order to maintain his battle against lead in the environment. A series of three prestigious scientific reports encapsulate his decades-long campaign. In 1971, the first comprehensive study of lead levels in 30 years was issued by a National Research Council panel for the National Academy of Sciences. The committee, which included six representatives from the lead industry, excluded Patterson entirely because he was considered too extreme and unwilling to compromise. The report concluded that the concentration of lead in urban air was rising slowly.

Nine years later, the National Research Council issued a second study called *Lead in the Human Environment*. This time, Patterson was invited to serve on the panel. Predictably, he disagreed with the committee's conclusions. In 20 days, he wrote his own 78-page, dissenting report and inserted it into the study as an appendix with a clear and dramatic illustration—the "Measles" cartoon.

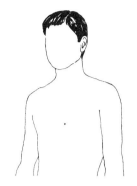 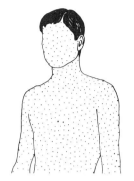 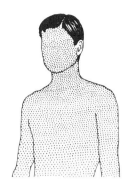

Preindustrial Lead Burden   Typical Lead Burden in 1965   Level of Acute Lead Poisoning

In Patterson's cartoon, nicknamed for obvious reasons "Measles," the pre-indus-trial man, shown on the left, has a single dot representing the level of naturally occurring lead. The average 1965 American, shown in the middle, has 500 dots, while the figure on the right has 2000 dots, the point at which symptoms of ob-vious lead poisoning appear. (*National Academy of Sciences. Lead in the Human Environment. National Academy of Sciences: Washington, D.C., 1980. Courtesy of the National Academy of Sciences*)

In his 1980 dissent, Patterson warned that "it is probable that (the mid-dle) person is also poisoned with lead, but in more subtle ways that have not yet been disclosed." He called for the phase-out of lead mining, smelting, and manufacturing, "a monumental crime committed by humanity against itself." Only two committee members, Cliff Davidson of the Carnegie Insti-tution and Jerome Nriagu of the University of Michigan, endorsed Patter-son's position.

Today Patterson's idea—that it is impossible to measure modern pollu-tion without establishing the level of natural, preindustrial contamination—is a basic precept of environmental chemistry. During the 1970s, however, it was not. Most scientists agreed that modern humans were naturally filled with lead, like the speckled figure in the middle of Patterson's cartoon. Few scientists could imagine that the person on the left, who lived before the advent of lead smelting, contained almost no lead at all. Thus, they were not alarmed that many Americans in the 1960s lived perilously close to the lead level on the right, a level that would gravely poison humans.

The third National Research Council report on lead, published in 1993, is nicknamed, "Patterson's Revenge." Patterson's former postdoctoral fellow, Russell Flegal, was appointed to the panel. "One of the first questions they asked me was whether I was going to cause problems like Patterson caused. I thought that was a peculiar question. I said I didn't plan on it. But the makeup of the committee was different. Everything Patterson said in his 1980 minority report, the 'Measles' picture, etc., we put in the official report ten years later." In all, it had taken more than 20 years to get Patterson's cartoon—summarizing his life's work—accepted in the body of a mainstream scientific report.

The third report was an unequivocal vindication of Patterson's work; lead exposure was "recognized to be among industrialized society's most important environmental health problems . . . Science and society have been remarkably slow to recognize and respond . . . but that is changing." The Centers for Disease Control's acceptable concentration of lead in children's blood had dropped from 60 to 10; lead had been removed from gasoline in the United States; and average blood levels had improved by more than 95 percent.

Efforts to get Patterson a Nobel Peace Prize proved unsuccessful, despite Saul Bellow's frequent nominations. However, Patterson was elected to the National Academy of Science; Asteroid 2511 was named for him; and he won both the Goldschmidt Medal of the Geochemical Society and the $150,000 John and Alice Tyler Prize for Environmental Achievement, the highest award for environmental science. Finally, with retirement nearing, he agreed to become a Caltech professor.

Thinking back on humanity's 2000 years of lead pollution, Patterson often asked himself, "What led us to poison the Earth's biosphere with lead?" He suggested that the brains of those involved in materialistic and utilitarian engineering might be different from those involved in aesthetic and scientific endeavors. Patterson's brain theory embarrassed many of his colleagues who regarded it as "off the wall stuff."

Patterson suffered the first of many severe asthmatic attacks after collecting acidic gas samples from a Hawaiian volcano in 1983. The steroids he took for the asthma exacerbated his inherited osteoporosis, and his frame shrank nine inches to five foot seven. He applied twice for funds to create a line of lead-free rats to study biological processes in uncontaminated mammals. After both applications were rejected, he frequently became depressed.

One day late in his life, Patterson telephoned one of his former postdoctoral students, Robert W. Elias, at the Environmental Protection Agency. The George H. Bush administration was attacking the agency, and Patterson knew how that kind of pressure felt.

"Are you okay?" Patterson asked Elias. "Are you going to be able to keep your job?"

Said Elias, "He was the only person who called, the only one who expressed any concern."

When Patterson died from asthma on December 5, 1995, few of his colleagues knew the enormous range of his research projects. Patterson's position in science was almost unique because he made important contributions in two quite separate areas of science: geochemistry and environmental science. George Tilton, for example, had worked with Patterson during the period when he determined the age of the Earth and the solar system, but Tilton said he had not realized the power and scope of Patterson's work until he wrote his obituary for the National Academy of Sciences. Tilton said, "I knew him over all the years, but I didn't realize what a really great person he was until I worked on this memoir. A lot of things happened without my knowing anything about them."

Patterson was the principal player in getting lead additives out of gasoline and lead solder from food containers. He discovered the difference between preindustrial and postindustrial lead levels in humans, and he argued the point until it was accepted universally. He was an Earth scientist who showed chemists how to analyze global environmental pollution, and he stimulated medical research into the effects of low-level lead pollution on human learning ability. With the removal of lead from gasoline, the amount of lead in the blood of Americans and the amount of lead falling on remote areas of the globe dropped dramatically during the 1990s. At the same time, medical research documented the effect of even extremely small amounts of lead on children's psychological performance.

When asked about Patterson, the eminent geochemist Gunter Faure said simply, "Patterson's a saint. The fact that we stopped using leaded gasoline is largely his doing, and he showed you can't study lead contamination in humans because there are no uncontaminated people anymore. I think he was a very brave man. As a man, he ranks right alongside Newton and Galileo."

POSTLUDE

The chemical roots of our modern way of life extend back to the bleaching fields of the eighteenth century and Nicolas Leblanc's momentous discovery for making pure washing soda. The strips of fabric that covered the bleaching fields are long gone, the land returned to other uses. The piles of noxious wastes that surrounded the Leblanc factories have been removed.

As a symbol of technology's bounty, washing soda has been replaced by an unprepossessing cable the width of a garden hose. Sheathed in protective steel or plastic, the cable winds its way for thousands of miles across the deep sea floor. Inside the cable are fibers that neither absorb light nor allow it to escape. As a result, each fiber can transmit light signals that simultaneously encapsulate five million telephone conversations. The first such cables were laid across the floor of the Atlantic Ocean in 1988, and today they form the backbone of long-distance telephone transmission around the world.

The key to the extraordinary power of these fibers is their fabulous purity. A triumph of modern chemistry, they are made of fused silica, essentially pure silicon dioxide, SiO_2. Thanks to this superpure glass, fiberoptic cables can snake their way across the ocean floor with virtually no discernible effect on their surroundings.

Two centuries ago, when Nicolas Leblanc opened his washing soda factory, such purity was unthinkable. Since then, however, scientists and engineers have learned how to manufacture needed goods without harming workers, the public, or the environment. At first, scientists could not even identify pollutants, much less get rid of them. When the public complained about emissions from the early Leblanc factories, no one could distinguish the damage caused by one factory from that of another, and manufacturers could blithely swear in court that hydrogen chloride gases in air and organic waste in drinking water were wholesome and healthful. Early advances in engineering and the recycling of waste products gradually reduced the pollution of the Leblanc factories until they were closed completely by the development of clean, new processes. German dye manufacturers limited pollution by confining their factories to a particular industrial region that workers entered at their peril. And Edward Frankland protected the public's drinking water by relying on ad hoc hypotheses until more scientific evidence became available.

Today, the scientific community can identify tiny trace amounts of chemicals in the environment. A quarter-century after Wallace Carothers introduced science-based industrial research to the United States, Clair Patterson adapted techniques developed for determining the age of the Earth to identify microtraces of global pollutants. Today scientists can analyze industrial contaminants in the parts per billion; in 1991 when a university scientist discovered in the atmosphere a harmful, low-level contaminant produced by the manufacture of nylon, industry volunteered within weeks to change production methods.

Ironically, despite all this scientific progress, modern fiberoptic cables went into service during a decade of chemical catastrophes more reminiscent of the old Leblanc factories than of optical fibers' superpurity. On December 3, 1984, a cloud of deadly methylisocyanate gas leaked from a Union Carbide plant in Bhopal, India; the gas killed more than 3000 people and injured up to 25,000. Two years later in Europe, a Sandoz chemical factory spilled 30 tons of chemicals into the Rhine River, killing fish for 120 miles downstream. In North America, the *Exxon Valdez* oil tanker spilled crude oil over 1000 miles of Alaskan coastline in 1989.

The public was outraged. It did not matter whether the pollution came from a chemical factory, power utilities, mines, petroleum, automobiles, or semiconductors; the chemical industry's reputation was in free-fall. In 1990, the U.S. Congress established the Super Fund, requiring industry to pay for cleaning up hazardous waste. Major chemical manufacturers banded together in a voluntary effort to reduce factory emissions to almost zero and to police themselves. At the opposite extreme, some environmentalists called for the elimination of all toxic substances.

Chemistry's relationship to the public is unique among the sciences. Chemistry's products become part of our everyday lives and are profoundly intertwined with society's tastes, needs, and desires. Fritz Haber's ammonia for fertilizing crops helped raise chemistry's prestige to such a peak early in the twentieth century that an adoring public supported the massive deployment of poisonous chemicals during World War I. Enthusiasm for DDT and Freon led to their overuse, far beyond anything envisioned by their inventors. Attempts to turn back the clock on technological development have failed or have had their own unintended consequences; stylish aristocrats flouted a French ban on dyed cottons, and popular bans on DDT helped malaria to reemerge in epidemic proportions in developing countries.

In the face of the public's overwhelming demand for new chemical products, the environmental movement and government regulation developed slowly. In the 1930s, Thomas Midgley, Jr., invented hugely popular products, including tetraethyl lead and Freon, untrammeled by public or scientific oversight. In the short run, taxpayers saved dollars by not funding lead research. In the long run, the imbalance between the underfinanced medical authorities who recognized the dangers of tetraethyl lead and the wealthy industry that conducted most of the lead research helped produce costly global pollution and widespread health problems. Even today, many modern consumers in industrialized countries distance themselves from pollution by using chemical products manufactured in developing countries with populations that lack the education, financial independence, and political power to monitor industry—much less the money to buy its products.

As a result of the growing sophistication of science and technology, a fundamental shift has occurred in the relationship between consumers and industrial pollution. Gone are the days when neighboring property owners were the first to complain about Leblanc pollution. Today the public is often unaware of problems until scientists discover them. The greatest concentration of resources and expertise for solving the public's environmental and safety concerns now resides—not among consumers at large—but in the science and engineering communities in industry, government, and universities. In fact, monitoring technology on behalf of the public requires as much scientific expertise as the manufacturing process does itself. It was Paul Müller who issued one of the early warnings against the overuse of his own invention, DDT; and when Rachel Carson alerted the public to the dangers of pesticides, she popularized research conducted by governmental and university scientists. Patterson raised his alert even before the public was aware of the existence of lead pollution or its potential for great harm.

In the end, the responsibility of citizens and industrial leaders is the same: to insist that the information provided by modern science and engineering is used wisely for the public good. By working together for the public welfare, we can enjoy the enormous benefits of industrial technology and protect Earth for coming generations.

ANNOTATED BIBLIOGRAPHY

Prelude

Claude-Louis Berthollet. *Essay on the New Method of Bleaching.* Dublin: Trustees of the Linen and Hempen Manufacture. 1790. English Translation.

William H. Brock. *Norton History of Chemistry* (titled *The Fontana History of Chemistry* in the United Kingdom). New York: W. W. Norton & Co., 1993.

Donald Cardwell. *Norton History of Technology.* New York: W. W. Norton, 1995.

Maurice Crosland. *The Society of Arcueil: A View of French Science at the Time of Napoleon I.* Cambridge, MA: Harvard University Press, 1967. A full-length biography of Berthollet.

Maurice Crosland. "Napoleonic Chemist." *Chemistry in Britain.* 9 (1973): 360–361. A brief biography.

M. Goupil-Sadoun. "Claude-Louis Berthollet, Un Savant Sans Ambition Politique." *Recherche.* 20 (Nov. 1989): 1382–1383.

L. F. Haber. *The Chemical Industry during the Nineteenth Century: A Study of the Economic Aspect of Applied Chemistry in Europe and America.* Oxford: Clarendon Press, 1958.

Barbara Whitney Keyser. "Between Science and Craft: The Case of Berthollet and Dyeing." *Annals of Science.* 47 (1990): 213–260. The watershed between dyeing as craft and as technology.

David Knight and Helge Kragh, eds. *The Making of the Chemist: The Social History of Chemistry in Europe 1789–1914.* New York: Cambridge University Press, 1998.

Michelle Sadoun-Goupil. *Le Chimiste Claude-Louis Berthollet 1748–1822: Sa Vie— Son Oeuvre.* Paris: Librairie Philosophique J. Vrin, 1977. A full-length biography of Berthollet.

Thomas G. Spiro and William M. Stigliani. *Chemistry of the Environment.* New Jersey: Prentice Hall, 1996.

CHAPTER 1 Soap and Nicolas LeBlanc

I would like to thank Bernadette Bensaude-Vincent, Jed Z. Buchwald, Otto T. Benfey, William H. Brock, Charles C. Gillispie, Jean Pierre Poirier, and J. B. Shank for reading this chapter and discussing it with me. Thanks are also due Susanne Hahn for her help during my visit to the Hoechst Corporate History Archives, Frankfurt, Germany.

Auguste Anastasi. *Nicolas Leblanc: Sa Vie, Ses Travaux et L'Histoire de la Soude Arti-ficielle*. Paris: Librairie Hachette et Cie, 1884. Sentimental biography by a descendant trying to get restitution for his ancestor's losses. Source for Leblanc's youth and education; National Academy quotation from 1856; coal explosion; and J. D. Dumas's academy report on Leblanc's invention and financial agreement with the duke.

T. C. Barker and J. R. Harris. *A Merseyside Town in the Industrial Revolution: St. Helens 1750–1900*. Liverpool: Liverpool University Press, 1954. Source for pollution in Leblanc towns and factories; industrial map of Europe; regulation and court suits; children, women, and Irish in work force.

Ernst Baeumber. *A Century of Chemistry*. Dusseldorf: Econ Verlag, 1968.

Sir Gavin de Beer. *The Sciences Were Never at War*. London: Thomas Nelson and Sons Ltd., 1960. Source for British and French scientists cooperation during wartime.

Bernadette Bensaude-Vincent. "Lavoisier: Une Révolution Scientifique." *Éléments d'Histoire des Sciences*. Michel Serres, ed. Paris: Larousse-Bordas, 1997, pp. 541–573.

———. "Between History and Memory: Centennial and Bicentennial Images of Lavoisier." *Isis*. 87 (Sept. 1996): 481–499. Source for Lavoisier. Bernadette Bensaude-Vincent and Isabelle Stengers. *A History of Chemistry*. Cambridge MA: Harvard University Press, 1996. Source for Leblanc as founder of industrial chemistry and for history of natural alkalis.

William H. Brock. *The Norton History of Chemistry*. (Titled in the UK: *The Fontana History of Chemistry*.) New York: W. W. Norton & Co., 1993. Source for history of nineteenth-century chemical industry; chemistry the rage of Europe; chemistry lags behind physics and astronomy; "a sordid, ugly town;" factory fumes; engineers reduce Leblanc pollution; social reformers; Solvay. In a private communication: how Leblanc's discovery made the first pure washing soda; and how Leblanc factories made the first vertically integrated chemical industry and began quality testing.

———. *Justus von Liebig: The Chemical Gatekeeper*. Cambridge, UK: Cambridge University Press, 1997.

Richard L. Bushman and Claudia L. Bushman. "The Early History of Cleanliness in America." *Journal of American History*. 74 (Mar. 1988): 1213–1238. Source for U.S. history of cleanliness; scabies; soap tax.

Donald Cardwell. *Norton History of Technology*. New York: W. W. Norton & Co., 1995.

André Castelot. *Philippe Égalité Le Régicide*. Paris: Jean Picollec, 1991. Almost the only biography of Philippe Égalité, and thus the source for him.

Archibald Clow and Nan L. Clow. *The Chemical Revolution: A Contribution to Social Technology*. London: The Batchworth Press, 1952. Source for sulfuric acid's role.

I. Bernard Cohen. *Revolution in Science*. Cambridge, MA: The Belknap Press of the Harvard University Press, 1985. Source for Lavoisier's scientific achievements.

John Thorne Crissey and Lawrence Charles Parish, *The Dermotology and Syphilology of the Nineteenth Century*. New York: Praeger, 1981. Source for history of scabies.

Maurice Crosland. "The Organisation of Chemistry in Nineteenth-Century France." In *The Making of the Chemist: The Social History of Chemistry in Europe*

1789–1914, David Knight and Helge Kragh, eds. Cambridge, UK: Cambridge University Press, 1998, pp. 3–14. Source for France pioneering environmental protections.

Maurice Daumas. *Histoire Générale des Techniques*, vol. 2. Paris: Quadrige/Presses Universitaires de France, 1996 edition of 1964 book. Source for vertical integration of the chemical industry.

A. S. Davidsohn. "Soaps and Detergents." *Encyclopaedia Britannica*. Chicago: Encyclopaedia Britannica, 1979. Source for soap black market.

T. K. Derry and Trevor I. Williams. *A Short History of Technology: From the Earliest Times to A.D. 1900*. New York: Dover Publications Inc., 1993. (Reprint of Oxford University Press edition 1961.)

J. B. Dumas. *Deux Pièces Historiques Concernant Les Opinions de Lavoisier au Sujet de la Formation des Êtres Organisés et Celles de N. Le Blanc au Sujet de la Théorie des Engrais*. Paris: Hachette et Cie., 1860. Source for Leblanc's manure studies.

Harold Donaldson Eberlein. "When Society First Took a Bath." *Pennsylvania Magazine of History and Biography*. 67 (1943): 30–48. U.S. history of cleanliness.

Reuben Friedman. *The Story of Scabies*. New York: Froben Press Inc., 1947. Source for scabies; Russian troops' smell.

Charles C. Gillispie. "The Discovery of the Leblanc Process." *Isis*. 48 (June 1957): 152–170. This is the antidote to Anastasi's sentimentalism and the source for Leblanc's method being only one of several; unsuccessful factory; sympathy of revolutionary government; process unprofitable if salt taxed; tiresome personality; French patents; demi-monde; and hero in 1860s.

Henry Guerlac. *Lavoisier: The Crucial Year 1772*. Ithaca, NY: Cornell University Press, 1961. Source for Lavoisier's importance.

L. F. Haber. *The Chemical Industry during the Nineteenth Century*. Oxford: The Clarendon Press, 1958.

J. L. Hammond and Barbara Hammond. *The Rise of Modern Industry*. New York: Haskell House Publishers, 1974. (Reprint from 1925 edition published by Methuen, London.)

Richard Hawes. "The Control of Alkali Pollution in St. Helens, 1862–1890." *Environment and History*. 1 (June 1995): 159–171. Source for Leblanc town pollution; failure of regulation and court suits; and Angus Smith.

Frederic Lawrence Holmes. *Lavoisier and the Chemistry of Life: An Exploration of Scientific Creativity*. Madison, WI: University of Wisconsin Press, 1985. Source for Lavoisier's scientific accomplishments.

Suellen Hoy. *Chasing Dirt: The American Pursuit of Cleanliness*. New York: Oxford University Press, 1995. Source for filthy Americans and the Civil War.

Karl Hufbauer. *The Formation of the German Chemical Community (1720–1795)*. Berkeley, CA: University of California Press, 1982. Source for Lavoisier's burning phlogiston at the stake.

Aaron J. Ihde. *The Development of Modern Chemistry*. New York: Harper & Row, 1964.

L'Académie Des Sciences Archives, Paris. The original Feb. 12, 1790, contract between Orléans, Leblanc, Shée, and Dizé.

Johannes Richard Lischka. *The Leblanc Alkali Process in Britain, 1815–1890: From Handicraft to Corporate Organization in the Chemical Industry*. Duke University Department of History Thesis, 1968. Source for closure of the last Leblanc factory.

Johannes Richard Lischka. *Ludwig Mond and the British Alkali Industry*. New York: Garland Publishing Inc., 1985.

Lois N. Magner. *A History of Medicine*. New York: Marcel Dekker Inc., 1992.

Adam Markham. *A Brief History of Pollution*. New York: St. Martin's Press, 1994.

Evan M. Melhado. "Scientific Biography and Scientific Revolution: Lavoisier and Eighteenth Century Chemistry." *Isis*. 87 (Dec. 1996): 688–694.

Stephen Miall. *A History of the British Chemical Industry*. London: Ernest Benn Ltd., 1931.

Ludwig Mond. "The Origins of the Ammonia-Soda Process." *Journal of the Society of Chemical Industries*. 4 (1885): 527–529.

A. E. Musson. "Science and Industry in the Late Eighteenth Century." *Economic History Review*. Second Series, 13, no. 2 (Dec. 1960): 222–244.

Ralph E. Oesper. "Nicolas Leblanc (1742–1806)." Parts One and Two. *Journal of Chemical Education*. 19 (Dec. 1942): 567–572 and 20 (Jan. 1943): 11–20. Source for Darcet.

Jean-Pierre Poirier. *Lavoisier: Chemist, Biologist, Economist*. Philadelphia: University of Pennsylvania Press, 1993. A biography that deals with Lavoisier's economic and governmental careers *and* with his chemistry and biology. Thus, the source for Lavoisier's nonscientific activities. Also the source for Morveau's quote; aristocratic chemistry; Marat; his personal life and wife; scientific achievements; terminology; Lavoisier's biology; promotion of new chemistry; mobs destroy customs wall first; and scientists work for revolutionary government.

William Allen Pusey. *The History of Dermatology*. Springfield, IL: Charles C. Thomas, 1933. Source for scabies.

Terry S. Reynolds and Stephen H. Cutcliffe. *Technology & the West: A Historical Anthology from Technology and Culture*. Chicago: The University of Chicago Press, 1997.

Charles E. Rosenberg. *No Other Gods: On Science and American Social Thought*. Baltimore: The Johns Hopkins University Press, 1997.

Michelle Sadoun-Goupil. *Le Chimiste Claude-Louis Berthollet 1748–1822: Sa Vie— Son Oeuvre*. Paris: Librairie Philosophique J. Vrin, 1977. Source for Orléans support of young scientists; and Berthollet takes Leblanc to inventory Lavoisier property.

L. F. Salzman. *English Industries of the Middle Ages*. London: Constable, 1913.

Michel Serres. "Paris 1800." *Éléments d'Histoire des Sciences*. Michel Serres, ed. Paris: Larousse-Bordas, 1997, 422–454.

John W. Servos. *Physical Chemistry from Ostwald to Pauling: The Making of a Science in America*. Princeton, NJ: Princeton University Press, 1990.

R. Norris Shreve. *Chemical Process Industries*. 3rd ed. New York: McGraw-Hill Book Co., 1967. Source for no Leblanc factory in U.S.

John Graham Smith. *The Origins and Early Development of the Heavy Chemical Industry in France*. Oxford: Clarendon Press, 1979.

Thomas G. Spiro and William M. Stigliani. *Chemistry of the Environment*. New Jersey: Prentice Hall, 1996.

F. Sherwood Taylor. *A History of Industrial Chemistry*. London: Heinemann, 1957.

Source for urine as cleaner; ancient and traditional soapmaking; free soda samples; pollution in Leblanc towns; and electrolytic process.

The Times: The Struggle for Supremacy: Being a Series of Chapters in the History of the Leblanc Alkali Industry in Great Britain. Liverpool: Gilbert G. Walmsley, 1907.

Georges Vigarello. *Concepts of Cleanliness: Changing Attitudes in France since the Middle Ages.* Cambridge: Cambridge University Press, 1988. History of cleanliness in France and Franklin's prancing.

Kenneth Warren. *Chemical Foundations: The Alkali Industry in Britain to 1926.* Oxford: Clarendon Press, 1980. Source for family shops changing to giant factories; Liebig quotation; plant sources of alkalis; Leblanc's experiment; Victorians like Leblanc factories; reduction in hydrochloric acid pollution; cost of pollution abatement; electrolysis; and 3 raw material units make 1 unit of product.

CHAPTER 2   Color and William Perkin

I am indebted to Anthony S. Travis for his careful reading of this chapter.

Tim Arnold. " 'Ein leichter Geruch nach Fäulnis und Säure . . . ' Wasserverschmutzung durch Färberei und frühe Farbenindustrie am Beispiel der Wupper." In *Das Blaue Wunder: Zur Geschichte der synthetischen Farben,* Arne Andersen and Gerd Spelsberg, eds. Köln: Kölner Volksblatt Verlag, 1990. Source for German dye industry pollution.

Isaac Asimov. *Asimov's Biographical Encyclopedia of Science and Technology.* Garden City, NY: Doubleday & Co., Inc., 1972. Source for Coumarin.

Ernst Baeumber. *A Century of Chemistry.* Dusseldorf: Econ Verlag, 1968.

———. *Die Rotfabriker.* Munich: Piper, 1988. Source for Hoechst history.

John Joseph Beer. *The Emergence of the German Dye Industry.* Urbana, IL: University of Illinois Press, 1959.

Bernadette Bensaude-Vincent and Isabelle Stengers. *A History of Chemistry.* Translated by Deborah van Dam. Cambridge, MA: Harvard University Press, 1996.

Erwin Bindewald and Karl Kapser. *Fairy Fancy on Fabrics: The Wonderland of Calico Printing.* Braunsweig: Georg Westermann Verlag, 1951. Source for public demand for printed cottons.

Franz-Josef Brüggemeier. *Blauer Himmel über der Ruhr: Beschichte der Umwelt im Ruhrgebiet, 1840–1990.* Essen: Klartext, 1992. Source for Ruhr River pollution.

Ana Carneiro and Natalie Pigeard. "Alsatian Chemists in the Nineteenth Century–A Network or School?" *Annals of Science.* 54 (Nov. 1997), 533–546.

T. K. Derry and Trevor I. Williams. *A Short History of Technology from the Earliest Times to A.D. 1900.* New York: Dover Publications, 1993.

Sidney Edelstein. "William Henry Perkin." *Dictionary of Scientific Biography.* New York: Charles Scribner's Sons, 1974: 515–517.

Simon Garfield. *Mauve: How One Man Invented a Colour that Changed the World.* London: Faber & Faber, 2000. A recent book recommended for further reading.

L. F. Haber. *The Chemical Industry during the Nineteenth Century: A Study of the Economic Aspect of Applied Chemistry in Europe and America.* Oxford: Clarendon Press, 1958.

John L. Hammond and Barbara Bradby Hammond. *The Rise of Modern Industry.* New York: Haskell House Publishers. 1974. (Reprint from 1925 edition published by Meuthen, London.)

David Knight and Helge Kragh, eds. *The Making of the Chemist: The Social History of Chemistry in Europe, 1789–1914.* New York: Cambridge University Press, 1998.

Charles C. Mann and Mark L. Plummer. *The Aspirin Wars: Money, Medicine, and 100 Years of Rampant Competition.* New York: Knopf, 1991. Source for early Bayer pollution.

Peter J. T. Morris and Anthony S. Travis. "The Chemical Society of London and the Dye Industry in the 1860s." *Ambix: Journal of the Society of the History of Alchemy and Chemistry.* 39, p. 2 (Nov. 1992): 117–126.

Christine Palochek, Costume Institute, Metropolitan Museum of Art, New York. Phone interview, May 5, 1999. Source for the effect of synthetic dyes on fashion.

William Henry Perkin. "Hofmann Memorial Lecture: The Origin of the Coal-Tar Colour Industry and the Contributions of Hofmann and his Pupils." *Journal of the Chemical Society.* 69, pt. 1 (1896): 595–626.

Letter to Heinrich Caro, The Chestnuts, Sudbery, May 25, 1891. *Kirkpatrick Papers L*, 1999, vol. 2.

Relating to William Perkin, Series One, Item 4, Museum of Science and Industry, Manchester, UK.

———. "The Story of the Discovery of the First Aniline Dye." *Scientific American.* 95 (Nov. 10, 1906): 342–343. Source for his childhood.

Anthony S. Travis. "William Henry Perkin: A Teenage Chemist Discovers How to Make the First Synthetic Dye from Coal Tar." *Textile Chemist and Colorist.* 20, no. 8 (1988): 13–18.

———. "Perkin's Mauve: Ancestor of the Organic Chemical Industry." *Technology and Culture.* 31 (Jan. 1990): 51–82. Ladies as an "all-powerful class."

———. "Science as Receptor of Technology: Paul Ehrlich and the Synthetic Dyestuffs Industry." *Science in Context* 3 (Autumn 1990): 383–408.

———. "A. W. Hofmann's Investigation of Aniline Red and Its Derivatives." *The British Journal for the History of Science.* 25 (Mar. 1992): 27–44.

———. "August Wilhelm Hofmann (1818–1892)." *Endeavour.* 16 (June 1992): 59–66.

———. *The Rainbow Makers : The Origins of the Synthetic Dyestuffs Industry in Western Europe.* Bethlehem, PA: Lehigh University Press, 1993.

Anthony S. Travis. "From Manchester to Massachusetts. via Mulhouse: The Transatlantic Voyage of Aniline Black." *Technology and Culture* 35 (Jan. 1994): 70–99.

CHAPTER 3   Sugar and Norbert Rillieux

I am greatly indebted to Christopher Benfey, Otto T. Benfey, John A. Heitmann, Robert Tracy McKenzie, and John Rodrigue for reading the draft of this chapter and for offering valuable advice.

Anonymous. *Norbert Rillieux, Commemoration du Centenaire de la mise en marche de la première installation d'évaporation dans le vide à triple effet à la Louisiane en 1834."* Lousiana State University Special Collections.

Herbert Asbury. *The French Quarter: An Informal History of the New Orleans Underworld*. New York: Alfred A. Knopf, 1936.

Christopher Benfey. *Degas in New Orleans*. New York: Knopf, 1997. Source for Degas in the United States.

————. "Norbert Rillieux, Chemical Engineer and Free Black Cousin of Edgar Degas." *Chemical Heritage*. 16:1 (Summer 1998): 10–11, 38–41.

J. P. Benjamin. "J. P. Benjamin's Address on Agriculture." *De Bow's Review 1* (Jan. 1848): 44–54.

————. *Black New Orleans, 1860–1880*. Chicago: University of Chicago Press, 1973.

William H. Brock. *Justus von Liebig: The Chemical Gatekeeper*. Cambridge: Cambridge University Press, 1997.

————. *The Norton History of Chemistry*. New York: W. W. Norton, 1992. Source for the sugar industry.

Alfred Chapman and Valentine Walbran Chapman. "Sugar." *Encyclopaedia Britannica*. New York: Encyclopaedia Britannica, (1911): 32–48.

David Brion Davis. *The Problem of Slavery in the Age of Revolution 1770–1823*. Ithaca, NY: Cornell University Press, 1975.

Noel Deerr. *The History of Sugar*. London: Chapman and Hall, 1949–1950.

T. K. Derry and Trevor I. Williams. *A Short History of Technology*. New York: Dover, 1960.

Eli N. Evans. *Judah P. Benjamin: The Jewish Confederate*. New York: Free Press, 1988.

John L. Hammond and Barbara Bradby Hammond. *The Rise of Modern Industry*. New York: Haskell House Publishers, 1974. (Reprint from 1925 edition published by Meuthen, London.)

John A. Heitmann. *The Modernization of the Louisiana Sugar Industry 1830–1910*. Baton Rouge LA: Louisiana State University Press, 1987. Source for federal tariffs; the relationship between railroad and sugar technology; the slow acceptance of Rillieux technology in Louisiana; French early thermodynamics; and railroad design.

Louisiana State University Library on-line exhibit about Louisiana sugar history. *http://www.lib.lsu.edu/special*.

George P. Meade. "A Negro Scientist of Slavery Days." *Scientific Monthly*. 62 (1946). (Reprinted in *The Negro History Bulletin* (Apr. 1957.)

Linda Nochlin. *The Politics of Vision: Essays on Nineteenth Century Art and Society*. New York: Harper & Row, 1989. Source for Degas as anti-Semite.

Frederick Law Olmsted. *A Journey in the Seaboard Slave States*. New York: Dix & Edwards, 1856.

J. A. Perkins. "The Agricultural Revolution in Germany, 1850–1914." *Journal of European Economic History*. 10 (1981): 71–144.

Proceedings of the Agriculturists and Mechanics Association of Lousiana containing . . . . The whole published by order of the association. 1846. Lousiana State University Special Collections.

Norbert Rillieux. "Rillieux's Sugar Machinery." *De Bow's Review*. V (1848): 291–293. His own description of his process.

Ferris C. Standiford. "Evaporation." *Encyclopedia of Chemical Technology*, 4th ed., vol. 9, pp. 959–981. Jacqueline I. Kroschwitz and Mary Howe-Grant, eds. New York: John Wiley & Sons, 1991.

J. Carlyle Sitterson. *Sugar Country: The Cane Sugar Industry in the South 1753–1950*. Lexington, KY: University of Kentucky Press, 1953.

Sugar Association Inc., Washington, DC. *http://www.dominosugar.com/dhtml/society/ index.html.*

T. Harry Williams. *Romance and Realism in Southern Politics.* Athens: University of Georgia Press, 1961: 17–43. Source for the unification movement.

Johannes Willms. *Paris: Capital of Europe from the Revolution to the Belle Epoque.* New York: Holmes & Meier, 1997. Source for Paris during the 1820s and 1830s.

CHAPTER 4   Clean Water and Edward Frankland

I am greatly indebted to William H. Brock and Colin A. Russell for their comments about this chapter and to Professor Russell in particular for locating an example of Frankland's notation.

Anonymous. "Sir John Eldon Gorst." *The Dictionary of National Biography.* Supplement for 1912–1921. Oxford: Oxford University Press, 1992. Source for Gorst's career.

Bernadette Bensaude-Vincent and Isabelle Stengers. *A History of Chemistry.* Cambridge, MA: Harvard University Press, 1996. Source for chemistry's positive image.

William H. Brock. "James Alfred Wanklyn." *Dictionary of Scientific Biography.* New York: Scribners, 1976. Source for Wanklyn.

———. *The Norton History of Chemistry.* New York: W. W. Norton & Sons, 1992. (In the U.K., this book is titled *The Fontana History of Chemistry.*) Source for the Johnsons; the Government Museum of Economic Geology; Manchester's polluters glad when he left; early years moonlighting and doing research in London; examining students; and Royal Society.

———. *Justus von Liebig: The Chemical Gatekeeper.* Cambridge: Cambridge University Press, 1997.

———. "A British Career in Chemistry: Sir William Crookes (1832–1919)." *The Making of the Chemist: The Social History of Chemistry in Europe, 1789–1914.* David Knight and Helge Kragh, eds. New York: Cambridge University Press, 1998: 121–129. Source for Crookes.

F.-J. Brueggemeier. "The Ruhr Basin 1850–1980: A Case of Large-Scale Environmental Pollution." In *The Silent Countdown: Essays in European Environmental History.* Peter Brimblecombe and Christian Pfister, eds. Berlin: Springer-Verlag, 19 (1990): 210–227.

Donald Cardwell. *The Norton History of Technology.* New York: W. W. Norton & Sons, 1995.

Rita R. Colwell. "Global Climate and Infectious Disease: The Cholera Paradigm." *Science.* 274 (Dec. 20, 1996): 2025–2031. Source for cholera and six pandemics.

Bruno Fortier. "The Control of Water." *Dix-Huitième Siècle.* 9 (1977): 193–202.

Stuart Galishoff. "Triumph and Failure: The American Response to the Urban Water Supply Problem, 1860–1923." In *Pollution and Reform in American Cities, 1870–1930.* Martin V. Melosi, ed. Austin: University of Texas Press, 1980. Source for Chicago pollution.

Christopher Stone Hamlin. *A Science of Impurity: Water Analysis in Nineteenth Cen-

tury Britain. Berkeley, CA: University of California Press, 1990. Source for moonlighting chemists and civil servants; clean water issues politicized; public looks to chemists for solutions; spa water analyzed; Frankland's radical position; "horrifying tables"; Frankland as expert witness combines "activism and authority"; Wanklyn; and Institute of Chemistry.

Christopher Hamlin. "Challenge to Public Policy between Knowledge and Action: Themes in the History of Environmental Chemistry." *Chemical Sciences in the Modern World.* Seymour H. Mauskopf, ed. Philadelphia: University of Pennsylvania Press, (1993): 296–321.

Frederic L. Holmes. "Liebig, Justus von." *Dictionary of Scientific Biography.* New York: Charles Scribner's Sons, 8 (1976): 333–338. Source for British look to chemistry for solution.

Aaron J. Ihde. *The Development of Modern Chemistry.* New York: Harper & Row, 1964. Source for cholera fatalities in England and liberals versus industrialists.

Nicholas D. Kristoff. "For Third World, Water Is Still a Deadly Drink." *The New York Times.* Jan. 9, 1997, pp. A1, A6. Third world statistics for 1990s.

Martin V. Melosi. "Environmental Crisis in the City: The Relationship between Industrialization and Urban Pollution." In *Triumph and Failure the American Response to the Urban Water Supply Problem, 1860–1923.* Austin: University of Texas Press, 1980.

I. Mieck. "Reflections on a Typology of Historical Pollution: Complementary Conceptions." In *The Silent Countdown: Essays in European Environmental History.* Peter Brimblecombe and Christian Pfister, eds. Berlin: Springer-Verlag, 19 (1990): 210–227. Source for clogged streets.

Frederick Law Olmsted. *A Journey in the Seaboard Slave States in the Years 1853–1854.* New York: G. P. Putnam's Sons, 1904. Source for breakfast claret.

John Ranlett. "The Smoke Abatement Exhibition of 1881." *History Today.* 31 (Nov. 1981): 10–13.

Colin A. Russell. *Edward Frankland: Chemistry, Controversy and Conspiracy in Victorian England.* Cambridge: Cambridge University Press, 1996. The definitive work on Frankland's adult life. The source for the Johnsons; Tyndall and Bunsen; early teaching positions; discovery of organometallic compounds and valency; lack of recognition for valency; Manchester years; consensus that disease caused by human and animal waste; Frankland's motto; outdoorsman; belief in bacterial cause; Frankland's new techniques; scope of Frankland's water analysis career; quotation that water's appearance is unimportant; Hagar's well; percolation data; sarcastic quotation; X-Club; money-grubbing; knighthood late; *Experimental Researches*; and death.

———. *Lancastrian Chemist: The Early Years of Sir Edward Frankland.* Milton Keynes, UK: Open University Press, 1986. The definitive work on Frankland's birth, youth, early education, and apprenticeship; Frankland's disparagement of Gorst's other children; and his two marriage certificates.

E. Schramm. "Experts in the Smelter Smoke Debate." In *The Silent Countdown: Essays in European Environmental History.* Peter Brimblecombe and Christian Pfister, eds. Berlin: Springer-Verlag, 19 (1990): 210–227.

Thomas G. Spiro and William M. Stigliani. *Chemistry of the Environment.* Upper Saddle River, NJ: Prentice-Hall, Inc., 1996. Use of chlorine and its replacement.

Joel A. Tarr, James McCurley, and Terry F. Yosie. "The Development and Impact of Urban Wastewater Technology: Changing Concepts of Water Quality Control, 1850–1930." In *Triumph and Failure: The American Response to the Urban Water Supply Problem, 1860–1923*. Austin: University of Texas Press, 1980.

Johannes Willms. *Paris: Capital of Europe from the Revolution to the Belle Epoque*. New York: Holmes & Meier Publishers, Inc., 1997. Source for Parisian cholera statistics.

CHAPTER 5   Fertilizer, Poison Gas, and Fritz Haber

Margit Szöllösi-Janze, author of the most authoritative biography of Haber, graciously read this chapter and discussed it with the author. I am greatly indebted to her for her help. I also want to thank Jean Colley for editorial assistance.

Tim Beardsley. "Death in the Deep." *Scientific American*. 277 (Nov. 1997): 17–20. Source for nitrogen-caused eutrophication and runoff pollution.

Bernadette Bensaude-Vincent and Isabelle Stengers. *A History of Chemistry*. Cambridge, MA: Harvard University Press, 1996. Source for history of nitrogen fixation.

Alan D. Beyerchen. "On the Stimulation of Excellence in Wilhelmian Science." In *Another Germany: A Reconsideration of the Imperial Era*, Joachim Remak and Jack Dukes, eds. Boulder, CO.: Westview Press, 1988, pp. 139–168. Source for role of technical schools; chemical companies employ more chemists than universities; funding of Kaiser Wilhelm institutes; and Memorial Service only protest.

Alan D. Beyerchen. *Scientists under Hitler*. New Haven: Yale University Press, 1977. Source for Jews leaving Germany 1933–1935.

Max Born. *My Life and My Views*. New York: Scribner's, 1978. Source for Born's quotation about Haber.

William H. Brock. *The Norton History of Chemistry*. New York: W. W. Norton & Co., 1993. Source for British Association president quotation and for nitrogen fixation experiment and its importance.

J. E. Coates. "The Haber Memorial Lecture. April 29, 1937." *Journal of the Chemical Society* (Nov. 1939): 1642–1672. Source for influential relative story; iron plates and streetcar currents; nitrogen fixation experiment; and Haber's authoritarianism during war.

James Franck. Taped interview with Maria Goeppert Mayer and Herta Sponer. July 12, 1962. American Philosophical Society Library. Source for quotation about discussions with Haber.

Morris Herbert Goran. *The Story of Fritz Haber*. Norman: University of Oklahoma Press, 1967. Source for Ostwald and the "pail of facts" and for legends about Haber. Goran interviewed many first-hand witnesses but unfortunately did not discriminate among gossip, legend, and fact.

Fritz Haber. *Les Prix Nobel, 1918 and 1919*. Stockholm: Nobelstifselsen Foundation, 1920. Source for his Nobel Prize speech.

Ludwig Fritz Haber. *The Chemical Industry during the Nineteenth Century: A Study of the Economic Aspect of Applied Chemistry in Europe and North America*. Oxford: Clarendon Press, 1958.

———. "Chemical Innovation in Peace and War." In *Science, Technology, and Society in the Time of Alfred Nobel*. Oxford: Pergamon Press, 1982.

Ludwig Fritz Haber. *The Poisonous Cloud: Chemical Warfare in the First World War*. Oxford: Clarendon Press, 1986. An authoritative history of chemical warfare by Fritz and Charlotte Haber's son. Source for Ypres; Haber's responsibility for poison gas; his authoritarianism during World War I; and failure of poison gas as weapon.

Otto Hahn. *My Life*. London: Macdonald, 1970.

Henry Harris. "To Serve Mankind in Peace and the Fatherland in War: The Case of Fritz Haber." *German History*. 10, no. 1 (1992): 24–38. Source for Haber's baptism; early Karlsruhe career; Hague Peace Conferences; Conant; Nationalism in 1900; wedding photo, and Haber as tragic hero.

Tony Harrison. *Square Rounds*. London and New York: Faber and Faber, 1992.

J. L. Heilbron. *The Dilemmas of an Upright Man: Max Planck as Spokesman for German Science*. Berkeley: University of California Press, 1986.

Erwin N. Hiebert. "Walther Nernst and the Application of Physics to Chemistry." In *Springs of Scientific Creativity: Essays on Founders of Modern Science*, Rutherford Aris et al., eds. Minneapolis: University of Minnesota Press, 1983, pp. 203–231. Source for Nernst's fight with Haber.

James B. Howard and Douglas C. Rees. "Structural Basis of Biological Nitrogen Fixation." *Chemical Review*. 96 (1996): 2965–2982. Source for nitrogen fixation today.

Jeffrey Allan Johnson. *The Kaiser's Chemists: Science and Modernization in Imperial Germany*. Chapel Hill, NC: The University of North Carolina Press, 1990. Source for German professorate; cold war atmosphere; Boer war; fight with Nernst; and Jewish participation in Kaiser Wilhelm institutes.

Kaiser Wilhelm Society. History of the Kaiser Wilhelm Institutes. http://www. fhi-berlin.mpg.de/history/found.html. Source for fact that Nazis politicized Haber's institute most of all society institutes.

D. J. Kevles. "Into Hostile Political Camps." *Isis*. 62 (1971): 47–60. Source for the reorganization of international science in World War I.

Wm. L. Langer. *An Encyclopedia of World History*. Boston: Houghton Mifflin Co., 1968.

Massimo Livi-Bacci. *Population and Nutrition: An Essay on European Demographic History*. Cambridge: Cambridge University Press, 1991. Source for how mortality rates dropped in the nineteenth century.

K. Mendelssohn. *The World of Walther Nernst. The Rise and Fall of German Science 1864–1941*. Pittsburgh: University of Pittsburgh Press, 1973. Source for joke about "before 35 . . . "; need for imported grain and guano; nitrogen fixation background; and fight with Nernst.

Timothy D. Moy. "Emil Fischer as 'Chemical Mediator': Science, Industry, and Government in World War One." *Ambix*. 36 (1989): 109–120. Source for German dependence on imported fertilizer.

David Nachmansohn. *German-Jewish Pioneers in Science 1900–1933: Highlights in Atomic Physics, Chemistry, and Biochemistry*. New York: Springer-Verlag, 1979. Source for percentage of Jews in universities and importance of baptism.

J. A. Perkins. "The Agricultural Revolution in Germany, 1850–1914." *Journal of European Economic History*. 10 (1981): 71–144. Source for fertilizer needs of beets and potatoes.

Max F. Perutz. "The Cabinet of Dr. Haber." *New York Review of Books*. 43, no. 8 (June 20, 1996): 31–35.

Fritz K. Ringer. *The Decline of the German Mandarins: The German Academic Community, 1890–1933*. Cambridge, MA: Harvard University Press, 1969. Source for German professorate.

Charles E. Rosenberg. *No Other Gods: On Science and American Social Thought*. Baltimore: Johns Hopkins University Press, 1997.

John W. Servos. *Physical Chemistry from Ostwald to Pauling: The Making of a Science in America*. Princeton, NJ: Princeton University Press, 1990. Source for physical chemistry as a new field.

Ruth Lewin Sime. *Lise Meitner: A Life in Physics*. Berkeley: University of California Press, 1996. Source for Meitner's quotation about "a lion" and Von Laue's about "spiritual suffering."

Thomas G. Spiro and Wm. M. Stigliani. *Chemistry of the Environment*. New Jersey: Prentice Hall, 1996. Source for bioengineering nitrogen-fixing ability into wheat and rice.

Fritz Stern. *Einstein's German World*. Princeton, NJ: Princeton University Press, 1999. Source for the richest English-language portrait of Haber the man. Source for Breslau patriots; Virchow and Max Planck; Einstein quotations; help with Einstein's divorce; Ostwald ignores Einstein; chess; and detective novels.

Dietrich Stolzenberg. *Fritz Haber: Chemist, Nobel Laureate, German, Jew*. To be published by Chemical Heritage Foundation, which kindly made the draft of its abridged English translation available to me. This book was originally published as *Fritz Haber, Chemiker, Nobelpreisträger, Deutscher, Jude: Eine Biographie* by Weinheim: New York, 1994. It was written by the son of one of Haber's chemical warfare colleagues. It is the source for Haber's youth; most friends were Jews; ox at the well; Haber's poem to Einstein; Haber's letter about his marriage; trip to United States and reports on it; Haber's treatment of students; ammonia made in power and coal gas plants; depletion of guano deposits; nitrogen-fixation experiment and BASF role; Haber's Kaiser Wilhelm Institute contract; Clara's despairing letter; poison gas warfare and Haber's responsibility for it; Haber's wartime authoritarianism; Clara's suicide; marriage to Charlotte; postwar gas research; water story; colloquia; sea gold; rise of Nazis; Haber quote about "one of the mightiest men"; Einstein "inner conflicts" letter; Haber's letter of resignation and letters to friend and Einstein, 1933; Haber and family after Aug. 8, 1933; and the Franklin Institute quotation.

Margit Szöllösi-Janze. *Fritz Haber 1868–1934: Eine Biographie*. Munich: Verlag C. H. Beck, 1998. This authoritative biography of Haber scrupulously sorts fact from fiction; unfortunately there is no English translation of this 928-page book. Source for facial scar; attempt to become reserve officer; role of sanitariums and Habers' stays in them; Clara as chemist and professor's wife; Haber's BASF contract; Reform Movement; Clara's despairing letter; Prussian ideals; Haber as Archimedes; his responsibility for poison gas and wartime authoritarianism; Clara and poison gas; Sackur; Haber leaves after Clara's suicide; Haber's postwar depression, Nobel Prize, postwar gas research, and help for Weimar Republic; April 1933 events to end; and Zyklon B.

———. "Losing the War, but Gaining Ground: the German Chemical Industry during World War I." Working Paper 5.56. Berkeley, CA: University of California Center for German and European Studies. 1997.

Ulrich Trumpener. "The Road to Ypres: The Beginnings of Gas Warfare in World War I." *Journal of Modern History.* 47 (1975): 460–80. Source for Ypres.

Barbara W. Tuchman. *The Guns of August.* New York: Bantam, 1989. Source for Belgium during World War I; manifesto and Einstein's countermanifesto; and the invasion of Belgium.

Trevor I. Williams. *A History of Technology,* vol. 6. Oxford: Clarendon Press, 1978.

Richard Willstätter. *From My Life: The Memoirs of Richard Willstätter.* Translated by Lilli S. Hornig. New York: W. A. Benjamin, 1965. Source for Haber's versification; rural Dahlem, and *danse macabre.*

CHAPTER 6 Leaded Gasoline, Safe Refrigeration, and Thomas Midgley Jr.

I would like to thank Thomas J. Clark, Stuart W. Leslie, Bernard A. Nagengast, Herbert L. Needleman, MD, and Harold Sheckter for reading and discussing this chapter with me.

I am also grateful for the help of Ruth Ann Bertsch, Mohinder Bhatti; James W. Caldwell, EPA; John Detrick; Marcia Goldoft, MD; William Holleran, curator of the GMI Alumni Foundation Historical Collection of Industrial History, Flint, Michigan; Dorothy Midgley; J. Darby Midgley; Jerome O. Nriagu, Walter Stolov, MD; Marcia Van Ness; Eric Weiss, MD; William Winegarner; Victoria Bergesen, Worthington Historical Society; Columbus Metropolitan Library; Ohio State University Archives; and Cornell University Archives.

In particular, I am indebted to Donald A. Henderson, MD, MPH, who directed the World Health Organization's eradication of smallpox, for his private e-mail communication, Nov. 23, 1999, explaining the effect of refrigeration on vaccination and smallpox.

Note: TEL is tetraethyl lead and Kettering is The Kettering University Archives, Flint, Michigan.

Oliver E. Allen. "Kettering." *American Heritage of Invention & Technology.* 12, no. 2 (Fall 1996): 52–63.

Anonymous. "Inventor Dies." *The Ohio State University Monthly.* 36 (Dec. 1944): 4. Source for Midgley's getting polio.

Bill Arter. "Man-Made Cavern." *Columbus Dispatch Magazine.* (Oct. 31, 1965): 5.

William F. Ashe. "Robert Arthur Kehoe, MD." *Archives of Environmental Health.* 13 (Aug. 1966): 138–142.

Associated Press. "Thomas Midgley Awarded Highest Chemical Honor." *Columbus Dispatch.* (April 8, 1941) Courtesy of the Columbus Metropolitan Library.

Kendall Beaton. *Enterprise in Oil: A History of Shell in the United States.* New York: Appleton-Century-Crofts, Inc., 1957. Source for TEL in World War II.

Mohinder S. Bhatti. "Historical Look at Chlorofluorocarbon Refrigerants." *ASHRAE Transactions.* 105, Part 1 (Jan. 23–27, 1999): 1186–1206. Source for Midgley

CFCs substitute for ozone destroyers; dangerous refrigerants; no hospital refrigerators; something spectacular needed; Midgley group discovers other CFCs and halons; lion's share; uses for CFCs; aerosols and halons in World War II.

———. "Riding in Comfort: Part 1: Evolution of Automotive Heating." *ASHRAE Journal*. 105 (Aug. 1999): 51–57.

———. "Riding in Comfort: Part 2: Evolution of Automotive Air Conditioning." *ASHRAE Journal*. 105 (Sept. 1999): 44–52. Source for auto air-conditioning; Greyhound, cars in Southwest; and drivers in shock.

Kathryn Black. *In the Shadow of Polio: A Personal and Social History*. New York: Addison-Wesley Publishing Co., 1996.

T. A. Boyd. "Gasoline Went to War and the Part Chemistry Had in It." *Record of Chemical Progress*. New York: Plenum. 8 (Jan.–Apr. 1947): 10–19. Source for Geoffrey Lloyd; Kettering at funeral.

———. "Pathfinding in Fuels and Engines." *SAE Quarterly Transactions*. 4 (Apr. 1950): 182–195. Source for knock; the public blames knock on self-starters; tomato can; U.S. Geological Survey; The Goat and aviation records; GM realizes exhaust danger; and doctors' opinions.

———. *Professional Amateur: The Biography of Charles Franklin Kettering*. New York: E. P. Dutton & Co., Inc., 1957. Source for how Kettering sells Midgley on knock and Midgley's World War I work.

———. "Some Recollections of Thomas Midgley, Jr. as Prepared in Response to Questions by Prof. Joseph J. Ermenc." Feb. 1966. Kettering file 19/77. Source of ice cube invention; fabulous memory; Henry Ford visit; cornea, and unstoppered bottle of TEL.

Seth Cagin and Philip Dray. *Between Earth and Sky: How CFC's Changed Our World and Endangered the Ozone Layer*. New York: Pantheon, 1993. Source for cemetery records of suicide; NRC recruiter; lead-lined lungs' letter; Dayton atmosphere; "fanatical health cranks"; "aura of Socialism"; "nose test;" Midgley irritates Frigidaire; and air-conditioned textile factory. Philip Dray graciously alerted me to Midgley's volumes of poetry in the New York Public Library and located his "lead-lined lungs" letter for me.

CDC's MMWR Weekly (Morbidity & Mortality Weekly Report). *Achievements in Public Health 1900–1999: Control of Infectious Diseases*. Atlanta, GA: Centers for Disease Control. 48, no. 29 (July 30, 1999): 621–629. Source for infant mortality rates.

Floyd L. Darrow. *The Story of Chemistry*. New York: Blue Ribbon Books, Inc., 1930. Source for TEL inventor as benefactor.

Barry Donaldson and Bernhard Nagengast. *Heat and Cold: Mastering the Great Indoors: A Selective History of Heating, Ventilation, Air-Conditioning and Refrigeration from the Ancients to the 1930s*. Atlanta: American Society of Heating, Refrigerating and Air-Conditioning Engineers, Inc. 1994. Source for "a lulu;" dangerous refrigerants, and air-conditioning public places.

John Duffy. *A History of Public Health in New York City*. vols. 1 and 2. New York: Russell Sage Foundation, 1968 and 1974. Source for horse pollution.

Anthony S. Fauci et al., eds. *Harrison's Principles of Internal Medicine*. 14th ed. New York: McGraw-Hill, 1998. Source for lead poisoning symptoms.

Fondation Gianadda Musée Automobile, Martigny, Switzerland. Private communication in 2001. Source for speeds of early luxury cars.

Frigidaire advertisements, 1920–1940. Kettering file 79-10.10.

George Sweet Gibb and Evelyn H. Knowlton. *The Resurgent Years: History of Standard Oil Company (New Jersey) 1911–1927*. New York: Harper & Bros. 1956. Source for development of TEL process; DuPont department heads meet; and Teagle warned.

August W. Giebelhaus. *Business and Government in the Oil Industry: A Case Study of Sun Oil, 1876–1945*. Greenwich CT: JAI Press, 1980. Source for Sun Oil; description of knock; and TEL added in factory.

William Graebner. "Hegemony through Science: Information Engineering and Lead Toxicology, 1925–1965." In *Dying for Work: Workers' Safety and Health in Twentieth-Century America*, David Rosner and Gerald Markowitz, eds. Bloomington, IN.: Indiana University Press (1987): 140–159.

Donald A. Henderson, MD, MPH. Private e-mail communication, Nov. 23, 1999: Effect of refrigeration on vaccination and smallpox.

David A. Hounshell and John Kenly Smith, Jr. *Science and Corporate Strategy: Du Pont R & D, 1902–1980*. New York: Cambridge University Press, 1988. Source for post-World War I auto industry; DuPont wants basic fuel research; Carothers talks to GM; German discovered TEL; few industrial toxicologists or U.S. researchers on worker health; public thinks chemicals harmless; German chemist's warning; GM has no alternative to TEL; Kettering upset and worried about publicity; DuPont criticizes Standard Oil but has problems too; DuPont releases sick workers; TEL adds "less lead" than paint; most electrified homes without refrigerators; and Cleveland hospital leak.

John Jewkes, David Sawers, and Richard Stillerman. *The Sources of Invention*. New York: W. W. Norton, 1969.

George B. Kauffman. "Antiknock and CFC Pioneer." *The World and I* (Nov. 1989): 358–367.

———. "Midgley: Saint or Serpent." *Chemtech* 19 (Dec. 1989): 716–725.

Robert A. Kehoe. His lead studies on humans include the following, arranged chronologically:

———. "On the Normal Absorption and Excretion of Lead". I–III. *Journal of Industrial Hygiene*. 15 (Sept. 1933).

———. "An Appraisal of the Lead Hazards Associated with the Distribution and Use of Gasoline Containing Tetraethyl Lead." *Journal of Industrial Hygiene and Toxicology*. 18 (1936): 42–68.

———. "A Spectrochemical Study of the Normal Ranges of Concentration of Certain Trace Metals in Biological Materials." *Journal of Nutrition*. 19 (1940): 579–592.

———. "Experimental Studies on the Ingestion of Lead Compounds." *The Journal of Industrial Hygiene and Toxicology*. 22 (Nov. 1940): 381–400.

———. "Lead Absorption and Lead Poisoning." *The Medical Clinics of North America* 26 (July 1942): 1261–1279.

———. "Responses of Human Subjects to Lead Compounds." *Industrial Medicine and Surgery*. 28 (Mar. 1959): 156–159.

———. "The Harben Lectures, 1960." *Journal of the Royal Institute of Public Health*. 24 (Apr. 1961): 81–97.

———. "Experimental Studies on the Inhalation of Lead by Human Subjects." *Pure and Applied Chemistry*. 3 (1961): 129–144.

Charles F. Kettering. "Midgley—Man of Marvels." *The American Weekly*. Mar. 25, 1945. Kettering file 12/34. Source for Midgley as World War II hero.

———. "Biographical Memoir of Thomas Midgley, Jr." *Biographical Memoirs, National Academy of Sciences*. 24 (1947): 361–80.

———. "Thomas Midgley, Jr., An Appreciation." Undated. Kettering 9/7. Source for knock's description and Midgley's photograph of knock.

———. "Keynote Address: How We Started the Antiknock Business." Undated. Kettering file 10/15. Source for TEL clogging cars.

Henrietta M. Larson, Evelyn H. Knowlton, and Charles S. Popple. *History of Standard Oil Company (New Jersey): New Horizons 1927–1950*. New York: Harper & Row, 1971. Source for aviation's need for antiknock and TEL added after Pearl Harbor

Stuart W. Leslie. "Thomas Midgley and the Politics of Industrial Research." *The Business History Review*. 54 (Winter 1980): 481–503. Source for Midgley's reading deeply; GM almost shuts down knock research; knocking related to fuel structure; Midgley can sit a while; unveils CFC; and Kinetic Chemicals.

———. *Boss Kettering*. New York: Columbia University Press, 1983. Source for Kettering's discoveries, hiring, and strong point; Ford hires mechanics; TEL on sale; public loves pep, not economy; TEL expands use of car; and Midgley loses interest in invention.

———. "Thomas Midgley, Jr." *American National Biography*. vol. 15. New York: Oxford University Press, 1999.

Alan P. Loeb. "Birth of the Kettering Doctrine: Fordism, Sloanism and the Discovery of Tetraethyl Lead." *Business and Economic History* 24 (1) (Fall 1995): 72–87. Source of the effect of TEL on public policy and government.

Harland Manchester. "The Magic of High-Octane Gas." *Harper's Magazine*. 184 (Feb. 1942): 286–293. Source for underpowered cars in 1920s traffic; TEL adds radios, heating, and heavy frames to cars; and TEL's effect on World War II planes.

"Medal to Midgley." *The Ohio State University Monthly*. 33 (Feb. 1992): 5.

Gerald Messadié. *Great Scientific Discoveries*. Edinburgh: Chambers, 1991. Source for knock's description.

Thomas J. Midgley, Jr. "Accent on Youth." *Chemical and Engineering News*. 22 (Oct. 10, 1944): 1646–1649. Kettering file 17/38.

———. "Bio Sheet, 1930." Cornell University Rare Manuscript Collections. Source for family background.

———. "Chemistry in the Next Century." *Industrial and Engineering Chemistry*. 27 (May 1935): 494–498. Source for easy physics and Methuselah.

———. "Critical Examination of Some Concepts in Rubber Chemistry." *Industrial and Engineering Chemistry*. 34 (July 1942): 891–896. Kettering file 17/38. Source for speech when received Gibbs medal; Pullman cars and mine air-conditioning; and rubber and rubber research.

———. "From the Periodic Table to Production." Speech on receiving Perkin Medal. *Industrial and Engineering Chemistry*. 29 (Feb. 1937): 241–244. Kettering file 19-103. Source for high school science; periodic table used in search for antiknock; how CFCs discovered; and how Freon discovered.

———. "The Chemist's View." *The Forum on the Future of Industrial Research*, sponsored by Standard Oil Development Company, Oct. 5, 1944. [Later published in *Chemical and Engineering News.* 22 (Oct. 25, 1944): 1756–1760.] Kettering file 17/38. Source for Midgley's last speech, delivered by telephone.

———. *Hobbies of 1926, Hobbies of 1927*, and *Hobbies of 1928.* New York Public Library. I am indebted to Philip Dray for calling my attention to Midgley's self-published poems.

———. "How We Found Ethyl Gas." *MoToR.* (Jan. 1925): 92–94. Kettering file 12/25. Source for trailing arbutus; aniline discovery; and tellurium smell.

———. "Introduction to Kettering." Speech to American Chemical Society, New York (Sept. 13, 1944). Kettering B4/184. Source for out of work; Kettering's door; Arabian nights; "throughout eternity;" and Freon discovery.

———. "Man-Made Molecules." *Industrial and Engineering Chemistry.* 30 (Jan. 1938): 120–122. Kettering file 17-38. Source for refrigeration industry's desire for air-conditioning, not refrigerators; "plots of boiling points . . . ," and "God's edict in Genesis."

———. "Organic Fluorides as Refrigerants." *Industrial and Engineering Chemistry.* 22, no. 5 (May 1930): 542–545. Source for how Midgley as an engineer explained refrigerant problem.

———. "Problem + Research + Capital = Progress." *Industrial and Engineering Chemistry.* 31(May 1939): 504–506. Kettering file 19/103. Source for the "tough, uncompromising problem;" bromine; TEL goes on sale in service stations and public response; and tractors with TEL.

———. Correspondence. I am indebted to his grandson, J. Darby Midgley, for these letters:

Aubrey D. McFadyen, March 11, 1936: Source for CFCs' advances in air-conditioning.

Newton Copp, Sept. 21, 1937: Source for a handicap without a Ph.D.

F. O. Clements, March 30, 1937. Source for predicted effects of TEL and doubts that TEL would increase car ownership.

———. Letter to Wilder D. Bancroft, Jan. 19, 1923. "Lead-lined lungs." Kettering Archives, GMI file 87-11.14-92. Portions of this letter first appeared in Seth Cagin and Philip Dray's book, *Between Earth and Sky: How CFC's Changed Our World and Endangered the Ozone Layer.* I am indebted to Philip Dray for locating the letter for me.

M. J. Molina, "Polar Ozone Depletion." 1995 Nobel Lecture. *Angewandte Chemie.* International English Edition, 35 (Sept. 6, 1996): 1786–1785.

Bernard Nagengast. *Heat and Cold: Mastering the Great Indoors: A Selective History of Heating, Ventilation, Air Conditioning, and Refrigeration from the Ancients to the 1930s.* Atlanta, GA: ASHRAE, 1994. Source for principle of refrigeration was long known.

———. "Refrigerants: 160 Years of Change." *ASHRAE Journal.* 37 (Mar. 1995): 54–56.

———. "A Historical Look at CFC Refrigerants." *ASHRAE Journal.* 30 (Nov. 1988): 37–39. Source for early history of refrigerants.

Herbert L. Needleman. "Clamped in a Straitjacket: The Insertion of Lead into Gasoline." Draft June 30, 1997. Source for Midgley can't find lead in exhaust; Indianapolis 500; Bureau of Mines emasculated; Kehoe says 18 percent staff sick;

TEL workers sick; House of Butterflies; and Midgley at press conference and New York World.

Jerome O. Nriagu. "The Rise and Fall of Leaded Gasoline." *The Science of the Total Environment.* 92 (1990): 13–28. An authoritative history of leaded gasoline. The source for airplane octane; lead industry pays Kehoe's salary; one of few environmentally unsafe products forced out of market place; one of top 10 chemicals in U.S.; Esso slogan; compression ratio and valve seat recession; Kettering about automobile at crossroads, Europe versus U.S.; 90 percent all U.S. gas and 80 percent worldwide; autos after 20 years of TEL; TEL drove U.S. transport; "lead" removed from "Ethyl" trade name and Ethyl's control of publications; and environment to be monitored by voluntary self-regulation, not legislation.

Oral History Project. All but one interview conducted by T. A. Boyd. Kettering. Interviews with:

John M. Campbell. Nov. 9, 1964.

James D. Carpenter. Aug. 10, 1960. Source for the tomato can.

Albert L. Henne. July 27, 1964. Source for the guinea pig test for CFCs.

Carroll A. Hochwalt. May 18, 1978. Source for no running water; hard-driving boss; airplane pistons in laboratory; team talk of abandoning search; TEL discovered and tested; and Hochwalt's and Midgley's lead poisoning.

Frank A. Howard, Sept. 14, 1960.

Robert A. Kehoe. Oct. 12, 1960. Source for how GM realizes exhaust danger and for Sloan's willingness to abandon TEL.

Richard K. Scales, Jan. 24, 1961. Source for Midgley's drawing more conclusions; golfs below 80; Kehoe hired and cares for Dayton victims; "Clear line of demarcation"; TEL "left . . . in our hands"; 1950 Cadillac; Midgley's love of driving; refrigeration industry wanted air-conditioning, not refrigerators; tunnels; and lawn.

George H. Willits. Dec. 19, 1960.

Joseph A. Pratt. "Letting the Grandchildren Do It: Environmental Planning during the Ascent of Oil as a Major Energy Source." *The Public Historian.* 2 (Summer 1980): 28–61. Source for Bureau of Mines studies of automotive exhaust, water pollution, and sulfur-rich petroleum; and environment to be monitored by voluntary self-regulation, not legislation.

Joseph C. Robert. *Ethyl: A History of the Corporation and the People Who Made It.* Charlottesville: University Press of Virginia, 1983. Source for DuPont's GM stock; conviviality and drinking; Midgley and impartial Bureau of Mines study; subnormal temperature March 15; two coworkers in Midgley lab die; Kettering's "calm intervention"; Sloan will abandon TEL; Kehoe founding father; Ethyl Corp. established; Ethyl threatened "with extinction"; and Ethyl's involvement with Surgeon General committee.

David Rosner and Gerald Markowitz. "Safety and Health as a Class Issue:, The Worker's Health Bureau of America during the 1920s." In *Dying for Work: Workers' Safety and Health in Twentieth-Century America*, David Rosner and Gerald Markowitz, eds. Bloomington, IN.: Indiana University Press (1987): 53–64.

———. "A Gift of God: The Public Health Controversy over Leaded Gasoline in the 1920s." In *Dying for Work, Workers' Safety and Health in Twentieth-Century America.* David Rosner and Gerald Markowitz, eds. Bloomington, IN.: Indiana University Press (1987): 53–64; 121–139. Source for GM sales strategy; Midgley's "serious consideration" given; "average street"; Bureau of Mines emasculated; TEL workers sick; Midgley at press conference and with New York World; labor's consultant a spy; Kehoe says lead studies to be paid for by industry concerned; and "Ethyl is Back" signs.

F. S. Rowland. "Stratospheric Ozone Depletion by Chlorofluorocarbons." 1995 Nobel Lecture. *Angewandte Chemie.* International English edition. 35 (Sept. 6, 1996): 1786–1798.

Kenneth J. Ryan. "Enteric Infections and Food Poisoning." *Sherris Medical Microbiology: An Introduction to Infectious Diseases.* 3d ed., Kenneth J. Ryan et al., eds. Norwalk, CT: Appleton & Lange, 1994.

Robert Schlaifer and S. D. Heron. *Development of Aircraft Engines and Aviation Fuels.* Cambridge, MA: Harvard Graduate School of Business Administration, 1950. Source for airplane fuel in 1920s. I am indebted to the Museum of Flight, Seattle, for this information.

Shellworth. *History of Frigidaire.* Unpublished manuscript. Kettering. File 79-10.1-41B. Source for air-conditioned restaurant and school.

David A. Shirley. *Organic Chemistry.* New York: Holt, Rinehart and Winston: 1964. Source for petroleum chemistry and TEL.

Walter Stolov. e-mail communication. Nov. 5, 1999. Source for lead poisoning's effect on polio.

U.S. Public Health Bureau. *United States Public Health Bulletin No. 158, Proceedings of a conference to determine whether or not there is a public health question in the manufacture, distribution, or use of tetraethyl lead gasoline."* Government Printing Office, August 1925. Source for industry at crossroads; 5 percent of fuel power; Kehoe says 18 percent staff sick; and the hearing.

Robert E. Wilson (Pan American Petroleum and Transport Company, NY). "The Medalist." *Industrial and Engineering Chemistry.* 29 (Feb. 1937): 239–241. Source for James Watt; Cornell academics; smoking car; and rubber research.

CHAPTER 7   Nylon, Polyester, and Wallace Hume Carothers

I am deeply grateful to Barbara Machetanz Osborn and to Jeffry B. Spencer for generously allowing me to read letters that Wallace Carothers wrote to Wilko Machetanz and Francis Gelvin Spencer, respectively. Wallace Carothers wrote Machetanz more than 125 letters during the course of their friendship, and I have drawn heavily on them, especially for Carothers' college and graduate student years. The Spencer letters are invaluable for Carothers' Du Pont years. Susan Kyle graciously permitted me to quote from Wallace Carothers' last letter to his mother. Robert M. Secor was exceptionally kind in setting aside work on his own full-length biography of Carothers to make the Osborn letters available to me and to speak with me about them and Carothers.

In the past, Carothers' health has been discussed only in terms of manic depression and alcohol. Among those experts who helped me in trying to understand his other medical problems were Peter S. Colley, MD; Leon Eisenberg, MD; Stephen A. Falk, MD; Gary Fujimoto, MD; Gerald N. Grob; Elaine Henley, MD; and Jonathan Q. Purnell, MD.

I am also very grateful to those who read and critiqued this chapter, including the late Arthur "Andy" Anderson, Otto T. Benfey, Jean Colley, Yasu Furukawa, Gerald N. Grob, Gilbert Haighat, David A. Hounshell, Joseph Labovsky, Robert M. Secor, John Kenley Smith, Jr., and Audrey Weitkamp.

Given the number of Carothers' letters and the space limitations of this book, I have grouped his letters and the data learned from them by location, rather than listing each letter individually. I hope that this enables scholars to locate sources of information about Carothers without making the book too expensive for general readers.

Interviews with the author (by telephone unless noted):

Polly Hill. Telephone interview, May 6, 2000. Source for Moore wrapping Carothers around finger; Hohman telling Carothers to marry; and agnosticism.

Joseph Labovsky. Interview, Feb. 28, 2000, Wilmington, Delaware, and e-mail Mar. 29, 2000. Source for Carothers' suits; lab formality; Du Pont hired postdoctoral students; music and literature; stop light; "damn, it's hot;" formal laboratory atmosphere; "95 percent . . . "; played squash like cobra; "within finite limits;" "where organic compounds begin . . . "; and Berchet personality.

Fred Machetanz. Telephone interview, May 6, 2000. Source for Carothers' high school song and verse for every occasion. Barbara Machetanz Osborn interview. April 26, 2000. Source of knife in poetry book and Isobel's salary.

Robert M. Secor. Telephone interviews, 2000–2001. Source for Sylvia Moore's background and end of their affair; club memberships; Julian Hill visits hospital and learns Carothers spent the night there before suicide; Carothers' grades and freshman chemistry class; Carothers rejects Neoprene medal; European doubts about Carothers' condensation polymers; and young Flory's opinion that polymers were of dubious scientific value.

Adeline C. Strange. Telephone interview, Feb. 28, 2000. Source for Du Pont visits to Helen Carothers and why Strange conducted interviews.

MANUSCRIPT SOURCES

Chemical Heritage Foundation, Philadelphia, PA

Joseph Labovsky. Interview with John K. Smith at Wilmington, Delaware, July 24, 1996, oral transcript #148. Source for how Coffman discovers nylon precursor.

Edgar W. Spanagel. Interview with John K. Smith at Wilmington, Delaware, May 9, 1997, oral transcript #158. Source for checking assistants every few days and Coffman's discovery.

University of Chicago

Wallace Carothers. Letter to Robert M. Hutchins, Nov. 4, 1934, Box 101, Folder 3, Presidential Papers. Source for Carothers' declining department chair.

University Of Illinois

Roger Adams. Letter to Frederic Woodward, Nov. 8, 1934, Presidential Papers 1925–1945, Box, 101, Folder 3, University of Illinois Archives, Joseph Regenstein Library, Urbana, IL. Source for "the best organic chemist" and good writer.

Roger Adams. Audiotape of interview at Chemist's Club, New York, 1964, RAP Box 9. Source for Carothers good at all science and "lovable."

Ira Carothers. Letter to Roger Adams, Dec. 2, 1937, RAP Box 54. Source for no hint of son's mental problems.

Mary (Molly) E. M. Carothers. Letter to Roger Adams, Nov. 23, 1937, RAP Box 54. Source for son's depression, "hard-headed business men," and Carothers last letter to her.

C. M. A. Stine. Letter to Roger Adams, Dec. 2, 1938, RAP Box 54. Source for why Du Pont hired Carothers and Bolton's opposition to basic research.

Three other letters between Roger Adams, Wallace Carothers, and John R. Johnson, RAP Boxes 7 and 54.

Osborn Papers

The Osborn papers, courtesy of Barbara Machetanz Osborn, include Wallace Carothers' letters to Wilko and Tort Machetanz as well as Tarkio College memorabilia. They are the source for Carothers' description of his father; penitentiary quote; his life at Tarkio and University of Chicago; appetite; thyroid operation; chemistry losing glamour and why; slime and dejection quotes; decision to teach at Tarkio; University of Chicago; college nickname; Tarkio teaching job and exhaustion; usual stage fright; why chose Illinois; "place in which to work"; South Dakota research; slavery; heavy teaching and class loads; bromine accident; fellowship; Adams' rest; kingly offer; misses university life; "saved just lightly more than nothing at all;" liquor consumption 1930; worries about neoprene; "a Group Leader . . . "; "social opinion means nothing. . . "; prayers; missed chemical arguments; and Carothers as professor.

Tarkio Yearbook, 1916 and 1917, are the source for Carothers' college teaching and nickname.

Wilko G. Machetanz. Letter to Miss Betty Jo Travis, Mar. 8, 1947. Source for exercise a torment; checked pulse; *Weltschmerz*; Prof's physical description; and grand march.

Wilko G. Machetanz. Letter to Clyde H. Canfield, May 12, 1958. Source for Tarkio student life.

Spencer Papers

Wallace H. Carothers to Frances Gelvin Spencer. These 14 letters, courtesy of Jeffry B. Spencer, are the source for "Even an Englishman"; Carothers credits Collins, not Nieuwland; "Hot air in wrong key"; neoprene "side issue"; Europeans' and Wilstätter's visits; Christmas Eve, 1931, and "you can imagine the state . . ."; Worries Du Pont spending on neoprene; "gaudy speakeasy. . . ."; "23, tall, slender, pretty . . ."; vagatonia; sports brighten; "balance in swivel chair. . . . Unfortunately alive"; "cock-roach-like"; "lordly"; prays daily; librarians' poem; "supefication"; Arden description and family relationship; "enough for one lifetime"; Bolton urges return to fibers; "it's a miracle"; and Isobel's performance.

Hagley Museum and Library, Wilmington, Delaware

Hagley Museum and Library is the richest repository of material about Carothers' scientific career. Marjorie McNinch was particularly helpful during my visit. Hagley's collection includes the correspondence between Carothers and Du Pont about his hiring, Carothers' notebooks, Carothers' letters to his close friend, John R. Johnson; and transcripts of interviews conducted with Carothers' associates by David A. Hounshell and John Kenley Smith, Jr., and by Adeline C. Strange.

Letters to and from Carothers, Charles M. A. Stine, Arthur P. Tanberg, and Hamilton Bradshaw outline Du Pont's job offer, Carothers' consideration of it; Carothers' outline of his research plan; Carothers' planning polymer experiments; 75 pounds of mercury; few purified chemicals; little known about polymers; course of action outlined; "little fantastic"; his interest in rubber; "dates of some events . . . "; and ordering supplies. These documents are contained in HML 1896 and HML Acc. 1784, Box 18.

Wallace H. Carothers. "Early History of Polyamide Fibers," addressed to Arthur P. Tanberg, Feb. 19, 1936, is the source for the discovery of superpolymer in the molecular still; "It should be noted that... "; obvious next step; putting amides on backburner was "foolish," but gives reasons; and Coffman's discovery. HML 1784, Box 18.

Miscellaneous letters include Ira Carothers' request for a yearly stipend; Carothers' letter to Pauline G. Beery about beginning Tarkio to study chemistry; why Carothers liked organic chemistry; and "You will understand that . . . "; Carothers' letter to Harry Bent about his racquet; Carothers to Elker K. Bolton about Carothers meeting with Midgley team on TEL; Carothers to Arthur Lamb resigning editorship; Arthur Lamb to Tanberg about Carothers' attacks at Harvard and reviewing weak article; Fred Machetanz correspondence with Hagley; Roger Adams to Wallace Carothers, "atrociously difficult"; and Willard Sweetman. HML 1896 and HML Acc. 1784, Box 18.

A few of Carothers' letters to Wilko Machetanz are in Hagley, HML 1850, Box 6. They are the source for "abulia" and paralysis of indecision; $70 income; "ideas of vast . . ."; romance with Fran and failure to confide in psychiatrists; and "My nervousness, moroseness. . . ."

Carothers' correspondence with his friend, John R. Johnson; correspondence is in Hagley, HML 1942 and 1784, Box 18. It is the source for thumbtacks; beating Fischer; "week of industrial slavery"; canceling St. Louis talk, cold feet; Wilmington train station; boulder hopping; "metaphorical explosion"; "galloping stage"; "condolences" on marriage; Philadelphia hospital and treatment; hiking in Bavaria; and priority argument.

Interviews in Hagley

Transcripts of interviews conducted by David A. Hounshell and John Kenley Smith, Jr., are in HML 1878. They were conducted with, among others:

Merlin Brubaker (source for vial of poison and suicide threat; DVA and explosions); Crawford H. Greenewalt (source for Bolton's focus on 6-6, and Carothers' calling Helen "Sylvia"); Julian Hill (source for small Midwest colleges; Du Pont's interest in hiring Carothers; shrewdness; bad hood; conducted few experiments; funniest man; stone wall; affronts; sees Collins discover neoprene; amides on back burner; chemists writing patents; future projects on polyfluorinated compounds and silicon chemistry; and "packed in cotton"); and Carl S. Marvel (source for "lower than snake belly"; seminars with beer; lifts him out of depression; Adams and Marvel recommend Carothers to Du Pont; and not enough sebacic acid) .

Adeline C. Strange conducted interviews during the 1960s with Gerard Berchet; Merlin Brubaker (source for vial of poison and suicide threat); Hal Cupery (source for how Carothers hired; no cross words; and toothbrushes); Virginia Duncan (source for how Carothers worked in library); Harry Dykstra (source for toothbrushes); Crawford Greenwalt (source for gentleness; Moore was "terrific . . . "); Julian Hill (source for Carothers' Friday musicals); John R. Johnson (source for publication of second article; no campus smoking; billiards/coffee; vial of poison and suicide threat; fishing; buys suicide book; and seashore plans); William Mapel (source for duets at parties and Black Forest thoughts of suicide); John and Libby Miles (source for tobacco mosaic virus interest); and Kenneth Reese (source for wooden blocks).

Articles and Books.

Roger Adams. "Wallace Hume Carothers." *Biographical Memoirs, National Academy of Sciences.* 20 (1939): 293–309. Source for Carothers' academic record; wide interests; best Illinois student; Conant on Carothers' teaching effectively; and nylon's significance.

American Psychiatric Association. *Statistical Manual for the Use of Hospitals for Mental Illnesses.* Albany, NY: Boyd Printing Co., 3rd ed., 1923; 4th ed., 1928. Source for the definitions of psychiatric problems in the 1920s.

Anonymous. "Chemists Produce Synthetic 'Silk.' " *The New York Times.* Sept. 2, 1931.

———. "Chemist Who Helped Make Real Rubber is D. M. Man." *Des Moines Register* (Nov. 4, 1931). Source for Ira's saying his son was slow learner.

———. "In Connecticut." *Time.* 19, no. 1 (Jan. 4, 1932): 44. Yale bank closures. Quoted in Hermes, *Enough for One Lifetime.*

———. "To Wed in New York Today." *Wilmington Journal-Every Evening* (Feb. 21 and 22, 1936): 23. Source for Carothers' marriage.

———. "In Connecticut." *Time.* 19 (Jan. 4, 1932): 44. Source for New Haven banks closing.

———. " 'Lu' of Radio Team Dies of Pneumonia." *The New York Times.* Jan. 9, 1937, p. 17.

———. "Dr. Carothers Is Found Dead in Hotel Room." *Wilmington Journal Every Evening.* Apr. 30, 1937a, p. 1.

———. "Dr. Carothers Poison Victim; Noted Chemist." *Wilmington Morning News.* Apr. 30, 1937b, p. 1.

———. "Nylon: From Test Tube to Counter." *Chemistry.* 37 (Sept. 1964): 8–23.

———. "Elmer Keiser Bolton." *McGraw-Hill Modern Men of Science.* New York: McGraw-Hill, 1966.

————. "Flory on Carothers and Du Pont." *CHOC News.* 1, no. 2 (1983): 9–10. Source for Carothers' influence and their office meeting.

Anonymous. "National Historic Chemical Landmark: The First Nylon Plant." American Chemical Society, 1995. Source for current nylon production.

K. E. Appel and E. A. Strecker. *Practical Examination of Personality and Behavior Disorders.* New York: Macmillan, 1936.

Bernadette Bensaude-Vincent and Isabelle Stengers. *A History of Chemistry.* Translated by Deborah van Dam. Cambridge, MA: Harvard University Press, 1996. Source for synthetic rubber and neoprene; early plastics; and Carothers' strategy.

Daniel Blain, "Twentieth Century Psychiatry—Living History in the Life of Kenneth E. Appel, M.D., 1896–1979." *Transactions & Studies of the College of Physicians of Philadelphia,* Series V. 2, no. 2 (June 1980): 144–154. Source for Appel.

Bruce Bower. "Pushing the Mood Swings: Social and Psychological Forces Sway the Course of Manic Depression." *Science News.* 157 (Apr. 8, 2000): 232–233.

Francis J. Braceland. "Memoriam, Kenneth Ellmaker Appel, 1896–1979," *American Journal of Psychiatry.* 137 no. 4 (Apr. 1980): 501–503. Source for Appel.

William H. Brock. *The Norton History of Chemistry.* New York: W. W. Norton & Co., 1993. Source for Lewis-Langmuir theory; early plastics; Staudinger controversy; available technology; carbon dioxide emissions, but relatively clean technology.

Jean Bruller (called Vercors). *21 Recettes Pratiques de Mort Violente.* Paris: Tchou, 1976. 50-Year Anniversary Reprint.

Robert F. Burk. *The Corporate State and the Broker State, The Du Ponts and American National Politics, 1925–1940.* Cambridge, MA: Harvard University Press, 1990. Source for Du Pont history.

Capital City Commercial Colleges Handbook. Iowa City, IA: State Historical Society of Iowa, 1908. Source for father's job and school descriptions.

Charles W. Carey, Jr. "Wallace Hume Carothers." *American National Biography,* vol. 4. John A. Garraty and Mark C. Carnes, eds. Oxford: Oxford University Press, 1999, pp. 425–426. Source for Carothers' strategy.

Wallace H. Carothers. "Polymers and Polyfunctionality." *Transactions of the Faraday Society.* 32 (1936): 39–53. Carothers' Cambridge speech is the source for polymers providing the bulk of living things; Collins' "cauliflower" mass; and no mention of nylon.

William H. A. Carr. *The Du Ponts of Delaware.* New York: Dodd, Mead & Company, 1964. Source for Du Pont family history.

J. McKeen Cattell and Jacques Cattell, eds. "Wallace Carothers." *American Men of Science,* 5th ed. New York: The Science Press (1933): 178.

Alfred D. Chandler. *The Visible Hand, The Management Revolution in American Business.* Cambridge, MA: Belknap Press of Harvard University Press, 1977.

William H. Conner. "Arden." *Sunday Morning Star.*

James B. Conant to Frederic Woodward, Nov. 13, 1934. PP, 1925–1945, Box 101, Folder 3, Harvard University Library. Source for Carothers' sweating.

Dorothy Detzer. *Appointment on the Hill.* New York: Henry Holt and Company, 1948. Source for Sylvia Moore's political milieu.

George Draper, "Psychoanalysis—The Inward Eye," *Scribner's Magazine.* Dec. 1931, 667ff. Source for public opinion of 1920s psychiatry, cited by Hermes.

John Dunning. *Tune in Yesterday: The Ultimate Encyclopedia of Old-Time Radio, 1925–1976.* Upper Saddle River, NJ: Prentice-Hall (1975): 136. Source for Isobel's radio program.

William S. Dutton. *DuPont, One Hundred and Forty Years.* New York: Charles Scribner's Sons, 1942.

Madeline Edmondson and David Rounds. *The Soaps, Daytime Serials of Radio and TV.* New York: Stein and Day, 1973. Source for Isobel's radio program.

Leon Eisenberg, MD, e-mail correspondence, May 9, 2000. Source for the effect of thyroid removal and electroshock therapy on mental health.

"Julius Arthur Nieuwland." *Encyclopaedia Britannica,* vol. 7, pp. 336–337. Chicago: Encyclopaedia Britannica, Inc., 1979. Source for his discovery of poison gas and getting credit for neoprene.

Paul J. Flory. Letter to Helen Carothers. Nov. 22, 1974. Source for polymers in 1930s considered poor scientific subjects. Courtesy of Joseph Labovsky.

———. *Les Prix Nobel en 1974.* Stockholm: Imprimerie Royale P. A. Norstedt & Soner, 1975. Source for his praise of Carothers and how Carothers interested him in polymers, and for the importance of polymers in biology.

Yasu Furukawa. *Inventing Polymer Science: Staudinger, Carothers, and the Emergence of Macromolecular Chemistry.* Philadelphia: University of Pennsylvania Press and Chemical Heritage Foundation, 1998. The most authoritative and scientific biography of Wallace Carothers. The source for Staudinger debates; WASP post-doctoral students; Carothers' effect on molecular biology and medicine; Carothers giving American polymer science a lead; Purity Hall virgins; supple prose; Hooke quote; "Well, gentlemen . . . "; nylon's significance; nylon development moved; meets Staudinger; National Academy; end of silk hosiery and world trade; polymer Nobels; and Carothers as prototypical industrial researcher.

Roland Gelatt. *The Fabulous Phonograph: From Edison to Stereo.* New York: Appleton-Century, 1965. Source for recorded music in 1930s.

Anne Geller. "Common Addictions," *Clinical Symposia.* NJ: Ciba-Geigy Corp. 48, no. 1(1996).

Malcolm Gladwell. "Well-to-do Teflon and Nylon Turn 50." *The Fresno Bee.* June 10, 1988.

Gerald N. Grob. *Mental Illness and American Society 1875–1940.* Princeton, NJ: Princeton University Press, 1983. Source for history of psychiatry.

Matthew E. Hermes. "Synthetic Fibers from 'Pure Science': DuPont Hires Carothers." In *Manmade Fibers: Their Origin and Development.* Raymond B. Seymour and Roger S. Porter, eds. London: Elsevier Applied Science, 1993.

———. *Enough for One Lifetime: Wallace Carothers, Inventor of Nylon.* Washington, DC and Philadelphia: American Chemical Society and Chemical Heritage Foundation, 1996. This book, a combination of factually reported and imaginatively recreated events, is the source for Carothers' deep reading; Babbitt; Harvard job offer; "partly Americanized class"; list of suicides; mushroom farmer; and $45,000 estate.

———. "How Dupont Hired Carothers." *Chemical Heritage.* 13:2 (Summer 1996): 4–5, 36–7.

J. W. Hill. *Proceedings of the Robert A. Welch Foundation Conferences on Chemical*

Research 20, American Chemistry Bicentennial. W. O. Mulligan, ed. Houston: Welch Foundation, 1977. Source for industrial labs solving practical problems.

Roald Hoffmann. "A Natural-Born Fiber." *American Scientist.* 85 (Jan.–Feb., 1997): 21. Source for rayon.

Leslie Hohman Biographical File, Alan Mason Chesney Medical Archives of The Johns Hopkins Medical Institutions. Source of undated Baltimore *Sunpapers* stories about Hohman.

Richard R. Holmes. "The Big Four." *Chemical Heritage.* 14, 2 (Summer 1997): 43. Adams' research.

David A. Hounshell. "Interpreting the History of Industrial Research and Development; The Case of E. I. Du Pont de Nemours & Co." *Proceedings of the American Philosophical Society.* 134 (Dec. 1990): 387–407. Source for Thome's saving Carothers' papers.

David A. Hounshell and John Kenly Smith, Jr. "The Nylon Drama." *American Heritage of Invention and Technology.* 4 (Fall 1988): 40–55. Source for condensation removing water; 12,000 molecular weight; patent argument; and toothbrushes.

David A. Hounshell and John Kenley Smith, Jr. *Science and Corporate Strategy: Du Pont R&D, 1902–1980.* New York: Cambridge University Press, 1988. The authoritative book about Du Pont's research, a classic in business history, and the work that brought Carothers to the attention of historians. Source for "reluctant inventor"; Du Pont switch from explosives to nonexplosives; profitability of switch; GM profits; universities did most basic research; Stine's background and dream; WASP postdoctoral students; Carothers' strategy; stone wall; Du Pont bonuses; patent argument; problems with polyester; Bolton background; the fiber hunt; nylon's significance; and nylon development transformed Carothers' lab.

John R. Johnson. "Wallace Hume Carothers, 1896–1937." *Journal of the Chemical Society* 143 (1940): 100–102.

John R. Johnson. "Carothers, Wallace Hume." *Dictionary of American Biography.* Supplement 2 (1958): 96–97.

George B. Kauffman. "Wallace Hume Carothers, Founder of American Polymer Chemistry." *Chemical Intelligencer.* 2:3 (July 1996): 49–51.

———. "Wallace Hume Carothers and Nylon, The First Completely Synthetic Fiber." *Journal of Chemical Education.* 65 (Sept. 1988): 803–808.

———. "Nylon at 50." *Chemtech.* 18 (Dec. 1988): 725–731.

Howard I. Kushner. *Self-Destruction in the Promised Land: A Psychocultural Biology of American Suicide.* New Brunswick, NJ: Rutgers University Press, 1989.

Joseph Labovsky. "Chemical Reminiscences." *Chemical Heritage Foundation.* Source for "Damn it, read it."

Frank M. McMillan. *The Chain Straighteners.* New York: Macmillan, 1979.

Herman F. Mark. "Polymers," *Encyclopaedia Britannica,* vol. 14, pp. 764–774. Chicago: Encyclopaedia Britannica, Inc., 1979.

———. "Polymer Chemistry in Europe and American—How It All Began." *Journal of Chemical Education.* 58 (July 1981): 527–534. Source for academics thought macropolymers' molecular weight under 1000; no U.S. macropolymer department; early plastics; Staudinger debate; and cold drawing discovered.

———. "Hermann: Father of Modern Polymer Science." 93–110. In *Pioneers in Polymer Science.* Raymond B. Seymour et al., eds. Dordrecht, Netherlands: Kluwer

Academic Publishers, 1989. Source for few academic chemists studied polymers; Staudinger controversy; available technology; and Carothers' high point of Faraday meeting.

———. "Remembering the Early Days of Polymer Science." In Raymond B. Seymour et al., eds. *Pioneers in Polymer Science*. Dordrecht, Netherlands: Kluwer Academic Publishers (1989): 29–41.

———. *From Small Organic Molecules to Large*. Washington, DC: American Chemical Society, 1993.

Herman Mark and G. Whitby, eds. *Collected Papers of Wallace Hume Carothers on High Polymeric Substances*. New York: Interscience, 1940. This contains Roger Adams' obituary of Carothers. The source for Carothers' conducting few experiments; discovering superpolymer in molecular still; "physical behavior of a molecular . . . "; and Carothers' description of cold drawing and making fibers.

Carl S. Marvel. "The Development of Polymer Chemistry in America—The Early Days." *Journal of Chemical Education*. 58 (July 1981): 535–539. Source for biological molecules have special properties; defined terms; clears up mystery; why amides put aside; and failure to make Dacron.

———. "Wallace Hume Carothers: Innovator, Motivator, Pioneer." In *Pioneers in Polymer Science*. 127–143. Raymond B. Seymour et al., eds. Dordrecht, Netherlands: Kluwer Academic Publishers, (1989): 29–41. Source for "hard driving . . . warm"; importance of Double Bond; older than other Ph.D.s; only universities did basic research; and Flory on Carothers.

Jeffrey L. Meikle. "Materia Nova: Plastics and Design in the U.S., 1925–1935." In *The Development of Plastics*. S. T. I. Mossman and P. J. T. Morris, eds. London: Royal Society of Chemistry (1994): 38–53. Source for designers liking plastic.

Herbert Morawetz. *Polymers: The Origin and Growth of a Science*. New York: John Wiley and Sons, 1985. Source for Staudinger controversy; available technology; and Carothers' strategy.

Peter J. T. Morris. *The American Synthetic Rubber Research Program*. Philadelphia: University of Pennsylvania Press, 1989. Source for synthetic rubber needed; German substitutes; neoprene properties and marketing.

———. "Synthetic Rubber: Autarky and War." In *The Development of Plastics*. S. T. I. Mossman and P. J. T. Morris, eds. London: Royal Society of Chemistry (1994). Source for neoprene not used for wartime tires, and for available technology.

S. T. I. Mossman and P. J. T. Morris, eds. *The Development of Plastics*. London: Royal Society of Chemistry, 1994. Source for Carothers inaugurating the age of polymers.

Frances R. Packard. *Some Account of the Pennsylvania Hospital from Its First Rise to the Beginning of the Year 1938*. Philadelphia: Engle, 1938. Source for description of the hospital.

Arthur M. Pardee to Roger Adams, enclosing "Contribution to the Biographical Memoir of Wallace Carothers," Feb. 19, 1938. RAP Box 54. Source for Pardee's opinion of Ira and Carothers at South Dakota.

Herbert T. Pratt. "Textile Mill Scale-Up of Nylon Hosiery, 1937–1938." In *Manmade Fibers: Their Origin and Development*. Raymond B. Seymour and Roger S. Porter, eds. London: Elsevier Applied Science, 1993. Source for marketing nylon and 80 percent of silk for hosiery in United States.

Percy Reboul. "Britain and the Bakelite Revolution." In *The Development of Plastics*. S. T. I. Mossman and P. J. T. Morris, eds. *The Development of Plastics*. London: Royal Society of Chemistry (1994):26–37. Source for early plastics.

David W. Ridgeway. "Interview with Paul J. Flory." *Journal of Chemical Education*. 54 (June 1977): 341–344. Source for throw-away economy; available technology; and Carothers' strategy.

Bruce Russell. "How Nylon Ushered in the Age of Synthetics." *San Francisco Examiner*. Jan. 17, 1988. Source for Hill's opposition to plastic throwaways.

A. Truman Schwartz. "The Importance of Good Teaching: The Influence of Arthur Pardee on Wallace Carothers." *Journal of College Science Teaching*. 10 (Feb. 1981): 218–221. Source for Pardee.

William Seabrook. *Asylum*. New York: Harcourt, Brace & Company, 1935.

John W. Servos. "History of Chemistry." In *Historical Writing on American Science: Perspectives and Prospects*. Sally Gregory Kohlstedt and Margaret W. Rossiter, eds. Baltimore: The Johns Hopkins University Press, 1985. Source for influence on molecular biology; soils studied; U.S. chemistry in the 1920s; and Adams' role.

Raymond B. Seymour, ed. *History of Polymer Science and Technology*. New York: Marcel Dekker, 1982.

Raymond B. Seymour and Charles E. Carraher. *Giant Molecules: Essential Materials for Everyday Living and Problem Solving*. New York: John Wiley & Sons, 1990. Source for polymerization as great technological feat; nylon's significance; and half of chemists in United States in polymers.

John K. Smith. "The Ten-Year Invention: Neoprene and DuPont Research, 1930–1939." *Technology and Culture*. 26 (Jan. 1985): 34–55. Source for discovery of superpolymer in molecular still; rubber as addition polymer; others condensation; Nieuwland; Collins assigned DVA problem; marketing Neoprene; and new products in Depression.

John K. Smith and David A. Hounshell. "Wallace H. Carothers and Fundamental Research at DuPont." *Science*. 229 (Aug. 2, 1985): 436–442. Source for Neoprene research "abundant in quantity"; Hill discovers fibers and cold drawing; problems with polyester; ring compounds; "it is expected to pay . . ."; and credit to Bolton for shrewd nudge.

Hermann Staudinger "Polyesterarbeiten und Gespraeche mit Carothers ueber die makromolecuklare Chemie." Lecture given at Du Pont, Wilmington, DE, Sept. 25, 1958. Deutsches Museum, Munich. HSP, B I 144. Source for Staudinger's praise of Carothers and Carothers gets United States to teach polymer science before Europe.

Jeffrey L. Sturchio. "Chemistry and Corporate Strategy at Du Pont," *Research Management*. 27 (1984):10–18. Source for transformation from explosives to non-explosives and for history of industrial labs.

D. Stanley Tarbell. "Organic Chemistry, 1876–1976." In *A Century of Chemistry: The Role of Chemists and the American Chemical Society*. Herman Skolnik and Kenneth M. Reese, eds. (1976): 339–350. Also appeared as "The Past 100 Years in Organic Chemistry." *Chemical and Engineering News*. 54 (Apr. 6, 1976): 110–123. Source for available technology.

D. Stanley Tarbell and Ann Tracy Tarbell. *Roger Adams: Scientist and Statesman*.

Washington, DC: American Chemical Society, 1981. Source for low-paid chemists; Adams as Illinois' chair; Adams' research, and hiking with Carothers.

Graham D. Taylor and Patrick E. Sudnik. *Du Pont and the International Chemical Industry.* Boston: Twayne Publishers, 1984. Du Pont quadrupled sales in Depression.

Arnold Thackray, Jeffrey L. Sturchio, P. Thomas Carroll, and Robert Bud. *Chemistry in America, 1876–1976.* Dordrecht, Netherlands: D. Reidel, 1985. Source for practical industrial lab research.

Mark H. Thiemens and William C. Trogler. "Nylon Production: An Unknown Source of Atmospheric Nitrous Oxide." *Science.* 251 (Feb. 22, 1991): 932–934.

William C. Trogler. e-mail communication, Sept. 25, 2000. Source for DuPont reaction to his nitrous oxide discovery.

Philip J. Wingate. "Why Carothers Joined DuPont: The Hopkins Mafia." *Chemical Heritage.* 15, 2 (1997): 44–46. Source for Hopkins praise of Carothers.

CHAPTER 8   DDT and Paul Hermann Müller

I am indebted to Frau Margartha Yaeggi-Müller for talking with me in Switzerland about her father. She is the source for comments about *Eigenbrötler*; asthma; blinders; family life; Läuger's phone call; her father's visit to the United States; wartime life; her mother's ironing; and the train trip to Stockholm.

I'm also indebted to Verena and David Brink for their hospitality during my stay in Switzerland and to Verena Brink and Thomas Papenbrock for their translations. Discussions with Christian Simon were particularly helpful.

Particular thanks go to those who read over the chapter in draft form: Verena Brink, Jean Colley, Darwin H. Stapleton, and Christian Simon. For DDT's effects on public health, I am indebted to Richard Fenske, MD.

Tina Adler. "Mauling Mosquitoes Naturally." *Science News.* 149 (Apr. 27, 1996): 270–271.

Anonymous. "DDT." *Journal for the Society of Dyers and Colourists.* 61 (Dec. 1945): 335–336. Source for Geigy's mothproofer; natural insecticides inadequate; key beetle experiment; DDT shirts; concentration camps; postwar uses of DDT; how DDT kills; Swiss potatoes saved; and Naples epidemic.

———. "Paul Müller." *Nature.* 208, no. 5015 (1965): 1043–1044. Source for Müller's methodical determination and outward reserve and his awards.

———. "Paul Hermann Müller." *Encyclopaedia Britannica*, vol. 6. Chicago: Encyclopaedia Britannica Inc., 1979. Source for 1968 DDT production and DDT's half-life in the environment.

Steven F. Arnold. "Synergistic Activation of Estrogen Receptor with Combinations of Environmental Chemicals." *Science.* 272 (June 7, 1996): 1489–1492.

Frank Augustin. *Zur Geschichte des Insektizids Dichlordiphenyltrichloräthan (DDT) unter besonderer Berücksichtigung der Leistung des Chemikers Paul Müller (1899–1965).* Dissertation A. Med., University of Leipzig, 1992. Source for Müller's childhood, youth, early career; reading in cottage, and the 350th compound.

William H. Brock. *The Norton History of Chemistry*. New York: W. W. Norton & Co., 1993. Source for Thalidomide and EPA.

James Ronald Busvine. *Disease Transmission by Insects: Its Discovery and 90 years of Effort to Prevent It.* New York: Springer-Verlag, 1993.

Frederick H. Buttell, "Socioeconomic Impacts and Social Implications of Reducing Pesticide and Agricultural Chemical Use in the United States." In *The Pesticide Question*, David Pimentel and Hugh Lehman, eds. New York: Chapman and Hall, 1993, pp. 153–182.

Andreas Buxtorf and Max Spindler. *Fifteen Years of Geigy Pest Control.* Basel, Switzerland: J. R. Geigy S.A., 1954. Source for Geigy woolen specialty; natural insecticides; delousing during World War I; pre-DDT insecticides; pyrethrum and rotenone as controls; and visit to United States.

Seth Cagin and Philip Dray. *Between Earth and Sky: How CFCs Changed Our World and Endangered the Ozone Layer.* New York: Pantheon Books, 1993. Source for aerosol sprays and Midgley.

Rachel Carson. *Silent Spring.* Boston: Houghton Mifflin, 1962.

Rita Colwell. "Global Climate and Infectious Disease: The Cholera Paradigm." *Science.* 274 (Dec. 20, 1996): 2025, 2031.

Alfred E. Cornebise. *Typhus and Doughboys: The American Polish Typhus Relief Expedition, 1919–1921.* Newark, DE: University of Delaware Press, 1982. The condon sanitaire.

Thomas R. Dunlap. "Science as a Guide in Regulating Technology: The Case of DDT in the United States." *Social Studies of Science.* 8 (Aug. 1978): 265–85. Source for why DDT research took so long; Clear Lake; impact of Rachel Carson; and peregrine falcons.

———. "The Triumph of Chemical Pesticides in Insect Control 1890–1920." *Environmental Review.* 2(1978): 38–47.

———. *DDT: Scientists, Citizens, and Public Policy.* Princeton, NJ: Princeton University Press, 1981. Source for undamaged potatoes; AMA for more studies; Wartime Production Board; postwar growth of pesticide sales and industry; WHO campaign; how DDT strays from spraying site; 1950s uses; Beech-Nut; radioactive fallout; and thalidomide.

Riley D. Dunlap and Angela G. Mertig, eds. *American Environmentalism. The U.S. Environmental Movement 1970–1990.* Philadelphia: Taylor & Francis, 1992.

Clive A. Edwards. "The Impact of Pesticides on the Environment." In *The Pesticide Question*, 13–47. David Pimentel and Hugh Lehman, eds. New York: Chapman and Hall, 1993. G. Fischer. "Presentation Speech to Paul Mueller." *Nobel Lectures, Physiology or Medicine, 1942–1962.* New York: Elsevier, 1964. Source for God-given substance; English journal article; and Swedish houseflies.

Harry Fiss. "The Interpreter." *New York Times Magazine.* May 2, 1999, p. 96. Source for typhus in Auschwitz.

Gaines M. Foster. "Typhus Disaster in the Wake of War: The American-Polish Relief Expedition, 1919–1920." *Bulletin of the History of Medicine.* 55 (1981): 221–232.

Donald E. H. Frear. *Chemistry of Insecticides, Fungicides and Herbicides.* New York: D. Van Nostrand Co., 1948.

Harold B. Friedman. "DDT: A Chemist's Tale." *Journal of Chemical Education*. 69, no. 5 (1992): 362–365. Source for bootlegger.

Marion Friedman. "Lt. Col. Theodore E. Woodward, M.C." *Maryland Medical Journal*. 44, no. 11 (Nov. 1995): 942-943, 977–978. Source for hand-spraying diagram; Mickey Finn drops; Naples epidemic; and Japanese occupation.

Victor Froehlicher. "The Story of DDT," *Soap and Sanitary Chemicals*. XX (July 1944): 115–119, 145. Source for Geigy-New York's reaction to DDT; tests in United States; caution; why DDT ignored; and Geigy hires Kettering Laboratory.

Geigy Co. "Dr. Paul Müller, 1899–1965." Obituary and short biography in Novartis Archives, Basel. For his retirement research. I am indebted to the Archives of the Novartis International AG, Basel, Switzerland, for this document.

Valerie J. Gunter and Craig K. Harris. "Noisy Winter: the DDT Controversy in the Years before Silent Spring." *Rural Sociology*. 63, no. 2 (1998): 179–198. Source for New York Times coverage of DDT.

Anne Hardy. "Urban Famine or Urban Crisis? Typhus in the Victorian City." *Medical History*. 32 (1988): 401–425. Source for the decline of typhus in Western Europe.

Samuel P. Hays. "From Conservation to Environment: Environmental Politics in the United States since World War II." In *Out of the Woods*. Char Miller and Hal Rothman, eds. Pittsburgh, PA: University of Pittsburgh Press, 1997, pp. 101–126. Source for Earth Day.

Margaret Humphreys. "Kicking a Dying Dog: DDT and the Demise of Malaria in the American South, 1942–1950." *Isis*. 87 (Mar. 1996): 1–17. Source for DDT in Bataan and New Guinea; MacArthur; and antimalarial successes in Europe.

———. "Water Won't Run Uphill: the New Deal and Malaria Control in the American South, 1933–40." *Parassitologia*. 40, no. 1–2 (June 1998): 183–191.

John Jewkes, David Sawers, and Richard Stillerman. *The Sources of Invention*. New York: W. W. Norton, 1969.

Linda Lear. *Rachel Carson: Witness for Nature*. New York: Henry Holt & Co., 1997. Her goals.

Robert Lips. *Globi im Urwald*. Zurich, Globi-Verlag, 1950. Children's verse. I am indebted to Andreas Berz of the Swiss National Library for this.

Massimo Livi-Bacci. *Population and Nutrition: An Essay on European Demographic History*. Translated by Tania Croft-Murray. Cambridge: Cambridge University Press, 1991.

John A. McKenzie. *Ecological and Evolutionary Aspects of Insecticide Resistance*. Austin, TX: R. G. Landes Co., 1996. Source for pests' resistance.

John A. McLachlan and Steven F. Arnold. "Environmental Estrogens." *American Scientist*. 84 (Sept.–Oct. 1996): 452–461.

Malaria Foundation International. "Worldwide Impact of Malaria." http://www.malaria.org.

Eliot Marshall. "African Malaria Studies Draw Attention." *Science*. 275 (Jan. 17, 1997): 299.

———. "A Renewed Assault on an Old and Deadly Foe." *Science*. 290 (Oct. 20, 2000): 428–430. This introduces a special section on malaria research, resurgent malaria epidemics, and increases in research.

Kenneth Mellanby. "With Safeguards, DDT Should Still Be Used." *Wall Street Journal*, Sept. 12, 1989, p. A26. Source for plague epidemics.

Paul Müller. "Histoire du D.D.T." *Les Conférences du Palais de la Découverte, Université de Paris*. Alençon: Maison Poulet-Manlassis, 1948. Source for mothproofing campaign; Swiss food shortages; typhus defined; and DDT not omnipotent.

———. *DDT Das Insektizid*. vols. 1 and 2. Basel: Birkhäuser Verlag, 1955.

———. "Dichloro-diphenyl-trichloroethane and newer insecticides." Nobel Prize For Physiology or Medicine speech 1948 and biography. *Nobel Lectures, Physiology or Medicine, 1942–1962*. New York: Elsevier, (1964): 147–176. Source for Müller's childhood; youth; early Geigy career; insecticide research plan, ideal insecticide, and DDT discovery; biologists' skepticism and caution about insecticides in complex ecological systems.

———. "Lebenslauf." Courtesy of Margartha Jaeggi-Müller. A brief autobiography. Source for his childhood, youth, and career.

M. D. Nettleman. "Biological Warfare and Infection Control." *Infection Control and Hospital Epidemiology*. 12, no. 6 (June 1991): 368–372. Source for typhus description.

Nobel Foundation Records. "Reports to the Nobel Committee for Physiology or Medicine for its 1945, 1946, and 1948 prizes," Stockholm, Sweden. Material from the Nobel Archives was kindly provided by the Nobel Committee for Physiology or Medicine. I am indebted to Nichole Sterling for her translation from the Swedish. Source for the key experiment and for Nobel prize nominations 1945–1948.

Elizabeth Olson. "DDT Complicates Debate on Pact to Ban Pesticides." *The New York Times*. Sept. 14, 1999. Source for current needs for DDT.

———. "Drug Groups and U.N. Offices Join to Develop Malaria Cures." *The New York Times*. Nov. 18, 1999, p. A5.

K. David Patterson. "Typhus and its control in Russia, 1870–1940." *Medical History*. 37 (1993): 361–381. Source for the Russian epidemic; Irish famine; known treatments; typhus defined; and laundresses.

John H. Perkins. "Reshaping Technology in Wartime: The Effect of Military Goals on Entomological Research and Insect-Control Practices." *Technology and Culture*. 19 (1978): 169–186. Source for entomologists' support of DDT; Wartime Production Board; postwar uses of DDT; Western apples and cattle; postwar increase in DDT tonnage and insecticide companies; citrus pests; and ridicule of cautious entomologists.

David Pimentel et al. "Assessment of Environmental and Economic Impacts of Pesticide Use." In *The Pesticide Question*, 47–84. David Pimentel and Hugh Lehman, eds. New York: Chapman and Hall, 1993. Source for India; $4 pesticides savings; and David Pimentel et al., "Environmental and Economic Impacts of Reducing U.S. Agricultural Pesticide Use." Source for cosmetic perfection.

Janet Raloff. "A New World of Pollutant Effects." *Science News Anniversary Supplement 1922–1997*. 1997, p. S19.

———. "Estrogen's Emerging Manly Alter Ego." *Science News*. 152 (Dec. 6, 1997): 356.

Kavita Ramamoorthy. "Potency of Combined Estrogenic Pesticides." *Science*. 275 (Jan. 17, 1997): 405.

Edmund P. Russell III. " 'Speaking of Annihilation' " Mobilizing for War against Human and Insect Enemies, 1914–1945." *Journal of American History.* 82 (1996): 1505–1529. Source for Farben's discovery of organophosphates and the War Production Board.

Ellen Ruppel Shell. "Resurgence of a Deadly Disease." *The Atlantic Monthly.* 280, no. 2 (Aug. 1997): 45–60. Source for flying syringes and use of DDT against resurgent malaria epidemics.

Christian Simon. "DDT—Forschung und Entwicklung zwischen Chemie und Biologie." *Chemie in der Schweiz,"* Thomas Busset et al., eds. Basel: Christoph Merian Verlag, 1997. Source for the 350th compound; note in calendar; Zeidler; spraying near toddlers; and controversies with Läuger, Martin, Geigy over priority and royalties.

———. *DDT: Kulturgeschichte einer Chemischen Verbindung.* Basel: Christoph Merian Verlag, 1999.

Thomas G. Spiro and William M. Stigliani. *Chemistry of the Environment.* Upper Saddle River, NJ: Prentice Hall, 1996. Source for how DDT kills; organophosphates, aldicarbs, and malathion; Sri Lanka; and pressure on Congress.

Darwin H. Stapleton. "The Short-Lived Miracle of DDT." *Invention and Technology.* 15 (Winter 2000): 34–41. Source for Geigy tests of DDT for typhus; Geigy tells Germany about DDT; DDT arrives in U.S.; early tests; dengue epidemic; marines sick; wartime red flags; five million lives saved; "Jekyll-Hyde" compound; FDA warning; DDT ban premature; 1999 pesticide usage; and DDT vs. resurgent malaria.

William N. Sullivan. "The Coupling of Science and Technology in the Early Development of the World War II Aerosol Bomb." *Military Medicine,* 136 (Feb. 1971): 157–158. Source for Sicily and African airbases.

Margit Szöllösi-Janze. *Lice, Mites. . . The Uses and Abuses of Modern Science: The Case of Fritz Haber 1868–1934.* London: Vortrag, 1999. Source for Haber's insecticides.

P. L. Trigg and A. V. Kondrachine. "Commentary: Malaria Control in the 1990s." *Bulletin of the World Health Organization.* 76, no. 1 (1998): 11–16.

Harry Wain. *A History of Preventive Medicine.* Springfield IL: Charles C Thomas, 1970. Source of Napoleon and typhus, and typhus description.

T. F. West, J. Eliot Hardy, and J. H. Ford. *Chemical Control of Insects.* London: Chapman & Hall, 1951.

James Whorton. *Before Silent Spring: Pesticides and Public Health in Pre-DDT America.* Princeton, NJ: Princeton University Press, 1974. Source for lead arsenate insecticide and Terres' article.

CHAPTER 9   Lead-Free Gasoline and Clair C. Patterson

I would like to thank Herbert Needleman, MD, Robert P. Sharp, and George R. Tilton for reading this chapter and commenting on it.

The Patterson Papers in the Archives of the California Institute of Technology contain the Patterson Papers ("PP" here) and Historical Files. I am indebted to the Archives for permission to quote from their holdings.

Interviews with the author, by telephone unless otherwise noted:

Leon Billings. Sept. 8, 1997. Source for Muskie's reaction to Patterson testimony and their continued cooperation.

Edward Boyle. June 17, 1997. Source for need for "really good data... obligation"; few bedrock values; and anthrosphere.

Thomas M. Church. Sept. 25, 1997.

Robert W. Elias. Sept. 26, 1997. Source for metalworker's restaurant; disappointed at Nobel; creationist; measles cartoon; and Sno Cat trip.

Samuel Epstein. Sept. 12, 1997.

A. Russell Flegall. Feb. 27, July 30, 1997. Source for CDC levels.

Sheldon Friedlander. Sept. 30, 1997.

Edward D. Goldberg. Sept. 13, 1997.

Todd Hinkley. Sept. 3, Oct. 27, Oct. 28, 1997. Source for microchemistry's power and his name on articles.

W. Barkley Kamb. Sept. 23, 1997.

Kathy Lima. Sept. 23, 1997. Source for his secretary.

James Morgan. Caltech, Aug. 6, 1997, and telephone, Sept. 16, 1997. Source for Caltech colloquium.

Herbert Needleman. Sept. 19, 1997.

Donald Nichol. Oct. 31, 1997, and private communication, Nov. 16, 1997. Background source for Muskie hearing.

Lorna McCleary Patterson. Sea Ranch, California, Oct. 4–5, 1997. Source for petition to Groves and the day the atomic bomb was dropped; penance for Oak Ridge; joggers' hair; Argonne and heart attack; seasick; running; MIT sabbatical; and Pit Diggers cartoons.

Dorothy M. Settle. Caltech, Aug. 6, 1997.

Robert P. Sharp. Sept. 20, 1997. Source for DuBridge phone call.

Lee Silver. Sept. 16, 1997.

George R. Tilton. Sept. 3, Oct. 27, 1997. Source for "Read it . . . "

Bibliography

Anonymous. "Dr. Patterson Returns, Puts Punch in Lead Hearings." *Environmental Health Letter*. June 15, 1966. In Caltech PP, Box 16.13.

———. "Obituary." *Los Angeles Times*. Undated. Caltech Archives Historical Files, Box Z31. Source of Manhattan Project as "crime."

William F. Ashe. "Robert Arthur Kehoe." *Archives of Environmental Health* 13 (Aug. 1966): 138–739.

Tim Beardsley. "Testing's Toll." *Scientific American*. 273 (Aug. 1995): 28. Source for bomb tests.

Bernadette Bensaude-Vincent and Isabelle Stengers. *A History of Chemistry*. Cambridge, MA: Harvard University Press, 1996.

James Bonner. "Arie Jan Haagen-Smit 1900–1977." *Engineering & Science*. XL, no. 4 (May–June 1977): 28–29. Source for smog experiment.

Claude F. Boutron and Clair C. Patterson. "Lead Concentration Changes in Antarctic Ice during the Wisconsin/Holocene Transition." *Nature*. 323 (Sept. 18, 1986): 222–225.

Claude F. Boutron et al. "Decrease in anthropogenic lead, cadmium and zinc in Greenland snows since the late 1960s." *Nature.* 353 (Sept. 12, 1991): 153–156.

Peter Bowler. *Norton History of the Environmental Sciences.* New York: W. W. Norton, 1993.

Edward Boyle. "Tyler Prize" talk. University of Southern California, April 28, 1995.

William H. Brock. *The Norton History of Chemistry.* New York: W. W. Norton, 1993.

Edmund G. Brown. Letter to Patterson, June 29, 1966. Caltech PP, Box 3.15.

Rudd Brown. Letter to Winslow Christian, May 3, 1966. Caltech PP, Box 3.15. Source for "Not a nut."

Stephen G. Brush. *Transmuted Past: The Age of the Earth and the Evolution of the Elements from Lyell to Patterson.* Cambridge: Cambridge University Press, 1996. Source for Rhode Island granite and unknown and uncited work.

Irene R. Campbell. "The House that Robert A. Kehoe Built." *Archives of Environmental Health.* 13 (Aug. 1966): 143–151. Source for Kehoe's volubility and for the financial background and international impact of the Kettering Lab.

James S. Chapman. "Katharine Boucot Sturgis, MD." *Archives of Environmental Health.* 22 (Feb. 1971): 189. Source for rejuvenated journal.

Tsaihwa J. Chow and C. C. Patterson. "The Occurrence and Significance of Lead Isotopes in Pelagic Sediments." *Geochimica et Cosmochimica Acta.* 26 (Feb. 1962): 263–308.

Thomas M. Church. "From Meteorites to Man: The Patterson Geochemical Heritage." Unpublished manuscript. Source for the impact of Patterson's Ph.D. thesis on geologists; few understood age of Earth work; ocean sediments; MIT sabbatical, Hardy and biology; Goldberg's tip; Schaule device; and lead-free rats.

——, ed. "The Clair C. Patterson Special Issue." *Geochimica et Cosmochimica Acta.* 58, no. 15 (Aug. 1994) 3139–3330. Source for especially Church "Foreword," 3139, and Patterson "Preface," 3141–3143, and "Delineation of Separate Brain Regions Used for Scientific versus Engineering Modes of Thinking," 3321–3327. Source of "Magnificent . . . vision"; excitement discovering Earth's age; "modern surge"; and depression about modern science.

Barry Commoner. *Science and Survival.* New York: Ballantine, 1963. Source for fallout history and power breakdown.

D.A.E. "Lead Hazard Discounted." *Science News.* 92 (Sept. 16, 1967): 278.

Samuel Epstein. "Introduction of Clair C. Patterson for the V. M. Goldschmidt Medal 1980." *Geochimica et Cosmochimica Acta.* 45 (Aug. 1981) 1383–1397. Source for Boucot's solicitation of manuscript.

Jonathon E. Erickson, Hiroshi Shirahata, and C. C. Patterson. "Skeletal Concentrations of Lead in Ancient Peruvians." *The New England Journal of Medicine.* 30 (Apr. 26, 1979): 946–951.

Gunter Faure. *Principles and Applications of Geochemistry.* Upper Saddle River, NJ: Prentice Hall, 1998. Source for characteristic isotopic values of gasolines.

A. Russell Flegal. "Clair C. Patterson (1922–1995)." *Nature.* 379 (Feb. 8, 1996): 487.

——. "Clair Patterson's Influence on Environmental Research." *Environmental Research.* 78 (Aug. 1998): 65–70.

Irwin Goodwin. "Fallout of Atmospheric Nuclear Tests in 1950s and 1960s Exposed More People to Iodine-131 than Chernobyl Accident." *Physics Today.* 50 (Sept. 1997): 54–55.

Alice Hamilton. *Industrial Poisons in the United States.* New York: The Macmillan Company, 1925. Source of medical knowledge of lead in the 1920s.

Yoshimitsu Hirao and C. C. Patterson. "Lead Aerosol Pollution in the High Sierra Overrides Natural Mechanisms Which Exclude Lead from a Food Chain." *Science.* 184 (May 31, 1974): 989–992.

Hu-Howard. "Knowledge of Diagnosis and Reproductive History among Survivors of Childhood Plumbism." *American Journal of Public Health.* 81 (Aug. 1991): 1070–1072. Source for third-generation effects of lead poisoning.

Robert A. Kehoe. "On the Normal Absorption and Excretion of Lead." *The Journal of Industrial Hygiene.* 15 (Sept. 1933): 257–272.

———. "An Appraisal of the Lead Hazards Associated with the Distribution and Use of Gasoline Containing Tetraethyl Lead." *Journal of Industrial Hygiene and Toxicology.* 18 (Jan. 1936): 42–68.

———. "Experimental Studies on the Ingestion of Lead Compounds." *The Journal of Industrial Hygiene and Toxicology.* 22 (Nov. 1940): 381–400.

———. "Responses of Human Subjects to Lead Compounds." *Industrial Medicine and Surgery.* 28 (Mar. 1959): 156–159.

———. "Experimental Studies on the Inhalation of Lead by Human Subjects." *Pure and Applied Chemistry.* 3 (1961) 129–144.

———. "Normal Metabolism of Lead." *Archives of Environmental Health.* 8 (1964): 232–243.

———. Letter to Editor. *Archives of Environmental Health.* 13 (Nov. 1965): 736–739. Source of his reply to Patterson's *Archives* article.

Robert A. Kehoe, Jacob Cholak, and Robert V. Story. "A Spectrochemical Study of the Normal Ranges of Concentration of Certain Trace Metals in Biological Materials." *Journal of Nutrition.* 19 (1940): 579–592.

M. Murozumi, Tsaihwa J. Chow, and C. Patterson. "Chemical Concentrations of Pollutant Lead Aerosols, Terrestrial Dusts and Sea Salts in Greenland and Antarctic Snow Strata." *Geochimica et Cosmochimica Acta.* 33 (Oct. 1969): 1247–1294. Source for details of polar field trips.

National Academy of Sciences. *Lead in the Human Environment.* Washington, DC: National Academy of Sciences, 1980.

National Academy of Sciences Committee on the Biological Effects of Atomic Radiation. *A Report to the Public on the Biological Effects of Atomic Radiation.* Washington, DC: National Research Council, 1960.

National Research Council. *Lead: Airborne Lead in Perspective.* Washington DC: National Academy of Sciences, 1972.

———. *Measuring Lead Exposure in Infants, Children, and Other Sensitive Populations.* Washington, DC: National Academy Press, 1993.

Herbert L. Needleman. "Clair Patterson and Robert Kehoe: Two Views of Lead Toxicity." *Environmental Research.* 78 (Aug. 1998): 79–85. A good summary of Patterson versus Kehoe.

Amy Ng and Clair Patterson. "Natural Concentrations of Lead in Ancient Arctic and Antarctic Ice." *Geochimica et Cosmochimica Acta.* 45 (Nov. 1981): 2109–2121.

Jerome O. Nriagu. *Lead and Lead Poisoning in Antiquity.* New York: Wiley, 1983. Source for ancient lead; leaded gasoline statistics; and Clean Air Act.

Jerome O. Nriagu. "The Rise and Fall of Leaded Gasoline." *Science of the Total Envi-*

ronment. 92 (Mar. 1990): 13–28. Source for Patterson versus Kehoe; Kehoe blames victims; and leaded gas sales.

Jerome O. Nriagu. "A History of Global Metal Pollution." *Science.* 272 (Apr. 12, 1996): 223–224.

Jerome O. Nriagu. "Clair Patterson and Robert Kehoe's Paradigm of 'Show Me the Data' on Environmental Lead Poisoning." *Environmental Research.* 78 (Aug. 1998): 71–78.

C. Patterson. "Contaminated and Natural Lead Environments of Man." *Archives of Environmental Health.* 11 (Sept. 1965): 344–360.

———. "Native Copper, Silver, and Gold Accessible to Early Metallurgists." *American Antiquity.* 36 (July 1971): 286–321.

———. "Silver Stocks and Losses in Ancient and Medieval Times." *Economic History Review.* Second Series. 25, no. 2 (May 1972): 205–235.

C. C. Patterson. Letter to Edmund S. Muskie. "Oct. 7, 1965." in Caltech PP, Box 16.13. Source for the letter about preparing to testify; surprise to medicine in 1920s; Kehoe is out of date, believes in "star-dust" and sharp line.

———. Letter to Edmund G. Brown, Oct. 27, 1965. Caltech PP, Box 3.15. Source for California State Dept. of Public Health and Ethyl Corp.; California's leadership.

———. undated note, "Educating the Calif. State Dept. of Public Health." Caltech PP, Box 3.15.

———. "An Alternative Perspective—Lead Pollution in the Human Environment: Origin, Extent, and Significance." *Lead: Airborne Lead in Perspective.* National Research Council, Washington DC: National Academy of Sciences (1972): 265–350. Source for measles cartoon.

———. "Silver Stocks and Losses in Ancient and Medieval Times." *Economic History Review.* Second Series, 25, no. 2 (May 1972): 205–235.

———. Letter to Senator Edmund S. Muskie. May 28, 1974. Caltech PP, Box 16.13.

———. Untitled poem. Caltech PP, Box 147.6.

———. Letter to Saul Bellow, May 31, 1987. Caltech PP, Box 2.9.

———. Letter to Dr. Herbert Needleman, Aug. 5, 1992. Caltech PP, Box 17.11. Source for harassment by Ethyl Corp. and "driven to prove."

———. "Duck Soup and Lead." Oral History by Shirley Cohen for Caltech Archives Oral History Project, March 1995. Archives of the California Institute of Technology. Source for most of Patterson's informal comments, e.g., Iowa, Grinnell, blip, zircon, duck soup, building Caltech clean lab; "dozen years literally"; funding ocean sediments; lead in oceans high; and wham.

Clair C. Patterson, T. J. Chow, and M. Murozumi. "The Possibility of Measuring Variations in the Intensity of Worldwide Lead Smelting during Medieval and Ancient Times Using Lead Aerosol Deposits in Polar Snow Strata." In *Scientific Methods in Medieval Archaeology.* Rainer Berger, ed. Berkeley: University of California Press, 1970, pp. 339–350.

C. C. Paterson, H. Shirahata, and J. E. Erickson. "Lead in Ancient Human Bones and Its Relevance to Historical Developments of Social Problems with Lead." *The Science of the Total Environment.* 61 (Mar. 1987) 167–200.

C. Patterson, G. Tilton, and M. Inghram. "Age of the Earth." *Science.* 112 (Jan. 21, 1955): 69–75

Joseph C. Robert. *Ethyl: A History of the Corporation and the People Who Made It.* Charlottesville: University Press of Virginia, 1983. Source for company background, sale, Kehoe's importance and founding father; reactions to conference and hearing; company financial difficulties and sale terms; changed image; GM decision; unchanged position.

John W. Servos. *Physical Chemistry from Ostwald to Pauling: The Making of a Science in America.* Princeton, NJ: Princeton University Press, 1990. Source for building U.S. chemistry departments.

Dorothy M. Settle and Clair C. Patterson. "Lead in Albacore: Guide to Lead Pollution in Americans." *Science.* 207 (Mar. 14, 1980): 1167–1176.

Robert P. Sharp. "Vignettes of Clair Patterson." Unpublished manuscript.

Herman Skolnik and Kenneth M. Reese, eds. *A Century of Chemistry and the American Chemical Society.* Washington, DC: American Chemical Society, 1976. Source for environmental division.

Thomas G. Spiro and William M. Stigliani. *Chemistry of the Environment.* New Jersey: Prentice Hall, 1996. Source for lead-halide particles; lead paint on school buses, highways, and bridges.

M. Tatsumoto and C. C. Patterson. "Concentrations of Common Lead in Some Atlantic and Mediterranean Waters and in Snow." *Nature.* 199 (July 27, 1963): 350–352. Source for extrapolation from sea surface to leaded gasolines and Lassen National Park.

Mitsonubu Tatsumoto and Todd Hinkley. Letter to Dr. Jerome B. Walker, Oct. 15, 1986. Source for Tyler Prize. Caltech Archives. Folder 20.

George R. Tilton. "Clair Cameron Patterson, June 2, 1922 – December 5, 1995." *Biographical Memoirs, National Academy of Sciences.* 74 (1998): 166–187. Washington, DC, National Academy Press, 1998. Source for Chicago lab pollution; importance of Ph.D. thesis; "wildman," and "trying situation."

U.S. Public Health Service. *Symposium on Environmental Lead Contamination.* Dec. 13–15, 1965. U.S. Department of Health, Education, and Welfare. FS2.2:646/4.

U.S. Senate, *Report of the Subcommittee on Air and Water Pollution of the Committee on Public Works.* Washington, DC, June 17–15, 1966. Source for Muskie hearings and Stockinger letter.

Index

About the Author

SHARON BERTSCH MCGRAYNE is a science writer and award-winning journalist. She has been a reporter for Scripps-Howard, Crain's, Gannett, and other newspapers covering education, politics, and health issues. She is a former science editor and writer for *Encyclopaedia Britannica* and the author of several books, including *Nobel Prize Women in Science.*